The Medieval Pilgrimage to St Patrick's Purgatory

The Medieval Pilgrimage to St Patrick's Purgatory Lough Derg and the European Tradition

edited by

Michael Haren & Yolande de Pontfarcy

Clogher Historical Society

ISBN 0 949012 05 X

Printed by R. & S. Printers, The Diamond, Monaghan.

Contents

Acknowledgements

Individual contributors wish to record the following obligations: without committing him to the interpretation advanced, Michael Haren thanks Art Cosgrove for reading and discussing Chapters VI and VIII; he also thanks Anthony Lynch for information derived from the Armagh registers. Próinséas Ní Chatháin thanks Yolande de Pontfarcy, Charles Doherty and Robert Mullally for assistance with Chapter IX. Yolande de Pontfarcy thanks Elizabeth Donnelly for drawing the maps.

The editors thank Rev. Noel MacTréinfhir for kindly agreeing to the Clogher Historical Society's use here of the reproduction of the Todi fresco, as published by him in *Clogher Record*, 1986. They acknowledge the generosity in granting permission of Prof. Marcello Castrichini, proprietor of Ediart, Todi, Italy. They pay tribute to R. & S. Printers and to Mr John Hughes, compositor, whose skill in setting much eased their task.

Finally and principally, the editors express with great pleasure their debt to Most Reverend Dr Joseph Duffy, Bishop of Clogher, Chairman of the Clogher Historical Society, whose suggestion the book was and who has with enthusiasm and assiduous organization nurtured its progress from inception to publication.

Contributors

Dorothy M. Carpenter, M.Phil., Dip. Psych., Dalkey, co. Dublin

Robert Easting, M.A., D.Phil., Department of English, Victoria University of Wellington, New Zealand

Michael Haren, D.Phil., F.R.Hist.S., Irish Manuscripts Commission, Dublin

Próinséas Ní Chatháin, M.A., Ph.D., Professor of Early Irish, University College, Dublin

Jean-Michel Picard, M.Phil., Dr de l'Université, Department of French, University College, Dublin

Yolande de Pontfarcy, M. ès L., Dr de l'Université, Department of French, University College, Dublin

Hugh Shields, M.A., Ph.D., F.T.C.D., Department of French, Trinity College, Dublin

List of Figures

Introduction

The massive Irish contribution to the enrichment of European civilization in the early middle ages is well known — the missionary work of exiled monks, their British and continental foundations, their own writings and their conservation and development of the literature of the classical past. Less well known is the fascination which the island itself exercised on the European mind throughout the middle ages. Three outstanding stories, written in Latin, in a continental milieu, helped to inspire and maintain that fascination. The first is the *Navigatio Brendani*, 'The Voyage of St Brendan', in which is related the quest of the saint who sailed across the ocean searching for the Promised Land. It was written in the first half of the tenth century in the kingdom of Lorraine (which at the time extended northwards from the present Lorraine and included the Netherlands). The second is the *Visio Tnugdali*, 'The Vision of Tnugdal', written in 1149 by the Irish monk Marcus in Ratisbon, the old capital of Bavaria in southern Germany. It narrates the vision experienced in Cork in 1148 by a knight from Cashel. The third is the *Tractatus de Purgatorio Sancti Patricii*, 'The Treatise on St Patrick's Purgatory', written in 1184 by an Anglo-Norman monk in England. It relates how the Lord revealed a cave or pit to St Patrick by means of which one could enter the otherworld as did the hero, Knight Owein. The consequences are a large part of the theme of the present book. The 'Treatise' not only aroused interest in the Purgatory on the part of the reading public but also attracted to it pilgrims from afar.

One point which these stories have in common is that their appeal was more to continental and English than to Irish readers. Few manuscripts containing them were written in Ireland and such as were are for the most part very late. But they were copied many times both on the continent and in England and were disseminated in most of the European languages. It is clear that this type of literature fulfilled a deep need of adventure and a dream that somewhere in the far western region of the world the impossible becomes possible. It was also charged with spiritual and theological

content, and in this reflects the currents of medieval religious
thought. Above all, it presented the afterlife as a concrete
reality. It had a deterrent import. It prompted towards
repentance, inviting readers to prepare for death by
renouncing vice. It encouraged pilgrimage, either in the
literal sense of leaving country, family and friends or in the
internal and figurative sense of conversion to a new life.

The cave alias pit named St Patrick's Purgatory was situated
on Station Island, one of the forty-six islands of Lough Derg,
in the modern county of Donegal. From the mid-twelfth
century, Station Island was the property of the Augustinian
priory of Saints' Island (Oileán na Naomh), located to the
north-west of Station Island and known also by the name of its
founder as St Dabeoc's Island. While the priory on the larger,
green island fell into ruin and the canons departed, the small,
rocky Station Island remained a place of pilgrimage, one of
the most unusual in the Christian world. Today it is
frequented mainly by Irish people and is hardly known outside
Ireland. In the middle ages by contrast and particularly in the
fourteenth and fifteenth centuries it attracted pilgrims from all
over Europe.

This book offers both to the general reader and to the
medievalist the history of the European-wide phase of the
pilgrimage to the Purgatory and a study of the visionary
literature which it generated. Chapters I and II discuss the
origins of the pilgrimage by sifting a rare blend of legendary,
literary, topographical and historical material. Chapter III
deals with the English tradition and in particular with the
account of Peter of Cornwall, with poetic reworkings of the
Knight Owein theme, with the pilgrimage of Sir William Lisle
and with the major English visionary produced by the
Purgatory, William of Stranton. Chapter IV examines how
the French popularized the legend and records the pilgrimage
of the Sire de Beaujeu and of Ghillebert de Lannoy. Chapter
V contains a full translation of the valuable account of the
Catalonian pilgrim, Ramon de Perellós. Chapter VI studies
the visits of two Hungarian pilgrims, George Grissaphan,
whose sojourn in the Purgatory and subsequent contacts
produced the largest single visionary treatise, and Laurence
Rathold of Pászthó, a high-ranking nobleman who made a

notable impression on fifteenth century Dublin. Chapter VII examines the tradition of the Purgatory in northern Italy and deals at some length with the account of Antonio Mannini. Chapter VIII brings the continental pilgrimage to a conclusion and discusses the context and implications of an entry in the *Annals of Ulster* for the year 1497, recording the closure of the cave. The episode has a number of puzzling features and poses questions which await additional evidence for their resolution. One salient fact is clear: the pilgrimage now entered a new phase. On the literary level, it generated a body of Irish poetry which is the subject of the final chapter.

The division of chapters according to the provenance of the pilgrims was dictated by the specializations required to treat subject matter of such wide linguistic and disciplinary range. However, the divisions have been handled freely and individual contributors have referred as necessary to material formally outside their main concern, in following sources and in drawing comparisons. A collaborative venture, organized thematically, inevitably entails some differences of interpretation and some overlap. Wherever possible, a common interpretation is advanced. Where the evidence is ambivalent there has been no attempt to achieve a specious uniformity. Such differences of presentation as result reflect real uncertainties and will, it is hoped, serve to stimulate further discussion. Overlap has been reduced to a minimum. What remains seemed a proper deference to the integrity of the subject. The book has in fact two powerful unifying features. One is its focus on the Purgatory, the cynosure of the travellers themselves. The other is its reflection of the broad cultural unity which characterises the European middle ages and which commends them so warmly as a study for our times. This unity in diversity at once demands and rewards the interdisciplinary approach which is the method of the book and which has enlivened for all the contributors their work on St Patrick's Purgatory.

MICHAEL HAREN
YOLANDE de PONTFARCY

The Argentine 'Ptolemy', 1513

Chronology of the Medieval Pilgrims (Historical and Literary) to St Patrick's Purgatory

Pilgrim	Provenance	Date of Visit, Attributed Visit or Account
Knight Owein	Ireland	c. 1146-7; H. of Saltrey's *Tractatus*, c. 1185
Anonymous Knight	Ireland	c. 1170; from Peter of Cornwall's Account, 1200
The Sire de Beaujeu	France	first half of fourteenth century
George Grissaphan	Hungary/Apulia	1353
Louis d'Auxerre	France	1358
Malatesta	Rimini, Italy	1358
Nicholas Beccari	Italy	1358
Taddeo Gualandi	Italy	c. 1360
John Bonham	England	1365
Guido Cissi	Italy	1365
Sir William Lisle	England	1394-5
Ramon de Perellós	Catalonia/Aragon	1397
William, 'lord of Corsy'	(?)England/France	1397; referred to by Ramon de Perellós
John of Brederode	Netherlands	1399
William of Stranton	England	(?)1409
Antonio da Focha	Italy	c. 1410

Antonio Mannini	Italy	1411
Laurence Rathold of Pászthó	Hungary	1411
Ghillebert de Lannoy	Wallonia	1430
Conrad von Scharnachthal	Switzerland	1446
Canon of Waterford	Ireland	mid-fifteenth century
Sir John de Banste	Bruges, Flanders	1460
Jean Garry François Proty Jean Burgey	Lyons, France	1485
John Bermyngham William Bramery	England	1489
Blasius Biragus	(?)	(?)c. 1490
Canon of Eymstadt	Netherlands	c. 1494-7
Nylanus O'Ledan	Ireland	1507
Anonymous Knight	France	1516
Francesco Chiericati	Italy	1517

I. The Historical Background to the Pilgrimage to Lough Derg

The *Tractatus de Purgatorio Sancti Patricii (Treatise on St Patrick's Purgatory)*, generally referred to as the *Tractatus*, is the earliest record of the pilgrimage to Lough Derg. It was written in Latin in 1184 by Brother H., a Cistercian Anglo-Norman monk of the abbey of Saltrey, in Huntingdonshire (England).[1] The story is centred on the journey in the otherworld undertaken by the knight Owein. The entrance to the beyond is a cave or pit named St Patrick's Purgatory. Henry of Saltrey, as the monk is commonly called, is at pains to prove the reality of his story. In the introduction he explains how the Purgatory (that is the cave) was revealed to St Patrick and what the ritual of admission to the cave was. In the conclusion he reveals how he came to know the story and claims that he is not the author but merely relates what he heard from Gilbert, a monk of the abbey of Louth (diocese of Lincoln) and ex-abbot of Basingwerk (North Wales). This Gilbert went to Ireland in 1148 to found a monastery which has been identified with Baltinglass.[2] To help him, the king (Diarmaid Mac Murchadha)[3], who offered him the land for the monastery, gave him also the knight Owein, who had just come back from St Patrick's Purgatory, as an interpreter. H. of Saltrey states:

> Gilbert was the cellarer of this house; as for the knight he was the external provider in everything and a devoted servant and most faithful interpreter.[4]

[1] Robert Easting, 'The date and dedication of the *Tractatus de Purgatorio Sancti Patricii*', *Speculum*, liii (1978), 778-783; Y. de Pontfarcy, 'Le *Tractatus de Purgatorio Sancti Patricii* de H. of Saltrey, sa date et ses sources', *Peritia*, iii (1984), 460-480.

[2] Fr Gwynn's review of A. Curtayne's *Lough Derg. Saint Patrick's Purgatory*, in *Studies*, xxxiii (1944), 552; R. Easting, 'Owein at St Patrick's Purgatory', *Medium Aevum*, lv (1986), 159-175.

[3] In later versions of the story, Owein has been made a knight in the service of King Stephen (the Norman Etienne de Blois, king of England between 1135 and 1154) and it was thought that Gilbert went to King Stephen for land to build a monastery. But H. of Saltrey only writes that it is in the days of King Stephen that Owein visited the Purgatory. In any case, the king who granted land in Ireland to build a monastery cannot in 1148 have been the king of England. If Baltinglass is the monastery founded by Gilbert, the king in question could only have been the king of Leinster, Diarmaid Mac Murchadha.

[4] J-M. Picard and Y. de Pontfarcy, *Saint Patrick's Purgatory* (Dublin, 1985), pp. 72-73. I am grateful to the publisher who allowed me to reuse J-M. Picard's translation of H. of Saltrey's account and my introduction to the text.

Gilbert remained two and a half years in Ireland and during his stay
the knight Owein told him about his experience and what he saw in
the otherworld. The text is therefore a story at second hand, told for
the first time between 1148 and 1150 by Owein, the Irish informant
and main character of the narrative, to the Anglo-Norman
Cistercian monk Gilbert who, some thirty years later,[5] related it to
an assembly of people among whom was H. of Saltrey who in 1184
put it into written form.

The anchoretic tradition

The introductory part of this famous tale of Owein's journey in
the otherworld is the sole record of the origin of St Patrick's
Purgatory. H. of Saltrey relates that the Irish refused to be
converted 'unless one of them could witness both the torments of
the wicked and the joys of the just' and that when St Patrick did
'vigils, fasts, prayers and good deeds' in order to win their
conversion Jesus appeared to him and took him 'to a deserted
place':

> There He showed to him a round pit, dark inside, and said to him that
> whoever, being truly repentant and armed with true faith, would
> enter this pit and remain for the duration of one day and one night,
> would be purged of all the sins of his life. Moreover, while going
> through it, he would see not only the torments of the wicked, but
> also, if he acted constantly according to the faith, the joys of the
> blessed. Thus, after the disappearance of the Lord from before his
> eyes, blessed Patrick was filled with spiritual joy not only because his
> Lord had appeared to him but also because he had shown him this pit
> by means of which he hoped the people would turn away from their
> errors.[6]

Then St Patrick built a church and placed Augustinian Canons
there.

> As for this pit, which is in the graveyard outside the west wall of the
> church, he had it enclosed within a wall and doors and had locks
> added so that nobody would dare enter by rash audacity and without
> permission. Furthermore, he commended the key to the prior of this

---

[5] In 1180 Gilbert was no longer abbot of Basingwerk. See *The Heads of Religious Houses,
England and Wales, 940-1216*, eds D. Knowles, C.N.L. Brooke, V. London (Cambridge, 1972).
[6] Picard and Pontfarcy, *Saint Patrick's Purgatory*, pp. 47-48.

community for safe keeping. And in the days of this blessed father, many people, driven by repentance, entered the pit and, on their return, testified that they had both seen the joys and endured the greatest torments. And blessed Patrick ordered that their accounts be recorded in the same church. So, because of the testimony of these people, the others began to accept the preaching of blessed Patrick. And since men were purged of their sins there, this place was called Saint Patrick's Purgatory. But the place of the church was called Reglis.[7]

After this H. of Saltrey explains the different steps that a pilgrim must undertake. He must obtain permission from the bishop in whose diocese the Purgatory is situated and choose of his own free will to enter the cave. The bishop tries to exhort the pilgrim to change his mind because many entered the Purgatory and never came back. If the pilgrim persists in his intention the bishop gives him letters and sends him to the prior who also tries to dissuade him. If all this is to no avail, the prior takes the pilgrim to the church — in which he will pray and fast for fifteen days — and then to the cave.

This type of penitential exercise is not out of line with what may have been practised in Ireland. In the eighth-century *Old-Irish Table of Commutations,* one reads that the commutations proper for clerics and nuns who have not slain a man are the following:

> . . . spending the night in cold churches or remote cells while keeping vigils and praying without respite, *i.e.* (without) leave to sit or lie down or sleep — as though one were at the very gates of hell — unless a little weariness chance to occur between two cycles of prayer, when one may sit.[8]

The penance of allowing oneself to be locked up in a cave seems also to have been practised. In the *Life of St Brendan* it is related that when the saint was ten years old he struck a little girl who wanted to mount the chariot on which he was sitting in order to play with him. Bishop Erc rebuked him and Brendan asked for a penance. Bishop Erc said to him: 'Go into this cave till morning . . . and remain there alone till I come to thee to-morrow'.[9] In the Irish life of St Rúadán,

---

[7] *ibid.,* p. 48.

[8] Ludwig Bieler, *The Irish Penitentials* (Dublin, 1963), p. 279, par. 8.

[9] C. Plummer (ed. and tr.), *Bethada Náem nÉrenn: Lives of Irish Saints* (2 vols, Oxford, 1922), i. and ii. 46, par. vii. See A. T. Lucas, 'Souterrains: the literary evidence', *Béaloideas,* xxxix-xli (1971-73), 186.

it is related that the saint dug a cave in his oratory in order to hide the king of Connacht, Aedh Guaire, who was flying from the wrath of the king of Tara. The monastery was known as *Poll Ruadháin* (Rúadán's Hole). One version of the Latin life explains this name in the following way: 'that is, Rúadán's cave, either because the saint made it to hide him *(Aedh)* or to punish himself'. This last remark shows that being voluntarily locked up in a cave was understood to be an ascetical practice.[10]

Yet this form of pilgrimage is most original. A careful analysis in the light of the medieval mentality of H. of Saltrey's account of the origin of St Patrick's Purgatory enables one to identify the existence of an anchoretic tradition in Lough Derg that the pilgrimage has adopted and preserved. Originally the idea of pilgrimage was associated in the first place with a journey outside one's kingdom within Ireland and in the second place with a journey overseas because the heroic quality of the torments of a voluntary exile and voyage, either without a specific aim or towards some famous shrine, was the means to reach an ascetic ideal. The literary examples of these voyages were recalled in the *immrama*. But under the influence of the anchoretic movement which inspired holy men and women to retire 'to the desert' or 'to a hard prison of stone',[11] that is to live in solitude (very often near a monastery) in order to give themselves up to the contemplative life, pilgrimage also became equivalent to a life in reclusion. In the *Old-Irish Penitential* (III, 6) one reads:

> As for him who desires to reach the pitch of perfectness, he distributes all he has to the poor and needy and goes on a pilgrimage, or lives in destitution in a communal church till he goes to Heaven.[12]

The *Annals of the Four Masters* have kept names of men and women who have opted for this type of pilgrimage:

---

[10] *ibid.*, 171-172, Lucas refers to *Vitae Sanctorum Hiberniae*, ed. C. Plummer (2 vols, Oxford 1910), ii. 246, n. 10.

[11] W. Stokes (ed. and tr.), 'Cuimmín's poem on the Saints of Ireland', *Zeitschrift für Celtische Philologie*, i (1897), 59-73. One reads with regard to St Molaise of Devenish: 'My Laise of the lake (Erne) loved to be in a hard prison of stone'.

[12] Bieler, *The Irish Penitentials*, p. 267. See Kathleen Hughes, 'The changing theory and practice of Irish pilgrimage', *Journal of Ecclesiastical History*, xi (1960), 143-151; John Ryan, *Irish Monasticism* (Dublin, 1986 reprint), pp. 261-262; Jean Leclercq, 'Monachisme et Pérégrination du IXe au XIIe siècle', *Studia Monastica*, iii (1961), 33-52; T. M. Charles-Edwards, 'The social background to Irish *peregrinatio*', *Celtica*, xi (1976), 43-59.

In 610: Gorman, (of) Mughdhorna *(the Mourne district)*, from whom are the Mac Cuinns, and who was a year (living) on the water of Tibraid-Fingin *(St Finghin's Well near Teampull Finghin, at Clonmacnois)*, on his pilgrimage at Cluain-mic-Nois, died.

In 704: Beg Boirche, King of the Ulidia, took a (pilgrim's) staff, and died on his pilgrimage at the end of twelve years afterwards.

In 834: Aedhagan, son of Torbach, Abbot of Lughmhadh *(Louth)*, died on his pilgrimage at Cluain-mic-Nois.

In 1063: Gormlaith, daughter of Cathal, son of Ruaidhri, died on her pilgrimage at Ard-Macha *(Armagh)*.

There are other examples.[13] And in every case pilgrimage ends by the (natural) death of the pilgrim, which means that a pilgrimage was undertaken for a lifetime. When stated, the places mentioned are (in order of popularity): Clonmacnois, Iona, Rome, Cologne, Armagh, Clonard, Lismore, Glendalough, Roscrea and Killaloe. The idea of a journey is retained as there is a movement from one place to another before entering a life of reclusion.

When H. of Saltrey states that many entered the cave but never came back, he in fact reveals the former existence of a pilgrimage that a recluse would enter upon for the rest of his life and accordingly would never be seen again. It is this reference to the anchoretic tradition which seems to have been misunderstood and to have left the door open to imaginative speculation. There are other instances in the *Tractatus* which prove the existence of an anchoretic tradition. The ritual of entering the pit, for example, is somehow similar to the ritual of entry into reclusion. H. of Saltrey relates that the pilgrim spends fifteen days praying and fasting in the Church. He continues:

> . . . the prior summons the neighbouring clergy and in the morning during the celebration of mass the penitent is strengthened by holy communion and sprinkled with holy water blessed at the same service. Then he is led to the door of the Purgatory accompanied by a procession and litany. As the prior opens the doors in front of everyone he warns him once again about the attacks of the demons and about the many persons lost in this pit. If, however, the penitent is firm in his intention, after receiving benediction from all the

---

[13] See the list compiled from the *Annals of the Four Masters* by John Ryan, 'Saint Patrick's Purgatory', *Studies*, xxi (1932), 450.

priests, he commends himself to the prayers of all, impresses the sign of the cross on his forehead with the correct hand, and enters. The prior immediately bolts the door. The procession then retires to the church and the next day, again in the morning, it returns from the church to the door of the pit and the prior opens the door. And if the man has come back, he is taken to the church in which he remains for another fifteen days intent on prayers and vigils. But if on the next day at the same hour he does not appear to have returned, the prior bolts the doors and they all withdraw, certain of his loss.[14]

The sixth-century description by Gregory of Tours *(History of the Franks,* VI, 29) of the entry into reclusion of a nun of the monastery of Ste Croix of Poitiers is quite enlightening:

The nun asked permission [from the Abbess St Radegund] to live there as a recluse. This was granted. All the other nuns assembled, with their lamps lighted. They sang psalms together and then their sister was taken in procession to the spot, the blessed Radegund leading her by the hand. They all bade her farewell and she gave to each the kiss of peace. Then she was enclosed in her cell and the door through which she had entered was bricked up.[15]

The later descriptions of entry into reclusion (the earliest written ritual dates from the twelfth century) do not differ greatly from these accounts. The candidate had to ask permission from the bishop or (if he lived in a monastery) the abbot. The ceremony was public and the first part was a Mass presided over sometimes by the bishop but more often by the abbot or a priest. The ritual was of a penitential nature and marked by the idea of death to the world. Then a procession accompanied the recluse to the cell, which was very often called a 'sepulchre'. The officiating cleric blessed the cell and the altar while prayers and hymns from the Mass of the dead were said and sung. The recluse was sprinkled with dust in the same way that earth is thrown on the coffin lowered into the grave. The door was then closed and either locked or sealed.[16]

The story of the prior with only one tooth, an account situated between the revelation of the Purgatory to St Patrick and the description of the ritual of admission to the Purgatory and which

---

[14] Picard and Pontfarcy, *St Patrick's Purgatory,* p. 50.

[15] Gregory of Tours, *History of the Franks,* tr. Lewis Thorpe (Harmandsworth, 1983).

[16] See Dom Louis Gougaud, *Ermites et Reclus* (Vienne, 1928), Chap. III: 'L'entrée en réclusion et son cérémonial', pp. 66-75.

appears out of place in the structure of the introduction, is in fact another testimony to the existence of an anchoretic tradition in Lough Derg. Henry relates that after the death of St Patrick there was an old prior of the community who 'had a cell arranged beside the canons' dormitory'. The explanation given was that this was 'in order not to seem to impose the annoyance of the infirmities of old age on the others'. From their dormitory the younger brothers often heard angels singing:

> 'Blessed are you and blessed is the tooth which is in your mouth, which has never been touched by delectable food.' For his food was dry bread and salt and his drink was cold water.[17]

This life of the prior with one tooth does not appear to be unlike the lives led by the old men on Station Island. In 1200 Peter of Cornwall, prior of Holy Trinity, Aldgate, London, reports:

> There is in that small island *(that is Station Island)* a small chapel, where old men dwell permanently living an anchoretic life, who drink nothing but water mixed with milk and in the Lenten season they always feed on oaten bread containing a third part of ashes.[18]

This suggests also that Reglis (also found written Regles or Rigles), the name of the Church that St Patrick is supposed to have built near the pit,[19] may well refer to this small chapel rather than to the church of the monastery.[20] It has often been understood as being the church of the priory because of the connection between *reglis* (Irish *reiclés)* and *regula*. It was indeed generally used of a church connected with a monastery.[21] However, it is thought to have been borrowed from the Latin *reclusum* and has in Irish two older meanings which are complementary. One is *'an oratory or small church* built by an Irish saint for his own use' and the other *'a*

---

[17] Picard and Pontfarcy, *St Patrick's Purgatory*, p. 49.

[18] Robert Easting, 'Peter of Cornwall's account of St Patrick's Purgatory', *Analecta Bollandiana*, xcvii (1979), 413, 59-61. S. Leslie, *St Patrick's Purgatory. A record from history and literature* (London, 1932), pp. 11-12, revised translation. This is the last part of the passage quoted below p. 18.

[19] See above pp. 8-9.

[20] See also Robert Easting, 'An edition of Owayne Miles and other Middle English texts concerning Saint Patrick's Purgatory', (unpublished D. Phil. thesis, University of Oxford, 1976), pp. cxxxviii-cxlv.

[21] In the *Annals* it was used with special reference to the monasteries of Armagh and Derry. See P. J. Dunning, 'The Arroasian order in medieval Ireland', *Irish Historical Studies*, iv (1945), 305-6.

monastic cell , the hut occupied by an Irish monk in a coenobitic settlement and in general an anchorite cell'.[22] The oratory of a recluse was either a little room adjacent to his cell or was situated in a corner of or a recess in the single room in which he lived.[23] Therefore Peter of Cornwall's statement reveals not only the existence of a cell-cum-oratory on Station Island but also a mode of life similar to that of the old prior with one tooth. When James Yonge — who gave an account of the pilgrimage made in 1411, by the Hungarian Laurence Rathold of Pászthó — declares in his description of Station Island that the main part of the island is called, in Irish, Regles,[24] this would refer to the fact that the meaning of *regles* includes also the plot or the enclosure around the oratory built by the saint.[25] Therefore H. of Saltrey did not realize that there were two different places — two islands to be precise — and that Station Island may have been used as 'a desert' for the monastery of Saints' Island. If the penitential beds (the low-walled circles of stone around which pilgrims gyrate) are remnants of beehive cells, they would be the archaeological proof of the existence of an anchoretic settlement on Station Island.

The pilgrimage to Lough Derg can be seen as an adaptation of the anchoretic life for a short period of time rather than for a lifetime. In this perspective, the entering into the cave appears to be a dramatization of the symbolic death that the recluse goes through, and the specified time of a day and a night to be spent in the cave can be understood as a metaphor of totality.[26] While penitential exercise for a short period of time is in accordance with the fact that pilgrimage was also a penance imposed for some sin and for a limited period[27] — in the penitential books, it was mentioned along

[22] Maud Joynt, *Contributions to a Dictionary of the Irish Language* (Dublin, 1944), Letter R, col. 31. See also J. Vendryes, *Lexique Etymologique de l'Irlandais ancien. Lettres RS* (Dublin/Paris, 1974), R 12. I thank Professor Próinséas Ní Chatháin for this reference.

[23] Gougaud, *Ermites et Reclus,* pp. 88-89.

[24] H. Delehaye, 'Le pèlerinage de Laurent de Pászthó', *Analecta Bollandiana*, xxvii (1908), 49, lines 9-10. See also below p. 162.

[25] Joynt, *Contributions to a Dictionary of the Irish Language,* Letter R. article *reiclés.*

[26] One is reminded in *Tochmarc Étaíne* (The Wooing of Étaín) of the trick that Dagda imagined so that his son, the Mac Óc, could get possession of the Brug of Elcmar. He suggested that the Mac Óc should threaten Elcmar's life and Elcmar would offer him something in exchange for his life. The Mac Óc should then ask Elcmar for the kingship for a day and a night, because 'it is in days and nights that the world is spent'. See Osborn Bergin and R. I. Best (eds and trs), *Ériu,* xii (1938), 146-147.

[27] Hughes, 'The changing theory', 150.

with exile, fasting and corporal punishment[28] — St Patrick's Purgatory is nevertheless a pilgrimage self-imposed like the entry into reclusion. This is emphasized in the ritual of admission and repeated in the account of Owein's undertaking. One reads:

> . . . as the bishop was scolding him on account of his sins and telling him that he had seriously offended God, he cried aloud the inner contrition of his heart and vowed to carry out a suitable penance at the bishop's pleasure. And as the bishop wanted to impose a penance according to the measure of his sin, Owein answered: 'Since you declare that I have so greatly offended my Creator, I will take on a penance more arduous than any penance. I will, with your encouragement, enter Saint Patrick's Purgatory'.[29]

It must have been this new opportunity to do penance as an anchorite which created the belief that it was the most arduous form of penance and therefore attracted the boldest pilgrims.[30] Without any doubt great torments, great spiritual happiness and perhaps visions were part of such an experience. Indeed the fact of being enclosed in a narrow dark place, the more so after having fasted for several days, would as psychological studies suggest have a disorientating effect on most people.

The modern pilgrimage to Lough Derg has been reduced to three days. But it is an extraordinary synthesis, extending even to our own days the medieval conception of pilgrimage. It includes a journey (represented by the voyage in the boat towards the island), a period of time spent in retirement (represented by the three days on the island), a symbolic death to this world (represented by the vigil in the church which has replaced the twenty-four hours in the cave) and penitential exercises which comprise fasting (tea or coffee and oatbread only once a day), walking barefoot, confessing one's sins and reciting specific patterns of prayers around the 'beds', around and in the church, and while standing or kneeling facing the lake.

Descriptions of the place of pilgrimage

Although H. of Saltrey offers the earliest description of the

---

[28] Cyril Vogel, 'Le pèlerinage pénitentiel', *Revue des Sciences Religieuses*, xxxviii (1964), 113-118.

[29] Picard and Pontfarcy, *St Patrick's Purgatory*, pp. 50-52.

[30] In Ireland there still exists the belief that this pilgrimage is for those who have committed some serious sin which needs to be atoned for in a special way.

pilgrimage, he is rather vague about the place of its happening. He does not name the diocese to which the Purgatory of St Patrick belongs nor the bishop Owein went to see. He does not mention any lake or any island. Fortunately two other authors gave more information. The first is Gerald of Wales in his *Topography of Ireland*, written about 1186. He approaches reality when he mentions a lake in Ulster as a place where extraordinary things happen:

> There is a lake in Ulster which contains an island divided into two parts.
>
> One part contains a very beautiful church with a great reputation for holiness, and is well worth seeing. It is distinguished above all other churches by the visitation of angels and the visible and frequent presence of local saints.
>
> But the other part of the island is stony and ugly and is abandoned to the use of evil spirits only. It is nearly always the scene of gatherings and processions of evil spirits, plain to be seen by all. There are nine pits in that part, and if anyone by any chance should venture to spend the night in any one of them — and there is evidence that some rash persons have at times attempted to do so — he is seized immediately by malignant spirits, and is crucified all night with such severe torments, and so continuously afflicted with many unspeakable punishments of fire and water and other things, that, when morning comes, there is found in his poor body scarcely even the smallest trace of life surviving. They say that if a person once undergoes these torments because of a penance imposed on him, he will not have to endure the pains of hell — unless he commit very serious sin.[31]

In the second version of the *Topography of Ireland*, written between 1187 and 1189, Gerald (certainly under the influence of H. of Saltrey's account)[32] adds that the place is named St Patrick's Purgatory. Although originally he did not know what the place was called, he is nevertheless the first person to situate it in Ulster and in a lake. But he mentions only one island. The fact that it is divided into two parts, one pleasant and one stony, may allude to the two islands. Though this division of Station Island will be confirmed in 1411 by James Yonge in his account of the pilgrimage of the

---

[31] Gerald of Wales, *The History and Topography of Ireland*, tr. J. J. O'Meara (Harmondsworth, 1982), p. 61.

[32] Pontfarcy, 'Le *Tractatus*', 463-464.

Hungarian Laurence Rathold of Pászthó,[33] it may indeed be a reminiscence of Gerald's account. The nine pits situated in the demonic part must be a reference to the penitential beds.[34] Gerald is the first to mention these beds or pits which play an important role in the penitential exercises of the pilgrimage, but his confusing them with the cave is interesting. St Kevin's bed at Glendalough is a grotto or a cave near the upper lake, to which the saint used to retire.

When in 1200 Peter of Cornwall started to assemble a collection of visions, his first item was H. of Saltrey's *Tractatus* which is followed by an account of what Peter heard about St Patrick's Purgatory.[35] In the first part of the account, Peter explains how he got his information from Bricius, an ex-monk of Mellifont and abbot of the monastery of St Patrick (tentatively identified with the monastery of Newry).[36] Bricius heard it in 1170 from a certain Walter, a monk of Mellifont, who learned about St Patrick's Purgatory while he was in Down, accompanying a certain bishop Laurence. Then follows a preliminary description of St Patrick's Purgatory in which appears the information known from H. of Saltrey about the cave *(fossa)* and the information given by Gerald of Wales about the penitential beds, which are no longer pits *(foveas)* but seats *(sedes)*. Peter, however, is not sure which of the two is Purgatory. He relates:

> Walter told Bricius, who told me, that opinions are divided concerning the entrance of the Purgatory itself. For some say that its entrance is through a door as is contained in the book . . . written

[33] See below p. 161.

[34] In 1517, Chiericati did not see any beds but mentioned three cells *(campana)* — dedicated to St Brigid, St Patrick and St Columba — that pilgrims must visit. (See M. Purcell, 'St Patrick's Purgatory: Francesco Chiericati's letter to Isabella d'Este', *Seanchas Ardmhacha*, xii, 2 (1987), 7-8). In the Appendix to the Introduction, note xvi, p. xl of the *Martyrology of Donegal* compiled in 1630 by Michael O'Clery, (eds J. Todd and W. Reeves, Dublin, 1864), one finds: *There are five beds of hard penance there, round which the pilgrims go, the Bed of Patrick, of Columcille, of Brigid, of Adamnan, and of Dabeog. This is the testimony of Fergal. But the bc.mi.* (sic) *says that he saw but two beds there, viz., Patrick's and Colum's. 48 (hours) without food, without drink. 9 days there altogether. A pilgrimage during the day, and prayers. The baking of bread must be without salt. Loch-gerc is its name.* In 1666, on Carve's Map of Station Island, (see below p. 186), the six penitential beds and the names of the saints attributed to them are as they are today. The larger one is dedicated to St Patrick and that adjacent to it dedicated to SS Dabeoc *(Abog* on the map) and Molaisse. The four others are to St Brendan, St Brigid, St Catherine and St Colmcille.

[35] R. Easting, 'Peter of Cornwall's account', 397-416. Dr R. Easting is the first to have studied and published this account, though the first half of it has been translated by Leslie, *Saint Patrick's Purgatory*, pp. 11-12.

[36] *ibid.*, 410, n. 1.

about the Purgatory of Patrick *(that is H. of Saltrey's* Tractatus). But others say there are certain seats outside the courtyard of an old man, who dwells there, and that they are set in some kind of a lawn or a garden. Whoever enters one of these seats, soon come Demons, as it appears to him, who lead him through diverse places or torments. It is possible that all that they say does not happen to him really in the body but spiritually in the imagination.[37]

Then follows the first description of the two islands, although Peter mentions a river *(flumen)* rather than a lake. This can be explained by the fact that Saints' Island is so near the shore that it was linked to it by a bridge. This unusual feature must have induced the belief that the water surrounding Saints' Island was a river. The description is preceded by an account of the geographical situation of St Patrick's Purgatory. The distance covered in a day seems very great when compared with that of the Hungarian pilgrim Laurence of Pászthó[38] and the Italian pilgrim Antonio Mannini.[39]

. . . the Purgatory is four day's journey distant towards the North from the City of Dublin, for it is one day's journey from Dublin to Mellifont and one day's journey from Mellifont to the Monastery of St Patrick [Bricius' monastery] and one day's journey from that Monastery to Armagh the See of the Archbishopric or Primacy, in which place the Schools of Ireland are customarily held. And from Armagh it is almost one day's journey to a certain Island, which is slightly large, called Mabeoch. Between this Island and the small Island in which is the Purgatory already mentioned, there is only a river, and people can pass from the larger Island to the smaller with a small boat. The larger Island is entirely surrounded by this river and this island is held in such authority and reverence amongst the natives that nobody dares injure another within the space of a day's journey from the water . . . There is a Church in this Island in which Canons serve God. Whoever wishes to enter the Purgatory will cross through this Island to the aforesaid small Island. There is in that small Island a small chapel . . .[40]

It should be pointed out that Gerald of Wales does not mention the cave and that Peter of Cornwall only reports (what he knows

---

[37] *ibid.,* 411-412, lines 26-37; Leslie's translation revised.
[38] See below pp. 159-160.
[39] See below pp. 181-2.
[40] Easting, 'Peter of Cornwall's account', 411-512, lines 39-51 and 57-65; Leslie's translation revised. For the remainder of this description see above p. 13.

from H. of Saltrey) that the entrance is through a door. Henry, therefore, is the first writer to have focused attention on the pit. But his description is rather vague. He declares that the pit — when shown by the Lord to St Patrick — was round and dark inside. Then the saint enclosed it within a wall and doors.[41] Owein, when locked into it, went on boldly for a very long time until a tiny glimmer began to shine from the opposite direction. It was not long before he arrived in a field where there was a hall.[42] For more details, one must wait for the descriptions of fourteenth- and fifteenth-century pilgrims.[43] The Hungarian George Grissaphan, who came in 1353, says that he descended by a spiral staircase into a pit which was over two miles deep. For a mile and a half the way was pitch-dark and then the light increased. At the end of the stairs there was a plain with a chapel,[44] as in the description of Owein. The Englishman Sir William Lisle, who came in 1395, went, according to Froissart, three or four paces down as if into a cellar. Hot vapour rose and forced him and his friend to sit on the stone stairs and they fell asleep.[45] The Catalan Ramon de Perellós, who came to Lough Derg in 1397, wrote that the cave was four cubits in length, with a turn to the left on the inside. After having felt sick and fallen asleep he was awakened by a great thunder and slid about six cubits downwards; then the cave widened and, going further down, he reached a large hall.[46] Ramon's description distinguishes between a cave of small dimensions with a turn near the surface (as pilgrims of the fifteenth century will testify) and a vast place further down (which accords with the descriptions given by Owein and George Grissaphan). One would be inclined to think that Ramon tried to reconcile what he saw with what he had read. Yet one should not forget that these testimonies of real experiences may express different levels of reality either factual or psychological.

The pilgrims of the fifteenth century give fairly consistent descriptions of the cave. The first part measured eleven palms in length, three in width and four in height, and the second chamber did not exceed nine palms by three by four for the Hungarian

---

[41] Picard and Pontfarcy, *St Patrick's Purgatory,* pp. 47-48.

[42] *ibid.,* p. 53.

[43] L. Bieler, 'St. Patrick's Purgatory. Contributions towards an historical topography', *Irish Ecclesiastical Record,* xciii (1960), 135-144.

[44] See below pp. 133-4.

[45] See below p. 67.

[46] See below pp. 114-5.

Laurence Rathold of Pászthó who came in 1411.[47] For the Italian Antonio Mannini, who also came in 1411, the cave is nine feet plus a southward turn of three feet in length, three feet in width and high enough for a man to kneel but not to stand upright.[48] For the Walloon Ghillebert de Lannoy, who came in 1430, the cave is nine feet and then turns for five feet towards the south-west, being about two feet in width and three in height.[49] A seventeenth-century drawing[50] shows that it was a gallery covered with stones. The last section of it is at an angle to the entrance. In 1727 John Richardson gave the following description of it (before it was demolished in 1780 because it had become unsafe for the large throngs of pilgrims):

> . . . 10 feet distant from the church; it was 22 feet long, 2 feet 1 inch wide, and 3 feet high. It hath a bending within six feet of the far end, where there is a very small window, or spike-hole, to let in some light and air to the pilgirms that are shut up in it. There is little or none of it under ground, and it seems never to have been sunk deeper than the rock. It is built of stone and clay, huddled together, covered with broad stones, and all overlaid with earth.[51]

In spite of divergences of perception all these pilgrims spoke about the same cave and visited the same place on Station Island. The case of the Dutch canon from Eymstadt, who came on a pilgrimage at the end of the fifteenth century, is more problematic. Having no money to give to the bishop, the local prince and the prior, he was eventually accepted. There is no evidence that he was brought to Station Island or even that he went to Saints' Island. Furthermore, the cavity into which he went appears to be quite different. The sacristan lowered him by a rope into a deep pit. Following his complaint to the pope (as he saw no devils), the cave was ordered to be closed.[52]

From all these descriptions it is not clear what the original purpose of this cave was. The most convincing suggestion — which

---

[47] See below pp. 162-3.

[48] See below p. 184.

[49] C. Potvin (ed.), *Oeuvres de Ghillebert de Lannoy* (Louvain, 1878), passage translated by Leslie, *St Patrick's Purgatory*, p. 39. See also below pp. 93-4.

[50] See Thomas Carve's map of Station Island, below p. 186.

[51] John Richardson, *The Great Folly, Superstition and Idolatry of Pilgrimages in Ireland; especially of that to Patrick's Purgatory* (Dublin, 1727), p. 8.

[52] See below p. 195.

was put forward in 1900 by Mac Ritchie[53] and supported by Lucas— is that it was a souterrain.[54] Indeed the following general description given by the latter explains the different features of the cavity visited by the pilgrims:

> A souterrain is an underground structure consisting of a low passage or a series of them . . . The passage is generally straight but is sometimes curved and, exceptionally, two adjacent ones lie at different levels, communicating with each other by an aperture partially concealed. Frequently the passage opens into one or more chambers, usually circular in plan and beehive in shape . . . Access to the chamber from the passage is normally to be gained only by creeping through a short low subsidiary passage. Chambers and passage are sometimes provided with narrow stone-built ventilation ducts opening on to the ground surface above . . . These structures vary greatly in size and complexity, some consisting of a single relatively short passage with or without a chamber . . .[55]

When one considers that a souterrain could have been entered either by the gallery or by the top (that is directly through a hole set in the roof of the chamber),[56] there emerges a possible explanation of the contradictory descriptions of, on the one hand, a vertical cavity (as seen by Grissaphan and the canon of Eymstadt, if the latter went to the same place) and, on the other hand, a horizontal descending cavity.

The pagan past and Lough Derg's first saints

Very little is known about the first period of monastic life on Saints' Island. The pagan past and the geographical situation of Lough Derg may have played a not insignificant part in attracting Christian settlements. It is located in the barony of Tír Aedha (Tirhugh) in the southern part of Cenél Conaill. But the range of mountains which surrounds it makes it appear as if turning its back to Donegal. It is easily accessible only from the north-east by the river Derg and from the south through the lower lands between Lough Erne and Lough Derg. The lake and the river Derg were

---

[53] D. Mac Ritchie, 'A note on St Patrick's Purgatory', *The Journal of the Royal Society of Antiquaries of Ireland*, xxx (1900), 165-167.

[54] Lucas, 'Souterrains', 189-191.

[55] *ibid.*, 165.

[56] I owe this information to Professor Michael Herity. See also Lucas, 'Souterrains', 174.

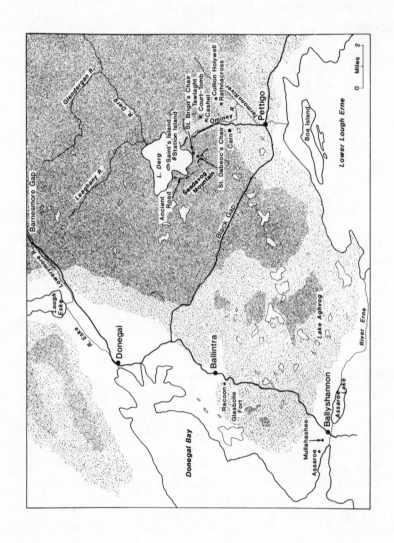

Map 1 : Lough Derg and its surroundings.

therefore an important link of communication between the Erne and the Foyle. The place names and ancient sites found precisely between Lough Derg and Lough Erne suggest that Christianity has superseded a strong pagan cult at this particular place. The countryside recalls the presence of St Dabeoc. A mountain in the south-west is called Seadavog Mountain. This name comes from the townland of *Suidhe Dhabheóg* where, on the top of a hill, turning its back to Lough Derg and set in front of a view of Lough Erne, there is the saint's seat which appears like a cairn-shaped eminence with a perpendicular trough in front of it.[57] A quarter of a mile northwards, on the shore of the lake, St Brigid has her Chair, which is a large rock looking like a reclining seat. On the 1932 Ordnance Survey Map, the words *Originally St Dabheoc's* are printed beside *St Bridget's Chair*.[58] But nothing of the kind is found on the 1907 Ordnance Survey Map. St Brigid is particularly venerated at Station Island where she has a penitential bed in her name and also her cross on a stone inserted in the outside of the wall of the church. Pilgrims, standing with their backs turned to it and their arms outstretched, three times renounce the world, the flesh and the Devil. She may well be the goddess Brigit whose cult may have been important in this area. But if the saint of Kildare has really superseded St Dabeoc, it might mean that her introduction in this area had a political meaning. K. McCone points out how, in the *Life of Tigernach* (the patron of Clones, whose life was written at the end of the eighth century), Brigid is shown as having a decisive influence on Tigernach's career. He understands this as expressing Clones' wish to be protected by the remote powerful church of Kildare in order to avoid the threatening power of its close neighbour, Armagh.[59] In this light St Brigid's Chair may have been a convenient landmark which delineated the extent of her power.

About a mile to the south-east of Lough Derg, that is in the direction of Lough Erne, there are very ancient sites. On the slope of Meenagassagh hill in the townland of Tawlaght there is a very large (34m) but much damaged cashel[60] and next to it near the head

[57] In 1903, D. O'Connor, in his *St Patrick's Purgatory, Lough Derg*, (Dublin, 1903) gave the following description (in a note p. 38): 'The cavity, or pit in front of "St Dabheoc's Seat", measures in length 3 feet; in depth it is 2 feet 8 inches; its average width is 2 feet; but the opening gradually slopes to a width of one foot at the bottom'.

[58] Leslie, *St Patrick's Purgatory*, the map at the end of the book.

[59] Kim McCone, 'Clones and her neighbours in the early period: hints from some Airgialla Saints' Lives', *Clogher Record*, xi (1984), 321-323.

[60] B. Lacy, *Archaeological Survey of County Donegal* (Lifford, 1983), par. 910.

of the Ominey (Owenea) River a court-tomb. This is a ceremonial courtyard set in front of a gallery divided into two chambers. The gallery is covered by a long cairn with the court at the east end.[61] A mile further south there is the Holy Well of Cullion[62] to which, according to O'Connor, pilgrims of the last century, after completing their Stations at Lough Derg, were accustomed to pay a visit, each one bringing with him from the shore of the lake a rounded pebble which he left at the well as a votive gift.[63] Next to the Holy Well of Cullion, on the summit of Drumawark hill, standing in the middle of a ring of raised earth, there was until 1880 the termonn-cross of Termonn-Dabeoc. On the 1907 Ordnance Map the place is called *Rathnacross*. At the beginning of the nineteenth century, a deep pit was dug in the eastern rim of this fort and 'about three or four feet from the surface, a regular floor or pavement of burnt stones was discovered'.[64]

It is therefore possible that the area between Lough Derg and Lough Erne was an important place of worship during pagan times. Furthermore the nearby Boa Island of Lough Erne bears perhaps the name of the war goddess Badhbh.[65] Máire MacNeill thinks that Lough Derg is not a Lughnasa site.[66] Since St Brigid's feast day is on 1 February, it may well have been an Imbolc site. Brigid's name derives from the root *brig 'high, exalted' and in the twelfth century Gerald of Wales attests the existence at Kildare of an inextinguishable fire attended by nuns.[67]

Considering the name given to the cave, it is tempting to think that St Patrick retired in this particular area, but there is no evidence either from history or tradition that he went to Lough Derg. The itinerary of St Patrick, as described by Tírechán[68] — who wrote towards the end of the seventh century, that is three hundred years after St Patrick — and as found in the two versions (one in

[61] *ibid.*, p. 14. The description of the Tawlaght court-tomb is given in par. 44. 'The gallery is about 6m long and is divided into two chambers by jambs. A fine lintel, 2.3m long, rests above the entrance jambs. The southern jamb is flanked by a single court stone. The structure is flanked by a large amount of cairn which seems to have been at least 23m long (E.W).'

[62] See below p. 46 n. 38.

[63] O'Connor, *St Patrick's Purgatory*, p. 53.

[64] *ibid.*, pp. 48-52.

[65] See P. W. Joyce, *The Origin and History of Irish Names of Places* (Dublin, 1871), p. 298, n.

[66] Máire MacNeill, *The Festival of Lughnasa* (Oxford, 1962), p. 525.

[67] Gerald of Wales, *The History and Topography of Ireland*, tr. J. J. O'Meara, pp. 81-82, pars 67-68. See also Francis John Byrne, *Irish Kings and High-Kings* (London, 1973), p. 155.

[68] L. Bieler (ed. and tr.), *The Patrician Texts in the Book of Armagh* (Dublin, 1979), pp. 160-161, par. 47.

Irish and the other in Latin) of the *Tripartite Life of St Patrick*,[69] written in the tenth century from oral sources, does not associate St Patrick and Lough Derg, though the saint moved in the vicinity. He entered Tír Conaill between Assaroe (near Ballyshannon) and the sea. At a place called *Rath-cunga,* identified with Racoon, situated south of Ballintra,[70] he founded a church. Then at *Ard-fotha* (identified with the massive hillfort of Glasbolie, situated south of Racoon)[71] St Patrick foretold the birth of King Domnal mac Aodha maic Ainmire who died in 642.[72] St Patrick afterwards came back towards the river Erne, near Assaroe, and the two versions of the *Tripartite Life* agree that at a place named *Síth-Aodha,* identified with Mullanashee fort, now in the west part of Ballyshannon town,[73] St Patrick blessed Fergus, Conall's son and predicted the birth of their descendant Colmcille. Then Tírechán, before mentioning that the saint moved northwards and went through the Gap of Barnesmore to the plain of *Mag Itha* (situated west of Derry), adds that St Patrick

> founded a church in *Mag Latrain* and the great church of *Sirdrommo,* which is held by the community of *Daminis* (Devenish) in *Doburbur.*[74]

These places are unidentified but on several occasions have been associated by modern critics with the old parish of Carn (Templecarn), situated on the ancient road between Pettigo and Lough Derg, because tradition holds that this church was founded by St Patrick.[75] If this was so, it is strange that the author of the *Tripartite Life,* who loves to recall so many folk traditions about St

---

[69] The Latin Version has been edited by Colgan, *Trias Thaumaturgae* (Louvain, 1647). He calls it the *The Vita Septima.* The passages relating to the movements of St Patrick in Donegal are found on pp. 144-145, pars 111-114. The Irish version *Bethu Phátraic* has been edited by W. Stokes, *The Tripartite Life of St Patrick with other documents relating to that saint* (2 vols, London, 1887), i. 148-151; ii. 328-329, Tírechán's text.

[70] E. Hogan, *Onomasticon Goedelicum* (Dublin/London, 1910), p. 570.

[71] Lacy, *Archaeological Survey,* art. 704, p. 115.

[72] See the *Annals of the Four Masters* at the year 639.

[73] Hogan, *Onomasticon,* p. 597.

[74] Bieler, *The Patrician Texts,* p. 161, par. 47(3).

[75] J. Healy, *Life and Writings of St Patrick* (Dublin, 1905) p. 299, thought that it was *Sirdrommo* which could be identified with the old church of Templecarn. P. Ó Gallachair in 'Patrician Donegal', *Donegal Annual,* v, 1 (1962) 74-75, suggests that *Mag Latrain* refers to the land where Templecarn was situated and that the old church site of Killadeas, on the eastern shore of Lower Lough Erne, may be identified with the Patrician foundation of *Sirdrommo,* because it is situated in tates of land which had belonged to the Devenish community.

Patrick, forgot to mention one of these places referred to by
Tírechán. But the reason is that tradition previous to the twelfth
century also fails to prove the passage of the saint on this lake. The
Latin version of the *Tripartite Life* recalls an extraordinary story in
which St Patrick is linked with an island, a cave and a monster. The
story takes place not in a lonely lake of Donegal, not even in Ireland
but in the Tyrrhenian Sea.

> At one time when St Patrick was in the Tyrrhenian Sea he come to a
> spot where there were three Patricks. They were in a solitary Cave
> between mountain and sea and he begged leave to remain with them.
> They answered that they would not unless he drew water from the
> neighbouring spring. In that place was a monster which caused the
> greatest havoc amongst men. Patrick assented and went to the
> spring, and the monster leaping at his sight showed signs of joy and
> showed itself gentle and tame to him. Afterwards he drew the water
> and returned home with benediction.[76]

It is again difficult to admit that if a story of this kind existed about
Lough Derg, the author of the *Tripartite Life* did not record it.

Tírechán's aim in recalling the itinerary of St Patrick is to
enumerate the churches that St Patrick founded and the clergy he
set in each place in order to prove that the 'successor' *(coarb)* of St
Patrick could claim almost the whole island as his *paruchia*. He
declares:

> However, my heart within me is filled with the (arrowing) love for
> Patrick, because I see deserters and arch-robbers and war-lords of
> Ireland hate Patrick's territorial supremacy, because they have taken
> away from him what was his and are afraid, for if an heir of Patrick
> were to investigate his supremacy he could vindicate for him almost
> the whole island as his domain.[77]

Thus Tírechán reveals bitter rivalries between churches. He writes,
for example, about bishop Assicus, a coppersmith of St Patrick,
who was buried at the Patrician place of Racoon:

> He (was) a monk of Patrick's, but the community of Colum Cille and
> the community of Ardd Sratha *(Ardstraw)* claimed him.[78]

---

[76] *Trias Thaumaturgae*, p. 122, par. 34; Leslie's translation, *St Patrick's Purgatory*, p. 3.
[77] Bieler, *The Patrician Texts*, pp. 138-139, par. 18(2).
[78] *ibid.*, pp. 140-141, par. 22.

This shows in this area a dispute as to the extent of the ecclesiastical power of St Colmcille's community, Ardstraw and Armagh. Lough Derg however is difficult to situate in a precise ecclesiastical jurisdiction. It lies on the one hand in the boundary limits of the political territories of Tír Aedha, of the Uí Fiachrach and of the Fir Luirg of Airgialla, and on the other hand in the boundary limits of the ecclesiastical territories of the community of Colmcille, Ardstraw and Clogher. This particular setting of St Dabeoc's monastery agrees, indeed, with the tendency in early Celtic society to build monasteries on boundary lands.[79] Whatever the reason may be, the Christian community at Lough Derg does not seem to have been, at the time of Tírechán, either under the authority of Armagh or in a disputed area from the point of view of ecclesiastical jurisdiction. Two or three hundred years later, the author of the *Tripartite Life* shows also that Lough Derg and its pilgrimage has not yet become embedded in folk tradition.

Although St Dabeoc is undoubtedly the saint of Lough Derg, the most ancient festilogy, *The Martyrology of Oengus* (which dates from the eighth century), does not associate any Dabeoc with Lough Derg. But one finds at 16 December a saint called *Mo Beóóc*, who is associated with Wexford[80] and who in the gloss, written at a much later period, is connected with Lough Derg. One reads:

> *My-Beóóc, i.e. Loch Garman. Or my Beóóc of Loch Gerg in the North.*[81]

It is perhaps the same saint about whom Cuimmín records the following austerities:

> My gifted Beóóc loved (this) according to the synod of the sages, when he was sorely abrased he would plunge his head into the well.[82]

The little known about Dabeoc is found in genealogies of Irish

---

[79] Pádraig Ó Riain, 'Boundary association in Early Irish Society', *Studia Celtica*, vii (1972), 12-29. I owe this reference to Mr Charles Doherty.

[80] W. Stokes, *The Martyrology of Oengus the Culdee* (Dublin, 1905), p. 252: 'the feast of my excellent Beóóc from lustrous Ard Cáinroiss'. This place is situated between Wexford and New Ross.

[81] *ibid.*, pp. 260-261.

[82] W. Stokes, 'Cuimmín's poem on the saints of Ireland', *Zeitschrift für Celtische Philologie*, i (1897), 59-73, par. 133. See also the *Martyrology of Tallaght*, ed. M. Kelly (Dublin, 1857), pp. 168-169, at the date 24 July and the *Martyrology of Donegal*, eds J. Todd and W. Reeves (Dublin, 1864), p. 201.

saints of the twelfth century. On the one hand, he appears as descending from Trichim of the Dál Fiatach (a people who dwelt in Co. Down). In the *Recensio major* of *The Book of Leinster* composed after 1152, his ancestors are given as follows:

> Dabeoc Glinni Gerg mac *(son of)* Luanin, maic *(son of)* Dibroga, maic Thola, maic Dorblusa, maic Dichon, maic Trichim.[83]

This entry does not exist in the *The Book of Glendalough* which was compiled c. 1120-1130 and which is the source of the *Book of Leinster*.[84] The reference to the place *Glenn Gerg* is omitted in the manuscript (TCD T.2.7), the text of which was composed around 1100.[85] The equivalence of Dabeoc of Lough Derg and Dabeoc of the Dál Fiatach — which may be right, for all we know, although it seems to have been made after 1152 — is interesting. It creates a link between Dabeoc of Lough Derg and St Patrick, since it is perhaps the conversion of Dabeoc's ancestor Dichú that Muirchú writes about in his *Life of St Patrick* (I, 11), a work composed in the seventh century. Muirchú relates that when St Patrick and his party entered Strangford Lough, they landed at Inber Sláne and went inland to rest:

> They were found by the swineherd of a man who was good by nature, although a pagan, whose name was Díchu *(Dichoin* in the Latin text). He lived in the place where there is now the barn named after Patrick. The swineherd, thinking they were thieves or robbers, went to tell his master Díchu (about them), and led him upon them unawares. Díchu had come with intent to kill them, but when he saw the face of holy Patrick the Lord changed his mind for the better, and Patrick preached the faith to him, and there and then he believed Patrick — the first man to do so — and the holy man stayed with him for a few days.[86]

On the other hand, from the *Mothers of Irish Saints*, a genealogy found also in the *Book of Leinster*, Dabeoc is associated with a saint called *Mobeoc*. He is the son of Dína, daughter of the king of the Saxons, and his father is Brachan, king of Brachaineoc (that is

---

[83] Pádraig Ó Riain, *Corpus Genealogiarium sanctorum Hiberniae* (Dublin, 1985): *Recensio major* 184; *Recensio minor* 501; *Recensio metrica: Náemshenchus naém Inse Fáil* 662. 148.

[84] *ibid.*, p. xxi and lxi.

[85] *ibid.*, p. xxxvii.

[86] Bieler, *The Patrician Texts*, pp. 78-79.

Brecon in South Wales). He has ten brothers, five of whom are associated with Wexford, two with Offaly, one with Wicklow, one with Ossory and one with Scotland.[87] The interesting fact is that Dína is said to have ten sons. *Mobeoc Glinne Gerg,* however, appears not only at the end of the list but in another sentence added after the enumeration of the ten sons. Mobeoc therefore is himself the eleventh. In the *Life of St Canocus,* Brachan and Dína have seventeen children — seven daughters and ten sons, the last of whom is Saint Mobeocus.[88] In the *Welsh Genealogical Tract* of Brachaineoc, Brachan has twenty-four or twenty-five daughters and eleven sons but none of these is named Mobeoc.[89] In the *Martyrology of Donegal,* in which at 1 January his Welsh family is given, Mobheoc has eleven brothers. Finally in the *Life of St Nectan,* a Cornish saint, Brachan has twenty-four children but none of them is named Mobeoc.[90] The alleged British ancestry of Dabeoc is perhaps borne out by the fact that the prefix *do-* comes from the archaic *to- tu-* and the suffix *-óc* is derived from a British suffix (Middle Welsh *-awc).* Thurneysen states that such a hypocoristic form is found in the names of Irish monks from the sixth century onwards.[91] This *do-* form is found alternating with *mo-* 'my'.

From the twelfth century onwards St Dabeoc is undoubtedly considered an ancient and important saint. In later lives of Colmcille, Dabeoc, as many other saints do, foretells the birth of Colmcille.[92] In the seventeenth-century Irish *Life of Brendan of Clonfert,* in a passage that the compiler has incorporated, a Dabheóg, following St Molaise of Devenish, is named among the chief saints of Ireland.[93] In 1647, Colgan writes in a note about St Mobeocus:

He is called *Dabheocus* in general, and often *Beoanus* in Latin. He is the patron of a very celebrated church in a certain lake of Ulster,

[87] Ó Riain, *Corpus Genealogiarum,* par. 722.89.

[88] J. Colgan (ed.), *Acta Sanctorum* (Louvain, 1640): 'De s. Canoco', pp. 311-312.

[89] P. C. Bartrum, *Early Welsh Genealogical Tracts* (Cardiff, 1966), 14-19.

[90] *ibid.,* p. 29. See also G. H. Doble, *The Saints of Cornwall* (Oxford, 1970), Part V, 65-79.

[91] R. Thurneysen, *A Grammar of Old Irish* (Dublin, 1946), par. 271. See also J. Vendryes, 'Sur les hypocoristiques celtiques précédés de *mo* ou de *to- (do-)*', *Etudes Celtiques,* ii (1937), 254-268. I owe these references to Professor Próinséas Ní Chatháin.

[92] *Trias Thaumaturgae,* 'Quinta Vita Columbae', Chap. x, pp. 390-391. See also *Betha Colaim Chille: Life of Columcille,* eds and trs A. O'Kelleher and G. Schoepperle (University of Illinois, 1918), par. 37.

[93] Plummer, *Bethada Náem nÉrenn. Lives of Irish Saints,* i. p. 88, par. 185; ii. p. 85; see also introduction i. p. xxii.

called *Loch-Gerg,* in which is that famous Purgatory of St Patrick, consequently, either the lake itself, or the place in which it lies, is called Gleann-Gerc, where in the adjacent country St Dabheocus is held in the greatest veneration to the present day . . .[94]

There are three feast days attributed to St Dabeoc or Mobeoc in the different festilogies: the 1st of January *(Martyrology of Tallaght* and *Martyrology of Donegal),* the 24th of July *(Martyrology of Donegal)* and the 16th of December *(Martyrology of Oengus* and also the *Calendar of Cashel* according to Colgan[95]). Undisturbed by the idea that these dates may refer to different saints, O'Connor confidently thinks that 'they commemorate three important epochs of (Dabeoc's) career — probably his birth, his installation as abbot and his death'.[96]

The political significance of Lough Derg in the twelfth century

Like the interest in the genealogy of St Dabeoc, the political importance of the monastery and the tradition of St Patrick at Lough Derg seems to have appeared during the eleventh/twelfth century. The third Irish version of the *Life of St Kevin* mentions the Cave of St Patrick as the centre of pilgrimage for Ulster, while the two other versions are silent. But this third version cannot be trusted. It was written in the eighteenth century and the copyist may have added that statement. There is very little known about the pre-twelfth-century history of the monastery of Saints' Island. The statement in the *Annals of the Four Masters* that in 721 Cillene of *Locha Gercc* died, signifies that he may have been an inmate or the abbot of the monastery or also some holy man living in solitude on an island of the lake. A Viking raid according to the *Annals of the Four Masters,* in 836 destroyed all the churches of Lough Erne. The Vikings may not have spared the monastery of Saint's Island. Monastic life, however, does not seem to have disappeared. The penitential beds are thought to be ninth-century *clochan.* But in the eleventh and early twelfth century the monastery seems to have acquired some political importance since Termonn Dabeoc was twice plundered. The *Annals of Ulster* relate for the year 1070, that it was pillaged by Ruaidrí Ua Canannáin. In 1111, according to the

---

[94] *Acta Sanctorum,* 'De S. Canoco', p. 313, n. 22.

[95] *ibid.,* p. 314, n. 22.

[96] O'Connor, *St Patrick's Purgatory,* p. 3.

Annals of the Four Masters, it was plundered by the king of Connacht, Toirdhealbhach Ua Conchobhair. Then a dramatic change occurred with the arrival of the Augustinian Canons who were introduced into Ireland in the 1140s by St Malachy[97] and installed in the monastery of Saints' Island which became a priory dependent for Augustinian Canons on the abbey of SS Peter and Paul, Armagh. They were certainly responsible for the creation of the pilgrimage under the patronage of St Patrick. H. of Saltrey declares this indirectly when he states that St Patrick gave the church and the care of the Purgatory to the Augustinian Canons.[98] This anachronism points to the time when a 'cave' was specifically used as a twenty-four-hour retreat during a short-term pilgrimage and therefore to the origin of to-day's pilgrimage.

St Patrick in all fairness can be considered as the initiator of pilgrimage under all its forms. He himself defines his life of exile among the Irish as a pilgrimage *(peregrinatio).* In the *Confession* (chap. 37) St Patrick explains how God triumphed in him against the arguments of his seniors:

> It was not grace of my own, but God, who is strong in me and resists them all — as He had done when I came to the people of Ireland to preach the Gospel, and to suffer insult from unbelievers, hearing the reproach of my journeying abroad *(peregrinatio)* and many persecutions even unto bonds, and to give my free birth for the benefit of others.[99]

In the *Letter to the Soldiers of Coroticus* (chap. 17) he writes:

> I have not laboured for nothing, and my journeying abroad *(peregrinatio)* has not been in vain.[100]

His retirement on Croagh Patrick associates him also with a short-term pilgrimage. Tírechán recalls:

> And Patrick proceeded to the summit of the mountain, climbing Cruachan Aigli, and stayed there forty days and forty nights, and

[97] Dunning, 'The Arroasian order', 297-315; M-T. Flanagan, 'St Mary's Abbey, Louth, and the introduction of the Arrouaisian observance into Ireland', *Clogher Record,* x (1980), 223-234.

[98] This was also the opinion of J. Lanigan, *An Ecclesiastical History of Ireland* (Dublin, 1882), i. 368.

[99] L. Bieler (tr.), *The Works of St Patrick* (London, 1953), p. 32.

[100] *ibid.,* p. 46.

birds were troublesome to him and he could not see the face of sky
and land and sea.[101]

Moreover at Assaroe tradition associates St Patrick with a cave —
partly natural, partly carved out — in which he dwelt during his
visit. It is also traditionally thought that the same cave was occupied
by St Colmcille.[102] It is not therefore incongruous that his memory
should be attached to the pilgrimage to Lough Derg and to the cave,
but highly appropriate if a pilgrimage of this kind was an innovation
introduced by the Augustinian Canons. It became a necessity to
justify it by the name of the highest ecclesiastical authority in
Ireland. Tradition is the guarantor of legitimacy.

The sole intention of the Augustinian Canons may have been to
give a new life to the monastery by opening a short pilgrimage in the
style of the anchoretic tradition. However the creation of a
pilgrimage to a St Patrick's cave appears to be very convenient in
the light of the ecclesiastico-political events of the time. In 1111, at
the synod of Rath Breasail, Ireland was divided in two
archbishoprics — Armagh and Cashel. But at the synod of Kells in
1152 two more archbishoprics were created: Dublin, taken from
Cashel, and Tuam, taken from Armagh. The pilgrimage to Croagh
Patrick which was previously in the archdiocese of Armagh was
included in the archdiocese of Tuam. Although on the one hand
Armagh was given the primacy, on the other hand its archbishop,
Giolla Mac Liag, found himself deprived of a famous place of
pilgrimage associated precisely with the saint of which he was the
coarb.[103] The matter of the extent of the diocese of Armagh seems
to have been a major concern for Giolla Mac Liag. His predecessor
in the see, St Malachy, had already diminished the extent of
Armagh by giving the territory of Louth to the diocese of Clogher.
It is known that Giolla Mac Liag, shortly before the synod of Kells,
tried unsuccessfully to reintegrate Louth in the diocese of
Armagh.[104] This attitude, showing how much the archbishop was
concerned with the extent of the power of Armagh, leads one to
assume that the new pilgrimage to St Patrick's Purgatory could have
been a welcome replacement for the lost pilgrimage to Croagh

---

[101] Bieler, *The Patrician Texts*, pp. 152-153, par. 38 (3).

[102] S. F. Milligan, 'Descriptive sketch of places visited in connection with the Ulster Meeting',
Journal of the Royal Society of Antiquaries of Ireland, xxvi (1896), 295.

[103] See Pontfarcy, 'Le *Tractatus*', 447, n. 4.

[104] A. Gwynn, 'Armagh and Louth in the Twelfth Century', *Seanchas Ardmhacha*, i-ii (1954),
5-7.

Patrick and a means of showing his power in the borderland of the dioceses of Raphoe, Clogher and Derry. It is again very difficult to determine to which diocese Lough Derg pertained in the twelfth century. It may have been in the diocese of Clogher, in which it is found in 1300. It may have been in the diocese of Derry, as it is claimed by Fógartach Ua Cerballáin (bishop of Tír Eoghain from 1185 to 1230)[105] in a testimony added to the long version of the *Tractatus de Purgatorio sancti Patricii*.[106] The first bishop of Ardstraw, which had been one of the seats of the diocese of Tír Eoghain, was called Eoghain, and perhaps it is significant that the first known pilgrim to St Patrick's Purgatory was named Owein, the English version of Eoghain and also the name of Owein Gwynedd (+1168), a generous benefactor of the abbey of Basingwerk, the abbot of which up to 1180 was Gilbert from whom H. of Saltrey heard of Owein's journey to the otherworld. The question is not answered. The fact nevertheless remains that the promotion of the pilgrimage to Lough Derg may have served the political interests of Armagh but would not have been sufficient to raise St Patrick's Purgatory to international fame without the contribution of the Anglo-Norman-Welsh.

Indeed between 1148-1150 when Gilbert heard the story and 1184, when Henry wrote it, some thirty-five years elapsed. Suddenly, along with H. of Saltrey, two other writers, independently and at the same period between 1184 and 1186, speak of the same place. They are Jocelin of Furness, who, in his *Life of St Patrick* (chap. 172), situates St Patrick's Purgatory on Croagh Patrick[107] and Gerald of Wales in a chapter of his

---

[105] See Picard and Pontfarcy, *St Patrick's Purgatory*, pp. 24-26.

[106] *ibid.*, pp. 74-75.

[107] He writes:

> On the summit of this mountain many have the custom of watching and fasting, thinking that after this they will never enter the gates of Hell. They consider that they have obtained this from God through the merits and prayers of Patrick. Some who have spent the night there relate that they have suffered the most grievous torments, which they think have purified them from all their sins. For this reason many call this place the Purgatory of St Patrick. (See E. Swift (tr.), *The Life and Acts of Saint Patrick*, London, 1809, pp. 189-190, translation revised.)

As is clear from information contained in the *Annals of Loch Cé* (which states that in 1113 a thunderbolt fell on the mountain on the eve of St Patrick and killed thirty pilgrims), Croagh Patrick was already a popular place for a short-term pilgrimage. In a paper (entitled 'Le Purgatoire de St Patrick') read at the meeting of the Centre International de Recherches et de Documentation sur le Monachisme Celtique (CIRDOMOC), in the abbaye of Landevennec on 10 July 1988, Bernard Merdrignac put forward the idea that the Purgatory of St Patrick was initially on Croagh Patrick.

Topography of Ireland.[108] This sudden interest can only be explained by the Anglo-Norman-Welsh activity in Ireland. Gilbert between 1155 and presumably 1180 was abbot of Basingwerk (North Wales). In 1169 the Norman-Welsh arrived in Ireland in response to the invitation of Diarmaid Mac Murchadha. In 1177 John de Courcy took possession of a territory covering the South of Armagh and the North of Down (the old domain of the Dál Fiatach). In the 1180s, he expressed an interest in St Patrick. He brought Jocelin from his monastery of Furness, established him in the monastery of Inch in Down and asked him to write the life of St Patrick. In 1186 he showed his readiness to support the bishop of Down for the Ceremony of the Translation of the Relics of St Patrick, St Brigid and St Colmcille to the main part of the Cathedral of Down. He does not appear to have had any connection with Gilbert or H. of Saltrey. It seems nevertheless, from the Anglo-Norman-Welsh point of view, a very happy coincidence that St Dabeoc of Lough Derg had ancestors precisely in Down and Wales. This close link with Down is again underlined in 1200, when Peter of Cornwall following information given to him writes, albeit erroneously, that St Patrick's Purgatory was situated in the diocese of Down.[109] One can therefore conclude that the encouragement of the pilgrimage to Lough Derg, its patronage by St Patrick and the interest in the ancestry and family of St Dabeoc had a crucial importance from the political point of view both of Armagh and of the Anglo-Norman-Welsh settlers. It must have been this interest in Ireland which brought back to Gilbert's memory and to the foreground the account of the knight's pilgrimage, but adorned and embellished with all the power of a clerical culture.

YOLANDE de PONTFARCY

---

[108] See above p. 16.
[109] Easting, 'Peter of Cornwall's account', 411, lines 15-16.

II. Accounts and Tales of Lough Derg or of the Pilgrimage

One of the most fascinating outcomes of the pilgrimage to Lough Derg is that it generated three types of tale which draw on Christian writings and/or on the rich lore of Irish tradition. The first type concerns the killing of a reptilian monster in Lough Derg by Fionn or Patrick.[1] This tradition in folklore and literary texts appears, under the influence of the pilgrimage, to be the crystallization of two separate motifs: the motif of St Patrick's being disturbed by demon-birds while retired on Croagh Patrick and the motif of the killing of a monster by a saint or a warrior. The second type of tale is represented by Peter of Cornwall's account of the experience of an unnamed knight in Purgatory. This unique version of a puzzling story, which appears like a parody of Owein's visit to the beyond, draws on the Irish tradition. The last type is represented by H. of Saltrey's account of Owein's journey to the beyond. In this story, the pilgrimage of the knight to St Patrick's Purgatory has been enhanced by the clerical and Christian tradition of visions of the otherworld.

Fionn, St Patrick and the Lough Derg monster

The defeat by a saint of a dragon symbolizing evil or paganism appears very early in Christian literature.[2] This influence can be seen in relation to St Patrick in Muirchú's *Life of St Patrick*, a work written in the second half of the seventh century. There the metaphorical killing of the dragon is an image of the missionary work of the saint. Muirchú writes that Patrick decided to celebrate his first Easter in Ireland in the great plain of Brega:

> . . . because it was there that there was the greatest kingdom among these tribes, the head of all paganism and idolatry; there, in the words of the Psalmist, he would smash the head of the dragon, and for the first time an irresistible wedge would be driven into the head

---

[1] See Dáithí Ó hÓgáin, ' 'Moch amach ar maidin dé Luain!' Staidéar ar an seanchas faoi ollphiasta i lochanna na hÉireann', *Béaloideas*, li (1983), 87-125.
[2] *ibid.*, 105-109.

of all idolatry with the hammer of brave action joined to faith by the spiritual hands of holy Patrick and his companions.[3]

Similarly, the defeat of an aquatic monster can express also the spiritual power of a saint.[4] Such is the meaning of the seventh-century story related by Adomnán in the case of St Colmcille and the Lough Ness monster. By raising his hands, making the sign of the Cross and ordering the monster to turn back, the saint saved one of his followers from being swallowed. The frightened beast disappeared under the water.[5] In this case the saint, by his spiritual power, is the counterpart of the warrior who can overcome the monster by his physical strength. The earliest example in Irish literature is the eighth-century account of the killing of a monster in Loch Rudraige by Fergus Mac Léti. As a result the water of the lake remained red for a month.[6]

The tradition, however, of St Patrick's fight against aquatic monsters is linked to his retreat on Croagh Patrick. According to Tírechán, who wrote at the end of the seventh century, the saint retired to the summit of this mountain for forty days and forty nights and 'birds were troublesome to him and he could not see the face of sky and land and sea'.[7] This motif was enlarged in the *Tripartite Life*, a work written in the tenth century and based on oral sources. The birds, now black, were demons in disguise. St Patrick chased them away by throwing his bell at them. The demons consequently disappeared from Ireland for seven years, seven months, seven days and seven nights. Afterwards an angel came to console the saint with white birds, the melodies of which comforted him.[8] In this text there is found for the first time an encounter between Patrick and a monster. The beast became tame and friendly at the sight of the saint. This event occurred in an island of the Tyrrhenian sea.[9]

With the political importance of Lough Derg which appears in the eleventh/twelfth century and the creation of the short-term pilgrimage under the patronage of St Patrick, folk tradition — in

[3] Bieler, *The Patrician Texts*, pp. 84-87, part I, 15(14).

[4] See Helen Waddell, *Beasts and Saints* (London, 1934).

[5] Alan O. Anderson and Marjorie O. Anderson (eds and trs), *Adomnán's Life of Columba* (London, 1961) ii. 27, pp. 386-389.

[6] D. A. Binchy (ed. and tr.), 'The saga of Fergus Mac Léti', *Ériu*, xvi (1952), 33-48. I thank Dr Dáithí Ó hÓgáin for this reference.

[7] See above pp. 31-2.

[8] *Trias Thaumaturgae*, 'Septima Vita S. Patricii', p. 138, par. 64. See also Stokes *Bethu Phátraic*, pp. 179-181.

[9] *ibid.*, p. 122, par. 34. See the passage quoted above p. 26.

order to explain the saint's presence in Lough Derg — elaborated on the story of St Patrick's fight with the demon-birds. When on Croagh Patrick St Patrick threw his bell at the demon-birds, they fled in panic into Log na nDeamhan, a hole in the northern part of the mountain. One — the devil's mother, Corra *(Caorthannach* 'Fiery One') — escaped. She flew into a lake (called ever since Loch na Corra) situated to the south of Croagh Patrick. The saint pursued her but she escaped to Lough Derg, where he eventually killed her. As her blood coloured the water of the lake, it was named Lough Derg (the Red Lake).[10]

Corra was seen several times at Lough Derg. Both Antonio Mannini and Laurence Rathold of Pászthó, who came in 1411, saw the bird. For Antonio Mannini, it has the shape of a heron but looks bigger. It is blacker than coal and has no feathers except for four or five on each wing. He names it *Corna.*[11] For Laurence, the demon is called (in the Irish language) *Cornu.* It looks like a heron, has no feathers and had been seen by many people.[12] Two centuries later Philip O'Sullevan Beare wrote that St Patrick drove all the venomous animals on to Croagh Patrick. From there he sent some into the sea, some into the cave on the side of the mountain, some into islands off the coast and some 'on the Island of the Swimmers to which they gave the name of demons'. He adds: 'The demoniac island in truth is girded by an inland lake. The lake is called Derg . . .'.[13] This tradition must have been in the twelfth century the source of Gerald of Wales' information when he writes that part of an island in an Ulster lake 'is abandoned to the use of evil spirits only'.[14]

The motif of the aquatic monster seems therefore a later addition to the initial motif of the demon-birds. This new element must have arisen from the motif of the fight of a saint or a warrior against a monster, a theme which was popular in twelfth-century Saints' Lives and found also in *Agallamh na Seanórach* 'The Colloquy of the Ancient Men'.[15] However, it is only in the late medieval period that the motif of the Lough Derg monster appears in the Ossianic lore. The fifteenth- or sixteenth-century lay called *Seilg na Féinne os*

---

[10] Máire MacNeill, *The Festival of Lughnasa* (Oxford, 1962), pp. 71-84, 502-511, 524.
[11] See below pp. 182-3.
[12] See below pp. 161-2.
[13] Philip O'Sullevan Beare, *Patritiana Decas* (Madrid, 1629), pp. 161 and 110v.
[14] See above p. 16.
[15] See Ó hÓgáin, 'Moch amach ar maidin dé Luain!', 99-104.

cionn Locha Deirg 'The Fenian hunt on the borders of Lough Derg', begins with Caoilte asking Patrick if he has heard of the chase by the Fianna over Loch Derg. Fionn's companion Albhaidh, a son of the king of Greece, who understood the language of all monsters, heard that this monster of Loch Derg demanded to be fed daily on fifty horses or fifty cows. Fionn accepted this demand thinking that it was preferable to the sacrifice of any of his warriors. That night the monster slept without food. When she came to the shore many warriors surrounded and attacked her. By midday the dead were more numerous than those who were still alive. The son of the king of Greece, Oisín, Dáolghus, Goll, Fionn mac Rossa, Conán Máol (The Bald), Diarmaid and Trénmhór were all swallowed by the monster, who was able to engulf as many as a hundred and one persons at once. But Fionn, who was not among the unfortunate, took the monster by one of her joints, gave her a violent twist and turned her on her back. His son Dáire was therefore able to plunge into the monster's throat and with his knife to open a way to freedom for himself and all who had been swallowed. All the rescued came out bald and naked. But Conán, who was already bald, emerged without a patch of skin left on his skull.

For a year, a month and three days afterwards the lake remained under some mystic darkness and its name changed from Fionnloch to Loch Dearg.

> Fionnloch dobh ainm don loch
> ar tús a chor a chléireach
>   do an Loch Dearg air ré a bheó
>   ó ár na Féine a n-énlo.

Fionnloch (White Lake) had been the lough's name in the beginning . . . Loch Dearg (Red Lake) became its name for ever by reason of that single day's slaughter of the Fian.[16]

There are in this story motifs which are common to other Fenian tales. The fourteenth-century poem called *The Chase of Sliabh Truim* tells of a fight between the Fianna and a monster in Loch Cuan (Strangford Lough in County Down). In this account the

---

[16] *Duanaire Finn*, Part II, ed. and tr. G. Murphy, Irish Texts Society, vol. xxviii (Dublin, 1933), 234-239; editorial explanations Part III, Irish Texts Society, vol. xliii (Dublin, 1941), 139-142. It is found also in the *Transactions of the Ossianic Society*, vi (Dublin, 1858), ed. and tr. John Daly (Dublin, 1861) 154-161. In this version the reciter is Oisín. The lay has also been edited with a summary in English by J. J. O'Kelly, *Leabhar na Laoitheadh* (Dublin, 1913), summary pp. x-xii; text pp. 18-21.

beast also demanded food. The Fianna are swallowed and it is Fionn
who cuts his way out through the side of the monster and liberates
everybody. This poem is a celebration of Fionn's deeds, for there is
a long enumeration of all the monsters/serpents/otherworld beings
that Fionn overcame all over Ireland. No mention however is made
of the Lough Derg monster.[17] The motif of the mark on the body, as
a result of a visit to the otherworld, occurs in other tales. In a late
medieval prose text, Fionn — from a swim in the water of the lake of
Slieve Gullion to recover a ring of red gold for a crying lady whom
he met on the shore of the lake — came back looking so old that his
dogs and companions failed to recognize him. When Fionn made
himself known, his companions forced Culann out of his dwelling
and obliged him restore Fionn's appearance. He did so by giving
Fionn a rejuvenating drink. Fionn, however, wished to keep half of
his hair white, while the other half returned to its original golden
colour.[18] In the sixteenth century *Bruidhean Chaorthainn* 'The
Rowantree Dwelling', Fionn and his companions got stuck on the
seats of this otherworld dwelling and Conán as a result lost the skin
of his buttocks.[19] Finally the colouring of the lake as a result of the
fight is also found in the tale of the killing of the monster of Loch
Rudraige by Fergus Mac Léti. Coincidentally, the motif of the fight
against a monster in Lough Derg is closely linked with fights against
monsters in two other lakes of the region of County Down, Lough
Cuan (Strangford Lough) and Loch Rudraige (Carlingford Lough
or Dundrum Bay).[20]

However the spirit of *The Fenian hunt on the borders of Lough
Derg* is quite different from these tales. Its originality lies in the fact
that its author has adapted the traditional Fenian themes to the
spirit of the pilgrimage. This is expressed in two ways. On the one
hand, Dáire, Fionn's son who delivers those who are swallowed, is
not himself swallowed but goes voluntarily inside the monster to
open her up and save others. There is here a father/son relationship
not unlike that of God the Father and Christ. In medieval
iconography hell is often represented as the open mouth of a

---

[17] *Duanaire Finn*, Part I, ed. and tr. Eoin MacNeill, Irish Texts Society vol. vii (Dublin, 1908),
75-80 and translation 187-194, editorial notes by G. Murphy in Part III, 59-63. See also the
Transactions of the Ossianic Society, vi, 102-127; and *idem*, ii ed. N. O'Kearney (Dublin 1855),
51-62.

[18] *Transactions of the Ossianic Society*, ii. 166-175.

[19] *Duanaire Finn*, Part III, pp. xxiv, xxvii; Dáithí Ó hÓgáin, *Fionn mac Cumhaill. Images of
the Gaelic Hero* (Dublin, 1988), pp. 213-216 and 288.

[20] Binchy, 'The saga of Fergus Mac Léti', 42, n. 9.

monster/dragon.[21] There seems also to be an allusion to the self-imposed death to this world that the pilgrim to Lough Derg undertakes. Sir Shane Leslie noticed that Conán's journey in the monster's belly was expressed in Irish by *turus Conáin*. Indeed *turus* means a journey, a (military) expedition and also a pilgrimage, a place of pilgrimage and a station[22] (turning around a dolmen, a cairn or a circular enclosure). On the other hand, nakedness and baldness express contact with the otherworld in the Christian tradition. The first consequence of the eating of the forbidden fruit appears in Adam and Eve's awareness of their nakedness. Baldness expressed by tonsure is a mark of priesthood and not only among Christians; the druids also were tonsured.[23] The return to this world in a hairless and naked state after having been swallowed is therefore a sign of contact with the otherworld and also an expression of metaphorical death and rebirth, since hairlessness and nakedness can represent the physical appearance of the newly born. Yet the main function of the lay is to explain the change in the name of the lake regardless of the fact that the real new-name of Fionnloch may rather have been Lough Derc (often found written *Gercc*),[24] as a reference to the anchoretic type of life led on the islands of this lake. Derc means a cavity and is found therefore in relation to a pit, a cave,[25] a grave,[26] a well or the socket of an eye.[27] This 'etymological' explanation would be of the same kind as that which inspired the motif of the reddening of the water of Loch Rudraige since *rua* also means 'red'.[28]

[21] In the *Vision of St Paul* — a third-century composition which was known in Ireland as early as the seventh century (See M. McNamara, *The Apocrypha in the Irish Church*, Dublin, 1975, p. 107.) — hell is a many-headed dragon which has its mouth forever open. (T. Silverstein, *Visio Sancti Pauli. The History of the Apocalypse in Latin together with nine texts*, London, 1935, pp. 66-69.) In the *Life of Maedoc of Ferns* (II, par. xxxv, 95), king Brandub saw himself near hell surrounded by many monsters ready to swallow him. (Plummer, *Bethada Náem nÉrenn: Lives of Irish Saints*, i, 216 and ii, 209-210).

[22] See David Greene and E. G. Quinn, *Contributions to a Dictionary of the Irish Language*, Letter to-tu (Dublin, 1948).

[23] Louis Gougaud, *Les Chrétientés Celtiques* (Paris, 1911), pp. 198-199.

[24] Leslie, *St Patrick's Purgatory*, p. 132, quotes John O'Donovan.

[25] Lough Derg meant for John O'Donovan 'the Lake of the Caves'.

[26] Sylvester Malone was of the opinion that Derg referred to a 'burial ground'. See S. Malone, *Church History of Ireland from the Anglo-Norman Invasion to the Reformation* (2 vols, Dublin, 1880), ii. 188 footnote.

[27] The lake of the Red Eye is the name of Loch Dergdeirc on the Shannon. See Mary E. Byrne and Maud Joynt, *Contributions to a Dictionary of the Irish Language*, degra - dodelbtha (Dublin, 1959).

[28] See Binchy, 'The saga of Fergus Mac Léti', 44, n. 3. See Ó hÓgáin. 'Moch amach ar maidin dé Luain!', 90-99, for the influence of the Book of Exodus, especially with regard to Moses and the Red Sea.

Folk versions have combined the tale of the *Fenian hunt on the borders of Lough Derg* with the participation of St Patrick. In a Galway folk-version St Patrick drove the monsters from Croagh Patrick but two escaped. One of the two, Bólán Mór, went to Lough Derg. St Patrick followed it, was swallowed but killed the monster from within with his crozier.[29] In a Tyrone version, at the end of Fionn's fight with the monster, St Patrick's horse overcomes the beast.[30] But the best known version of this kind, related on several occasions by scholars from the seventeenth century onwards, shows a gathering of many motifs.

There once lived in Ireland an old hag who had a giant as a son. The witch, who knew the virtues of every herb, used to brew in a silver pot a powerful poison, in which her son digged the point of his arrows and which inflicted a mortal wound. She was called the Hag with the Finger because she had but one long and pliant finger on each hand.

At this time the king of Ireland was called Niall. He called his druids and asked them to find a means of getting rid of the witch and her son, as both spent their time doing all kinds of mischief. The druids answered that it was only one of the Fianna who could kill the hag and that she would have to be shot with a silver arrow. The king sent for Fionn mac Cumhaill who with his companions undertook to hunt the pair. They found them gathering deadly herbs on a hill in East Munster. She had with her the pot in which she boiled the herbs. Goll mac Morna shot an arrow at her, missed, overturned the pot and spilled the poisonous mixture. To escape the attack the giant threw his mother on his shoulder but Fionn sent a silver arrow which pierced the heart of the old hag. Carrying his burden the giant flew with astonishing speed until he came to the mountains of Donegal where, stopping to take breath, he discovered that all that remained of his mother were her legs, her backbone and her two arms, the rest having been torn apart in his flight through the woods. The giant threw down the remains of his mother, continued his flight and was never seen again.

Some years later the Fianna came hunting in that part .of the country where the bones of the hag lay. While Oisín stood moralizing over her remains, a little red-headed dwarf made his appearance. He told them not to touch the old hag's bones because in the thigh bone was concealed a worm which, if it once got out and could find water

[29] Douglas Hyde, *Legends of Saints and Sinners* (Dublin, 1915), pp. 287-289; MacNeill, *The Festival of Lughnasa*, pp. 505-506, H 6.

[30] E. Ó Tuathail (ed.), *Sgéalta Mhuintir Luinigh: Munterloney folk-tales* (Dublin, 1933), pp. 111-115.

enough to drink, would be likely to destroy the whole world. The dwarf disappeared but his counsel was disregarded. Conán Máol broke the thigh bone with his hunting spear and a long hairy worm crawled out. He took it on the end of his spear and defiantly threw it into the lake. Immediately there rushed out an enormous beast, so terrible that all the Fianna hid themselves from its fury. The monster overran the country, spreading destruction and swallowing hundreds of people at a mouthful.

In this extremity, Fionn mac Cumhaill sucked his thumb and discovered that the beast was vulnerable only in one spot — a mole on its left side. Therefore he attacked the monster and jumped into its throat. Inside the beast he met two hundred live men and women. He found the mole about twenty yards below the heart. With his weapon he opened a hole about the size of a coach-house door and came out with the captives. Then he left the beast struggling and bleeding on the shore of this same lake, ever since named the Red Lake (Lough Derg). The beast lay writhing and bellowing with pain until Saint Patrick came and found it and, to show the power of the faith he was preaching, ordered it to go to the bottom of the lake where he effectually secured it. When the lake is ruffled by a storm, the monster is still sometimes seen rolling among the waves.[31]

At the beginning of the seventeenth century the rocks about the entrance to Station Island were reported to be the entrails of a great petrified serpent.[32]

This story is a folk version of the lay *The Fenian hunt on the borders of Lough Derg*, to which is added a long introduction which serves to magnify Fionn's deeds. He saves the country from a hag, a giant and a monster. He appears as a skilled archer, as a fearless attacker of monsters and as the good leader helping his king and re-establishing the cosmic order threatened by the mistakes of his companions. St Patrick only perfects Fionn's work. The two parts of the story are connected through the relationship between the hag, her son the giant and the monster. Indeed the monster is somehow the offspring of the hag since it lived under the form of a worm in her

[31] This story was told by Bishop Henry Jones, *St Patrick's Purgatory: containing the Description, Originall Progresse and Demolition of that superstitious place* (London, 1967), p. 2; Richardson, *The Great Folly*, pp. 181-191; A. C. Otway, *Sketches in Ireland* (Dublin, 1827), pp. 181-91. I have followed in a simplified way the version given by Thomas Wright, *St Patrick's Purgatory* (London, 1844), pp. 2-4, who omits Fionn's visit inside the beast that Otway gives in great detail. This story was still being told in 1935: see MacNeill, *The Festival of Lughnasa*, p. 507, H 8.

[32] Bishop Henry Jones, *Account of St Patrick's Purgatory;* Messingham, *Florilegium Insulae Sanctorum* (Paris, 1624), p. 96; Richardson, *The Great Folly*, p. 3.

thigh bone. It replaces the giant who has fled. The dwarf's warning to the Fianna (not to touch the hag's bones for fear of a worm which can turn into a monster if it can drink water) reminds one of the warning (not to go under the water of Loch Rudraige) that the chief leprechaun (elf) gave to Fergus Mac Léti together with the gift of passing under seas, pools and lakes.[33] This folk story is therefore a synthesis of many motifs relating to Fionn's fight against monsters of every shape, to Fergus Mac Léti's encounter with the beast of Loch Rudraige and to the participation of St Patrick.

Peter of Cornwall's account

The Latin story of the experiences of an unnamed knight in Purgatory was related in 1200 by Peter of Cornwall but heard by his informant Bricius in 1170. It seems therefore that this tale existed orally at a time when Owein's story was not yet written by H. of Saltrey but known orally, at least by Gilbert of Louth. However, the unnamed knight's adventure betrays a knowledge of Saltrey's text. One assumes that the place of the happening of the knight's experiences is Lough Derg, because of the reference to Purgatory as a place which one enters and a description of the entry to the otherworld as a hall as in Saltrey's text. Although related through Latin and a religious milieu, this story has a secular rather than a clerical spirit. It is as follows:

> At the time of Henry II, a certain knight entered Purgatory. He arrived in a splendid hall as if in a palace. Gulinus, the king, was absent but soon returned from hunting with a great commotion, as if all the earth were shaking. He learnt that the knight was looking for hospitality and gave it to him.
>
> Gulinus had a daughter who seemed to the knight the most beautiful girl he had ever met. He instantly fell in love and willingly accepted the king's offer of her hand in marriage. A servant went to prepare the couch but just as the knight was about to enjoy her his eyes opened. He saw that he was embracing an old, dried, awful tree-trunk. His virile member, stuck in a hole in this trunk, was for most of the day severely tortured by one of Gulinus' servants with a hammer and nail. When the knight was brought to the edge of death by the excruciating pain, Gulinus asked that he be brought to him and then enquired how he felt. The knight spoke of his pains and Gulinus, in order to relieve them, offered a warm bath. The knight accepted

---

[33] Binchy, 'The saga of Fergus Mac Léti', 43, par. 8.

but the water was boiling and he was as if melting. Again King Gulinus asked how he felt and proposed a cold bath to temper the heat. Willingly the knight entered the bath, the water of which turned out to be icy cold. He was pierced by icy points harder and sharper than nails. King Gulinus, very sorry for the pains of his son-in-law, offered him in compensation a good time playing with his servants in his 'sports-centre'. The room was made of stone and in the walls sharp stones were inserted in such a way as to stick out. Above there was a beam from which hung a cord. The servants tide the knight by the feet, with his head hanging down. They played with him like a ball, sending him from wall to wall against the sharp stones until his limbs were lacerated and his brain fell out. As dawn approached, King Gulinus, his servants, the hall, the vision and the torments disappeared and the knight found himself back at the entrance to the Purgatory. He was in such a poor state that he thought he would die.

According to Peter of Cornwall, this story was told to him by Bricius who heard it from Walter, a monk from Mellifont, who obtained knowledge of it from the knight himself when he accompanied a certain bishop Laurence to his new see of Down.[34]

This pilgrimage has features of the visit of Owein to Purgatory. The arrival of the unnamed knight in a hall which looked like a palace and the coming of Gulinus with great noise as if all the earth were shaking, is the counterpart of Owein's arrival in the hall which looked like a cloister and also of the arrival of the demons with an uproar as if all the earth were shaking.[35] The outstanding characteristic of Gulinus is the fact that he cannot be trusted; he lies constantly. This is also the main characteristic of the demons in H. of Saltrey's story. Owein was warned by the fifteen messengers who greeted him in the hall. They told him:

> They (the demons) will promise to lead you unharmed to the door through which you entered if you agree to turn back; they will try to see if you can be deceived even by this ruse. If you are in any way either defeated by the agony of their tortures or terrified by their threats or taken in by their promises and if you offer them your consent, you will die body as well as soul. . .'[36]

[34] Easting, 'Peter of Cornwall's account', 413-416. Dr Easting is the first to have edited this text.

[35] Peter of Cornwall writes: '. . . quasi totus mundus concuteretur'. (See Easting, 'Peter of Cornwall's account', 414, 1. 73-74.). In the manuscripts containing the short versions of the *Tractatus* one finds: '. . . quasi totus commoveretur mundus'. See K. Warnke, *Das Buch vom Espugatoire S. Patrice der Marie de France und seine Quelle*, Bibliotheca Normannica, IX (Halle/Saale, 1938), p. 58, par. 3, lines 28-29.

[36] Picard and Pontfarcy, *St Patrick's Purgatory*, p. 54.

Lough Foyle

Raphoe •   • Derry

Strangford
Lough

Lough Derg

Clogher
•
Armagh   • Downpatrick   Inch
         •
Lough Erne

Newry •
Slieve Gullion ▲   Dundrum
Dundalk •   Bay

Mellifont ‡   Carlingford Lough
Drogheda •

▲ Croagh Patrick

Tuam •

Dublin
      •

‡ Baltinglass

▲ Brandon Mt.   Cashel •

Wexford •

0   Miles   50

Map 2

Later, when Owein was told by the devils that the well full of flames was the entrance to hell, other devils came to him and said:

> Our companions told you that this was meant to be hell. They were lying. It is our habit always to lie so that we can deceive through lies those we cannot dupe through truth . . .'[37]

Tortures of the sexual organs, torments of heat and cold and excruciating pain caused by sharp objects inserted into the flesh are part of the paraphernalia of the torments of hell. There is however a big difference. The unnamed hero does not expiate any sins but appears like an innocent fool who has not learned to distrust his host and willingly gives himself into the hands of his torturers. The spirit of this story is totally secular. The similarity with the *Tractatus* may have been introduced by Peter of Cornwall.

Gulinus, the name of the king, may be related to Culann, the great artificer who is supposed to have his forge on Slieve Gullion and from whom the mountain got its name. This, from the linguistic point of view, is apparently wrong[38] but tradition has its own logic. Slieve Gullion (which is situated some five miles north-west of Dundalk, and some five miles south-west of Newry) is a hill rich in mythological tradition.[39] On it there is a lake. The late medieval prose story of how Fionn became old looking after having dived into the water has already been related. It was Culann who restored Fionn's appearance.[40] There is also a cave on Slieve Gullion. In the fifteenth century *Adventure on Slieve Gullen,* Oscar, Oisín's son, was brought into it for a year to recover from his wounds.[41] And there is a passage grave on the southern top of the mountain. It is known as the Cailleach's House. The Cailleach Bhéara is an ugly

[37] *ibid.*, p. 64.

[38] P. W. Joyce, *Irish Names of Places* (2 vols, Dublin, 1871), i. 513-514. He adds: '. . . if this were the case, the ancient name should be written *Sliabh-Culainn;* whereas we know that in the oldest and best authorities, it is *Sliabh-Cuillin,* which admits of one only interpretation 'the mountain of holly'. Incidentally, Holly would be the name also of the holy well near Lough Derg, which is known as the holy well of Cullion, as if Cullion were the name of a person.

[39] See T. G. F. Paterson, *Country Cracks. Old Tales from the County of Armagh* (Dundalk, 1939), p. 44 footnote; Michael J. Murphy, *At Slieve Gullion's Foot* (Dundalk 1940 and 1975 reprint). I thank Dr Séamas Ó Catháin for these references.

[40] See above p. 39. N. O'Kearney thinks that Sliebh Cuillinn refers to the moat of Castletown, to the north of Dundalk. See *Transactions of the Ossianic Society,* ii. 169 note.). The Irish form of Slieve Gullion, however, happens to be Sliebh Cuillinn. (See above Joyce note 38). Ó hÓgáin assumes also that the adventure of Fionn happened in the lake of Slieve Gullion. (See *Fionn mac Cumhaill,* p. 23).

[41] See *Dunaire Finn,* Part II [248-297], verse 100, 276-277.

old woman with supernatural strength, a sort of witch who has the bad reputation of having caused the death of many young men.[42] She is also the one who laments her youth in fine poems and in the embrace of the rightful king, becomes of greatest beauty. It seems therefore that behind the name Gulinus there may be a reference to Culann. The forge is a demoniacal image in Christian iconography.[43] Behind the name Gulinus there is also a tradition which can be related to Slieve Gullion as a place where one can gain access to the otherworld.

Two motifs of Peter of Cornwall's account are common to the Fenian tales. One is the love relationship between a visitor from this world and the daughter of a lord of the otherworld. In the lay of *Caoilte's Urn,* for example, written about 1200, Fionn and eight of his companions are led while hunting a boar to a fairy hill *(sidh)* dwelling. All are welcomed and well entertained. Royal gifts are offered to them. Fionn falls in love with the beautiful daughter of the house, offers to marry her and is accepted by father and daughter. When the couch is ready, the girl asks for a harp. She plays magic music which puts the Fianna to sleep. When they rise from sleep they are back in this world with their gifts but Fionn is very disappointed.[44] Like the unnamed knight, Fionn does not enjoy the pleasure he expects with his betrothed. Each girl deceives her lover, one by putting him to sleep and the other by changing herself into an old tree-trunk. The metamorphic process which occurs when the rightful king embraces the old hag is reversed in the otherworld. The beautiful girl is changed into a dead tree. Deception is also a motif found in the *bruidhean* tales in which one reads of how Fionn and his companions are enticed to a magic dwelling *(bruidhean)* and how they suffer ill-treatment. In the twelfth century lay *The Headless Phantoms,* Fionn, Caoilte and Oisín discover a house (near Ballyvourney in county Cork) and, having sought entertainment, are tormented by a grey-haired giant, a three-headed hag, a headless man with one eye in his chest and nine bodies with nine heads separated from them. At dawn the

---

[42] A. H. Krappe, 'La Cailleach Bheara. Notes de mythologie Gaélique', *Etudes Celtiques,* i (1936), 292-302.

[43] In Isaiah (LIV, 16) the devil is represented as a smith. In the *Voyage of St Brendan* there is an evil island of smiths. (See *The Voyage of St Brendan,* tr. J. J. O'Meara (Dublin, 1978), chap. 23). In the *Vision of Tnugdal* the worst torment in superior hell is represented by Vulcan and his forge. (See J-M Picard and Y. de Pontfarcy, *The Vision of Tnugdal,* Dublin, forthcoming).

[44] *Dunaire Finn,* Part I, 38-45 and 140-149. Ó hÓgáin, *Fionn mac Cumhaill,* p. 136.

house disappears and Fionn and his companions arise unharmed.[45] In a later tale, *The dwelling of little red Eochaid,* Fionn and sixteen of his companions find themselves one Halloween trapped in the magic dwelling of Eochaid. They are challenged by various hostile visitors coming one after another. Thus Conán is tackled by a hag who overcomes him and ties him up. Then a strange warrior carrying a trough of water challenges the best man of the Fianna to wash his hands and feet in it. Conán puts his little toe into the water and it is burnt to a cinder. Afterwards there comes a warrior with a boar on his shoulders. He throws it on the floor as a present from Eochaidh but they have to cook it themselves. Conán attempts to do so but is scalded. Eventually all ends well, for on each occasion (and there are other challenges) the Fianna manage to overcome their foes.[46]

G. Murphy thinks that the original *bruidhean* was an otherworld dwelling equivalent to the Greek Hades and that that theme which was in origin mythological has been preserved in Ireland mainly by folk tradition.[47] Therefore one can draw the conclusion that Peter of Cornwall's account of the experiences of an unnamed knight is the clerical rendering of the motif of the *bruidhean.*

H. of Saltrey's 'Treatise on St Patrick's Purgatory'

H. of Saltrey, who provided the first description of the pilgrimage to Lough Derg, related also the first tale of a physical journey to the otherworld. This may have contributed to the popularity of the account. This popularity appears in the numerous manuscripts in which are kept copies of the *Tractatus* — one hundred and fifty manuscripts of the Latin text and as many translations in different European vernaculars — and also in the widespread interest in the story all over Europe, as the circulation of the texts (whether in Latin or translated into vernacular languages) shows.

After the dedication — in which Brother H. offers his work to the abbot H. of Sartis (the old name of Wardon, mother abbey of Saltrey) — comes a long introduction composed of six parts. Henry starts with a theological survey concerning the otherworld. He

[45] *Dunaire Finn,* Part I, 28-30 and 127-130; Textual analysis *Duanaire Finn,* Part III, I follow the summary given by G. Murphy, *The Ossianic Lore and Romantic Tales of Medieval Ireland* (Dublin, 1961), pp. 22-23.

[46] Ó hÓgáin, *Fionn mac Cumhaill,* pp. 207-211 and 288-289.

[47] Murphy, *The Ossianic Lore,* p. 16.

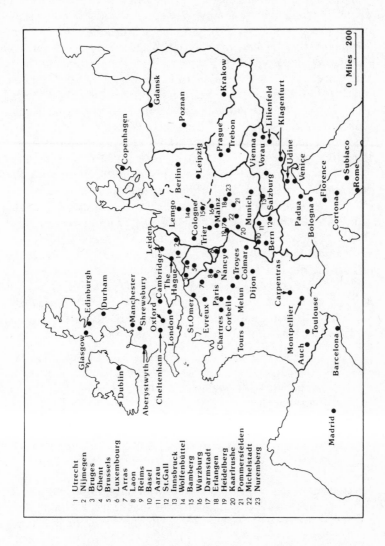

1 Utrecht
2 Nijmegen
3 Bruges
4 Ghent
5 Brussels
6 Luxembourg
7 Arras
8 Laon
9 Reims
10 Basel
11 Aarau
12 St.Gall
13 Innsbruck
14 Wolfenbüttel
15 Bamberg
16 Würzburg
17 Darmstadt
18 Erlangen
19 Heidelberg
20 Kaarlrushe
21 Pommersfelden
22 Michelstadt
23 Nuremberg

0 Miles 200

Map 3: Present locations of St Patrick's Purgatory texts in Latin and the vernacular languages (not shown is Yale University Library, Ms 395).

refers to St Gregory's *Dialogues* and to St Augustine and draws without saying so on Hugh of St Victor's *De sacramentis*.[48] His main aim is to emphasize the reality of the otherworld. He then relates how St Patrick preached to the pagan Irish in order to convert them, frightening them by the torments of hell and strengthening them by the promise of paradise. He interrupts his narrative to relate a story that Gilbert gave as an example of Irish savagery. One day an old man came to confession to Gilbert and never mentioned that he had killed five people and had wounded many more because he had not known that this was a sin. Coming back to St Patrick, Henry explains how the Irish refused to be converted and how the Purgatory (meaning the cave) was revealed by Jesus to the saint.[49] Then follows the story of an old prior of the place who was accustomed to being visited by angels who blessed him because his only tooth never touched food except for cold water, bread and salt.[50] And the introduction ends with an account of the ritual that should be observed in entering St Patrick's Purgatory.[51]

The main narrative begins with the story of Owein. It is related how in the days of King Stephen a knight called Owein went to confession 'to the bishop in whose diocese this Purgatory was located'. And, sorry for his sins, he decided to enter the Purgatory. He followed the ritual and before entering the cave the prior explained to him what he was going to find:

> 'You will walk for some time through an underground cavern until you emerge in a large field where you will find a hall built with wonderful art. When you enter it you will immediately be met by messengers from God who will explain carefully what will be done to you or what you will suffer. They will then depart and leave you alone there and demons will arrive soon afterwards to tempt you. We understand it happens thus from those who have entered before you. As for you, be constant in the faith of Christ'.[52]

Owein thus entered the cave 'armed with faith, hope and justice, confident in God's mercy and stronger than iron'. He went along the cavern in darkness and arrived in the field and the hall which

---

[48] R. Easting, 'Purgatory and the Earthly Paradise in the *Tractatus de Purgatorio Sancti Patricii*', *Cîteaux*, xxxvii (1986), 23-48.

[49] See above p. 8.

[50] See above p. 13.

[51] See above pp. 11-12.

[52] Picard and Pontfarcy, *St Patrick's Purgatory*, p. 52.

looked like a monk's cloister. He sat and waited. After a while came 'fifteen men who looked like monks recently shorn and dressed in white clothes'. The one who looked like their prior welcomed Owein and advised him as to how he should behave among the devils:

> If however you firmly and faithfully place absolute hope in God so that you do not yield to their tortures, threats or promises but steadfastly despise them as being nothing, not only will you be purified of all your sins but you will even see the torments which are in store for sinners and the place of rest in which the just rejoice. Always remember God and when they torture you call upon the Lord Jesus Christ, for through the invocation of his name you will immediately be delivered from the torture.[53]

Soon after the departure of the messengers, Owein heard a loud roar 'as if the entire earth was shaking' and there arrived a multitude of 'hideously misshapen demons' who rushed to welcome him but also to mock him because he had not even waited to die before coming to them. They offered to bring him back to the door so that he could enjoy life a little longer. As Owein made no answer, he was dragged off by the demons, tied hand and foot and tossed into a huge fire. But he invoked the name of Jesus and the fire was quickly extinguished.

He was then taken across a waste land shrouded in darkness in the direction of the place 'where the sun rises in midsummer'. They turned right and went southwards and heard most pitiful moans. He saw, in a plain full of beings of both sexes and all ages, people pinned face downwards to the ground by red-hot nails through their hands and feet. They were also ceaselessly beaten by devils.[54] The devils offered Owein the opportunity of turning back. When he refused they tried to nail him down but failed because he invoked the name of Jesus.

In another plain full of greater misery Owein saw people pinned down with their backs to the ground. But this time flaming dragons,

---

[53] *ibid.*, p. 54.

[54] In the *Vision of Adomnán* and the *Vision of Laisrén,* sinners have red-hot nails through their tongues. See C. S. Boswell, *An Irish Precursor of Dante. A Study on the Vision of Heaven and Hell ascribed to the eighth-century Saint Adamnán, with translation of the Irish Text* (London, 1908), p. 41, par. 27 and for Laisrén, p. 171.

fiery serpents and huge toads were gnawing at them[55] and eating their hearts. Devils were beating them with whips. This plain was so big that Owein could not see its confines. Once more the name of Jesus saved the knight.

In a third plain Owein again saw people pinned to the ground by red-hot nails, this time through all parts of their bodies. There were so many nails that not so much as the space of the tip of a finger could be found between them. The pains were so excruciating that the only sound that people could utter was a noise like those who are about to die. As well as being beaten, they suffered from a cold and at the same time a burning wind.[56] Owein, threatened by the demons, was saved by calling upon the name of Jesus.

Owein was dragged to a fourth plain where he saw all kinds of tortures. Some people were hanging by different parts of their bodies, others were burned in furnaces, roasted on grills or toasted on molten metal.[57] Owein escaped the tortures by invoking the name of Jesus.

Moving away, Owein was brought before a blazing iron wheel on which people were hooked. Half of the wheel was in the air and the other half in the earth going through fire.[58] The devils spun the wheel with such speed that Owein could not distinguish those hanging on it. Thrown by the demons on to the wheel, the knight was lifted into the air but called upon the name of Jesus and came down unharmed.

Afterwards he was conducted towards a large house. The heat coming from it was so fierce that he stopped but the demons forced him to go on. In the building there were in the ground many round pits full of molten metal in which people were immersed up to different parts of their bodies.[59] The devils tried to throw Owein into one of the pits but failed when they heard the name of Jesus.

Owein was dragged towards a mountain on which there was a multitude of naked people who were crouched and turned towards the north. They were waiting in a state of terror. Suddenly a

[55] The same torment as in the *Vision of Saint Paul*. See H. Brandes (ed.), *Visio Sancti Pauli. Ein Beitrag zur Visionslitteratur mit einem deutschen und zwei lateinischen Texten* (Halle, 1885); T. Silverstein, *Visio Sancti Pauli. The History of the Apocalypse in Latin together with nine texts* (London, 1935).

[56] The suffering from heat and cold is found in the *Visio Pauli* and in the *Vision of Drycthelm* (in Bede's *History of the English Church and People,* Book V, chap. 12.).

[57] The same torment as in the *Vision of St Paul.*

[58] *ibid.*

[59] *ibid.*

powerful whirlwind arose and carried the multitude, the demons and Owein into a fetid and icy river in which they suffered from the most unbelievable cold. Those who tried to get away from the river were pushed back into it by demons running on the surface of the waters. Thanks to the name of Jesus, Owein found himself on the opposite bank.

Then Owein was dragged towards the south. He was brought near a dark stinking well from which horrible flames shot up full of naked people who kept falling back into the well and the fire.[60] The demons told Owein that this pit was the entrance to hell where they lived. They pulled him into the pit which got wider and wider. The pain he suffered was so intense that he almost forgot the name of Jesus. But when he called upon the name of Jesus the flames lifted him up and carried him on the edge of the pit where he stayed alone for a while. Then demons came and told him that the others had lied and that they were going to show him the true hell.

They took the knight to a wide stinking river blazing with sulphurous fire and swarming with more demons. They told him that below this river was the entrance to hell. Above there was a perilous bridge that he would have to cross. Not only did the devils warn Owein that they would cause a wind to blow him off the river but the bridge was also unbelievably slippery, narrow and high. Owein called upon the name of Jesus and the bridge became so wide that two carts could have passed each other on it.[61] Furious, the devils roared to such an extent that the terror of their noise was more horrible than all the pains already endured by the knight. Unsuccessfully they threw their hooks at him and Owein reached the other side unharmed.

A homily on the lightness of the pains of this world compared to those of the otherworld and the necessity of the intercession of the living for the dead links the episode of purgatory with that of earthly paradise. This was a place situated on the other side of the perilous bridge behind a large wall. It was so full of perfume that Owein forgot all his sufferings. Two archbishops welcomed him and guided him around a most beautiful land full of flowers, music and

[60] A similar torment as in the *Vision of St Paul, Vision of Drycthelm* and the *Vision of Tnugdal*, chap. XIII.

[61] The sources here are the *Dialogues* (IV, 37) of Saint Gregory, where there is the first reference in Christian literature to the bridge that links hell and paradise. The motif of the bridge is found also in the *Vision of Saint Paul, The Vision of Adomnán* and the *Vision of Tnugdal*.

happiness.[62] It was peaceful and neither hot nor cold. The two archbishops explained that this was a place of rest after having been purified and that here people were not yet worthy of the higher joy of the saints. Then they took Owein to the top of a mountain and showed him in the sky the door of celestial paradise. Another homily is inserted inviting people to remember the joys of the blessed and the torments of the sinners. Owein, after having received some celestial food which filled him with the most delightful happiness, was told to go back to earth. He therefore reluctantly went back the same way and the devils, ashamed, 'fled into the air like terrified birds'. At the hall he was welcomed by the fifteen messengers and at the gate by the prior who conducted him to the church where he spent fifteen days in prayer. Afterwards he took the Cross, left for Jerusalem and returned.

In conclusion we are told how Gilbert was sent by Gervais of Louth (Lincoln) to Ireland to ask the king for the land that the king (who must be Diarmaid Mac Murchadha)[63] had granted to Gervais in order to found an abbey. As Gilbert could not speak Irish, the king gave him the knight Owein as interpreter. Gilbert learned the story from Owein. They stayed together for two and a half years. Then Gilbert went back to Louth and afterwards became abbot of Basingwerk.

Gilbert, as an extra testimony to Owein's story and as a proof that the knight experienced everything in the flesh and not in the imagination, adds that when he was in his previous monastery (that is Basingwerk) he himself knew a monk who was one night kidnapped by devils and badly beaten. 'He lived for fifteen years afterwards, but his wounds could not be healed by any medicine.'

H. of Saltrey gathered other testimony in order to validate the story of the Purgatory (cave). He consulted two abbots from Ireland, one who had never heard anything of the kind in his country and the other who certified that everything was true. Then he talked to bishop Florentianus[64] who said that everything was true and that the Purgatory lay in his diocese. Florentianus added a story of a hermit living nearby who at sunset is visited by devils appearing to him as naked women. Not daring to enter his cell they remain at

---

[62] A similar description of earthly paradise is found in the *Vision of Drycthelm* related by Bede in his *History of the English Church and People* (V, 12). See also Easting 'Purgatory and the Earthly Paradise', 23-48.

[63] See above p. 7 n. 3.

[64] Fógartach Ua Cerballáin, bishop of Tír Eoghain (1185-1230).

the door. As they talk freely, the hermit knows the secret life of many people of the province. The chaplain of the bishop happened to know this holy man and related that his cell is 'a hundred miles from the foot of St Brendan's mountain'. This holy man told the chaplain two stories that he had heard from the demons. In one instance they were rejoicing because a certain hermit not too far away was not really living like a hermit and the devils congratulated themselves on having been able to seduce him so easily. In the other story, the devils were bringing with them lots of food because a rich peasant refused charity to two poor clerics and said that he had nothing to give them. In consequence of his perjury he lost what he had. The chaplain finally told the story of a priest who severed his genitals rather than fall into the trap that the devils had set for him, in the form of an abandoned baby girl whom he had reared. Henry finished his story with an epilogue in which he says that he wrote the story to obey his abbot and asks for prayers from his readers.

The original copy of Henry's story has been lost. From the study of a certain number of manuscripts, however, two versions have emerged — a short one (known as the α text) based on Owein's journey and a long one (known as the β text) which possesses extraneous items (the long prologue, the old Irishman's confession, the two homilies and the testimonies added at the end of Owein's story). Scholars have argued as to which of the two is the closer to the original composition. Opinions differ. According to Warnke, the long version represented by the manuscript — British Library, Royal 13 B viii[65] — is an expansion of the short text.[66] R. Easting thinks that the long version is closer to the lost original.[67] A study of the sources on which the *Tractatus* is based reveals that Saltrey may be the author of two versions — a short version written in 1184 while H. of Sartis (to whom he dedicates his work) was still abbot and, between 1186 and 1188, another version expanded with homilies and anecdotes.[68]

To begin with, it seems that Owein's account given to Gilbert of Louth must have been merely a description of pains suffered due to the hardship of this pilgrimage. Jocelin refers only to torments endured on Croagh Patrick.[69] Gerald of Wales, referring to this

---

[65] This is the version translated by J-M. Picard and the one related above.

[66] Warnke, *Das Buch vom Espurgatoire S. Patrice.*

[67] Easting, 'An edition of Owayne Miles', pp. lxix-xc.

[68] See Pontfarcy, 'Le *Tractatus,* 464 and 470-472.

[69] See above p. 33 n. 107.

lake of Ulster, mentions only tortures by evil spirits.[70] These pains were easily turned into infernal torments, taken in the main from the *Vision of St Paul*, a third-century text which is the source of most medieval legends of hell. A further stage occurred when the description of torments was balanced by a description of the delights of earthly paradise and when this was included in a four-fold partition of the otherworld — hell, underneath a river; celestial paradise, very high up above; and in between a two-sided intermediary state, one hellish which will eventually be called purgatory and the other the earthly paradise which will later disappear from the topography of the otherworld. This new stage came about through the influence of the *Vision of Drycthelm*. This addition to the initial description is visible in the manner in which the author created the passage from purgatory to earthly paradise and in the way he created the awareness of celestial paradise. Traditionally the number of the pains of hell was nine.[71] This number is found for example in the *Elucidarium* of Honorius Augustodunensis, a work written in England at the beginning of the twelfth century and used for the training of clerics.[72] In the *Tractatus* there are nine torments including that of the pit full of flames said to be the entrance to hell. By the use of the same device as that contained in the *Vision of Drycthelm* — that is, the hero believes he is seeing hell but is then informed that hell is elsewhere — the number was brought to ten, which is an untraditional number of pains but which allows the author to introduce the motif of the bridge across the terrible river of hell which leads to the shore of earthly paradise. As in the *Vision of Drycthelm*, the hero, when he thinks that he is in celestial paradise, is told that it is only earthly paradise. Was it Gilbert of Louth's idea to balance a description of torments by a vision of earthly paradise and to have reused the fourfold partition of the otherworld? One cannot answer with certainty but one must not dismiss Gilbert's participation in the literary creation of this story.[73] This is the basis of a short version that H. of Saltrey may have written in 1184. But soon afterwards he produced an extended version. One of the most ancient

[70] See above p. 16.

[71] See E. Becker, *A Contribution to the Comparative Study of the Mediaeval Visions of Heaven and Hell* (Baltimore, 1899), p. 30.

[72] See Y. Lefèvre, *L'Elucidarium et les Lucidaires* (Paris, 1954), pp. 59, 218, 221.

[73] See H. Shields, 'An Old French Book of Legends and its Apocalyptic Background' (unpublished Ph.D. thesis, Trinity College, Dublin 1967), pp. 344-345.

manuscripts containing the *Tractatus* — British Library, Royal 13 B viii — dates from the last ten years of the twelfth century. It contains the story in its fully developed form and its structure bears witness to the manner in which the story was composed. A chapter is allotted to each torment while the delights of earthly paradise are in a single long chapter. This manuscript also contains the third edition of Gerald of Wales' *Topographia*.[74] Gerald wrote the first edition at the same time as Henry wrote his *Tractatus*. One can therefore assume that Henry may have done similar work on his text and that he may also be the author of the long version. Consequently one must speak of two lost originals, a shorter and a longer version.

The scope of H. of Saltrey's story on the theological and literary planes is also extremely important. It was an expression of Cistercian spirituality and made a contribution towards the definition of Purgatory as a place.[75] It is not a vision but a journey to the otherworld undertaken by a real person. Therefore this tale of adventure has also an historical value. This helps to explain the interest aroused by the story.

One cannot overemphasize the significance of these tales. On the one hand they bore witness to the importance of Lough Derg as a place of pilgrimage. On the other hand they contributed to its fame. At home, through the medium of tales based on folk lore, they enshrined the pilgrimage in the tradition of the country. Abroad they carried the not yet extinct pagan idea that somewhere, across the ocean in the most western land of the world, access to the beyond was possible and the extent of this fame is evident from the daring journeys that bold knights from afar undertook to come there.

YOLANDE de PONTFARCY

[74] J. F. Dimock (ed.), *Giraldus Cambrensis. Opera* (London, 1867) v. p. lii.
[75] See Jacques Le Goff, *Le Naissance du Purgatoire* (Paris, 1981); Easting, 'Purgatory and the Earthly Paradise', 23-48.

III. The English Tradition

A thousand tymes have I herd men telle
That ther ys joy in hevene and peyne in helle,
And I acorde wel that it ys so;
But, natheles, yet wot I wel also   *(know)*
That ther nis noon dwellyng in this contree
That eyther hath in hevene or helle ybe,
Ne may of hit noon other weyes witen,   *(know)*
But as he hath herd seyd, or founde it writen;
For by assay there may no man it preve.   *(experience/prove)*

(Geoffrey Chaucer, *Prologue* to *The Legend of Good Women*)[1]

It is interesting that Chaucer does not mention St Patrick's Purgatory, though he had more than likely heard of it, especially if he knew the so-called 'Auchinleck' manuscript, which contains an account of Owein's visit.[2] We may be certain that he would have been sceptical of the claim that the Purgatory was a physical entrance to the otherworld. In the *Tractatus*, Gilbert is reported as acknowledging such scepticism with the just assertion, 'There are people who say that when they enter the hall at the beginning they fall into ecstasy and they see all these things in their minds.'[3] Yet until the late fifteenth century Lough Derg's European fame rested precisely on the notion that here a pilgrim might prove the otherworld *by assay*, as Owein claimed he had done. To be sure, you were likely to witness only a glimpse of heaven and hell, but many clearly expected to experience the pain of purgatory and the joys of the Earthly Paradise in deed. The combination of a specific physical site in this world with the expectation of obtaining a physical sight (or at least a spiritual vision) of the otherworld

[1] *The Works of Geoffrey Chaucer*, ed. F. N. Robinson, 2nd ed. (London: Oxford University Press, 1957), p. 482, Text F.

[2] For the claim that Chaucer used and possibly even owned this collection of romances and religious tales, see L. H. Loomis, 'Chaucer and the Auchinleck Manuscript: *Sir Thopas* and *Guy of Warwick*', in *Essays and Studies in Honor of Carleton Brown* (New York, 1940), pp. 111-128. It has been argued, though not, I think, conclusively, that Chaucer knew the story of Owein from 'St Patrick' in the *South English Legendary;* see M. A. Stanford, 'The Sumner's Tale and Saint Patrick's Purgatory', *Journal of English and Germanic Philology*, xix (1920), 377-81, and Theodore Spencer, 'Chaucer's hell: a study in mediaeval convention', *Speculum*, ii (1927), 177-200.

[3] *Saint Patrick's Purgatory*, Picard & Pontfarcy, p. 73.

fuelled interest in St Patrick's Purgatory across the Continent for over three centuries.

This chapter centres on the visit to Lough Derg in the early fifteenth century by William of Stranton from County Durham, but first treats some of the earlier accounts of the Purgatory in the English tradition.

Authors of Latin texts working in England were the first to make St Patrick's Purgatory known outside Ireland.[4] In the eleven-eighties Jocelin of Furness and Gerald of Wales briefly offered varying information on the site of the Purgatory, and H. of Saltrey in the *Tractatus* gave us the first extended account of its founding and the earliest story of a person's visit. His narrative of the knight Owein was probably taken up in the early thirteenth century by John of Cella, the likely forerunner of Roger of Wendover, whose chronicle version was subsequently copied by Matthew Paris at St Albans. It was Owein's story that most subsequent pilgrims had 'heard said' or 'found written'.

Another English author, Peter of Cornwall, writing in Latin in 1200, gave us the first accurate information on the site of the Purgatory. After H. of Saltrey, he was also the next to tell of a visit to the otherworld at Lough Derg. Peter's material appears to have existed in only a single copy prepared under his supervision. It is found in a work entitled *The Book of Revelations (Liber Revelationum,* now Lambeth Palace Library, MS. 51), a very large collection of visions of the otherworld, compiled to demonstrate the existence of the soul and the reality of the afterlife. It is not surprising, therefore, to find that a copy of the *Tractatus* is the first text in the collection.

Peter tells of an encounter in the Purgatory about the year 1170 between an anonymous knight and a certain demonic king named Gulinus. The tale is unusual for it is quite independent of the *Tractatus*. It sounds exactly like one of the legends that must have circulated in local tradition about Station Island, the kind that Gerald of Wales spoke of when he said that if anyone should venture to spend the night in any one of the nine pits on the island,

he is seized immediately by malignant spirits, and is crucified all

---

[4] This is true at least of texts that survive. The assertion that David Scottus, an Irishman in Würzburg, wrote *De Purgatorio Patricii* in c. 1120 remains tantalizingly uncorroborated. See James F. Kenney, *The Sources for the Early History of Ireland: Ecclesiastical. An Introduction and Guide,* with addenda by L. Bieler (New York, 1966), pp. 354-6 and p. 620 n. 324.

night with such severe torments, and so continuously afflicted with
many unspeakable punishments of fire and water and other things,
that, when morning comes, there is found in his poor body scarcely
even the smallest trace of life surviving.[5]

In keeping with such legends, the knight in Peter's account does
not progress from purgatory to the Earthly Paradise, and does not
even witness the punishment of souls in purgatory. Instead, he
himself suffers an appalling sequence of tortures at the hands of
Gulinus's ministers. First, he is invited to go to bed with the king's
beautiful daughter. When he most willingly does so, she is
transformed into a disgusting old tree-trunk, and his penis, stuck
in a hole in this trunk, is battered by one of Gulinus's aides with a
nail and hammer.[6] To 'refresh' him, he is next offered a warm
bath, which turns out to be of boiling water, hotter than any fire,
and thereafter a cold one — of piercingly sharp ice. He is finally
offered relief in what we might now call a recreation-centre. Here
he becomes the plaything of Gulinus's fiendish household.

> On all sides in a circle on the walls of this house there were sharp
> stones sticking out a little. And there was a beam above placed
> across the walls, to which was fastened a cord, which hung down.
> To this rope the officers tied the knight's feet, with his head hanging
> down. Drawing him up a little, they flung him back and forth like a
> ball from wall to wall, and these officers did not cease from this
> game until all the limbs of the knight were dashed and sliced off by
> the foresaid sharp stones, and his head struck, broken and crushed,
> until his brains poured out. The foresaid knight said that this same
> affliction was incomparably more intolerable than all his
> aforementioned torments. When he had thus been played with for a
> very long time, and early dawn was approaching, all those ministers
> of wickedness disappeared with Gulinus their king, and all his
> torments vanished even with his vision, and the knight found
> himself in the entrance to the Purgatory from which he had first
> entered into purgatory, and he saw nothing of those he had seen.
> Then he suffered such infirmity or debility of body that he thought
> he would completely expire.[7]

---

[5] Gerald of Wales, *History and Topography*, tr. O'Meara, p. 61.

[6] For a possible context for this demonic sexual encounter, see Hans Peter Duerr,
Dreamtime: Concerning the Boundary between Wilderness and Civilization, translated by
Felicitas Goodman (Oxford, 1985), chapter 3. St Patrick's Purgatory is noted on page 211.

[7] Translated from the edition of this text in Easting, 'Peter of Cornwall's account', p. 415
lines 132-50.

No-one, says Peter, leaves the Purgatory without some debility or loss of mind.

We are a long way here from the spiritual comfort eventually attained by Owein and by latterday pilgrims!

Thus the first two visitors to Lough Derg, of whom *we* hear tell, were knights, and the element of knightly quest clearly contributed to the popularity of the story of Owein with secular audiences. This set the pattern for many later members of the European nobility whose pilgrimages are recounted in this book. H. of Saltrey says very little about his hero's background, however, and this was clearly felt to be a lack of the chroniclers mentioned above. When they incorporated a reduced version of an α text of the *Tractatus*[8] into their works, they also expanded on Owein's sinful nature:

> . . . a knight named Owen, who had for many years served under king Stephen, obtained the king's licence, and went to visit his parents in Ireland his native country. After spending some time there, he began to call to mind his wicked life, which had been employed from his cradle in plunder and violence. He particularly repented of the violation of churches, and invasion of ecclesiastical property, besides other enormous sins of which he had been guilty.[9]

There is no warrant for this in the *Tractatus*, but it is an early indication of how subsequent retellers of the story were to adapt that text for their own purposes.[10]

At the period when these Latin accounts were produced in England, French dominated English as the literary language of the educated laity. The earliest vernacular accounts of the Purgatory are the Anglo-Norman verse translations of H. of Saltrey's prose *Tractatus*. There survive no less than five independent Anglo-Norman translations, which amply testify to the story's popularity in England among the ruling class.[11]

The first notice of the Purgatory in the English language is the translation of the *Tractatus* which appears under 'St Patrick' in the

[8] For parallel editions of the α and β redactions of the *Tractatus*, see Warnke, *Das Buch vom Espurgatoire S. Patrice*, and see above p. 55.

[9] *Roger of Wendover's Flowers of History*, translated by J. A. Giles, Bohn's Antiquarian Library (2 vols., London, 1849), i. 511.

[10] For fuller discussion of the historical details involved, see Easting, 'Owein at St Patrick's Purgatory'.

[11] See the discussion by D. D. R. Owen, *The Vision of Hell: Infernal Journeys in Medieval French Literature* (Edinburgh and London, 1970), pp. 64-75.

South English Legendary,[12] a widespread collection of saints'
legends in verse dating from the second half of the thirteenth
century. The poem 'St Patrick' is a rendition with elaborations of
the essential story of the founding of the Purgatory and Owein's
visit, taken from an α text of the *Tractatus*.[13] Except for the
opening, which deals with Christ's revelation to St Patrick of the
purgatorial entrance, the bulk of the poem is devoted to Owein's
pilgrimage; this was clearly the most popular story connected with
the saint to be circulating in late thirteenth-century England.[14] It
makes a fitting companion in the *Legendary* for that other Irish
otherworld adventure, the voyage of St Brendan.

There were subsequently two further translations of Owein's
story into Middle English verse, one in the early fourteenth
century and another maybe a century later. The earlier of these is
much the most interesting of the three English versions, and I shall
give a brief account of it here. It is based on one of the
Anglo-Norman texts,[15] and is preserved in a unique copy in the
famous Auchinleck manuscript that Chaucer may have known
(now Edinburgh, National Library of Scotland, MS. Advocates',
19.2.1).[16]

Sir Walter Scott first published extracts from this anonymous
poem in the introduction to the 'Lyke-Wake Dirge' and notes to
'Clerk Saunders' in his *Minstrelsy of the Scottish Border* in 1802.
The poem's title and opening have been excised from the
manuscript, probably for the sake of a miniature; Scott called the
poem *The Legend of Sir Owain*, but since its first complete

[12] The most recent and accessible text is in *The South English Legendary*, ed. Charlotte
D'Evelyn and Anna J. Mills, Early English Text Society, 235 (1956), 85-110.

[13] For a full discussion see Robert Easting, 'The *South English Legendary* "St Patrick" as
translation', forthcoming in *Leeds Studies in English*.

[14] Manfred Görlach has written of this poem, 'In the case of *Patrick* it is noteworthy that the
"Z" translator did not choose *Vita III*, the text most commonly known in England and
therefore adapted for English breviaries (L. Bieler, *The Life and Legend of Saint Patrick*
(Dublin, 1949), p. 125), but that he deliberately selected the most *popular* text.' *The Textual
Tradition of the South English Legendary* (Leeds, 1974), p. 225 note p. 44.

[15] The Anglo-Norman source has not previously been recognised: it is the version contained
in Cambridge University Library, MS. Ee.6.11 and a fragment in British Library, Lansdowne
MS. 383. This new source-identification fits the pattern for many other texts in the Auchinleck
manuscript that are also translated from French.

[16] See the facsimile, *The Auchinleck Manuscript*, with an Introduction by Derek Pearsall &
I. C. Cunningham (London, 1977).

printing in 1837[17] it has usually been known as *Owain* (or *Owayne*)
Miles, i.e. 'Sir Owain', a title taken from one manuscript of the
later translation. (For convenience I shall refer to the Auchinleck
poem as OM1.)

The manuscript numeration shows that OM1 is still in its
original place, following the lives of St Margaret and St Katherine
and followed by *The disputation between the body and the soul* and
the *Harrowing of Hell,* a perfect position for a poem that combines
elements of saint's life with an adventure story that echoes Christ's
victory over the otherworld.

In the presentation of purgatory the poem takes a more overtly
moral and didactic line than its Anglo-Norman source and the
Tractatus; OM1 adds passages detailing the sins punished (one
should say purged) by each of the torments Owein encounters. In
this way most of the seven deadly sins are accounted for in a
sequence of befitting punishments: the slothful are nailed to the
ground; gluttons are eaten; hot lechers are cooled by a cold wind;
the covetous whirl on the fiery wheel; and the pit is reserved for
the sin of pride. Envy and anger are probably to be accounted for
in the fourth field of torment, which is reserved for thieves,
backbiters, blasphemers and false witnesses and by the fiery wind
for *nithe and ond,* 'spite and malice' (stanza 95 line 2). In addition,
usury is purged in the hall of pits, and Owein himself is accused in
his progress of pride, lechery, gluttony, covetousness and usury. It
is clear that the impetus for the inclusion of these elements has
come from a Middle English version of another famous
apocalyptic text, the *Vision of St Paul.*[18] This similarly lists the sins
punished in hell, but the enumeration is not as thorough as in
OM1.

The OM1 poet also forcefully distinguishes between purgatory,
whence redeemed souls pass safely across the narrow bridge to the
Earthly Paradise, and hell beneath the bridge. This was a
distinction that apparently needed persistent elucidation, for the

---

[17] *Owain Miles and Other Inedited Fragments of Ancient English Poetry* [ed. David Laing
and W. B. D. D. Turnbull and others] (Edinburgh, 1837). It was subsequently published by E.
Kölbing, 'Zwei mittelenglische Bearbeitungen der Sage von St. Patrik's Purgatorium',
Englische Studien, i (1877), 98-112. There is a modern prose translation of OM1 in M. H.
Shackford, *Legends and Satires from Medieval Literature* (Boston, 1913), pp. 33-49. Both the
later Middle English versions have been edited anew in my forthcoming volume for the Early
English Text Society.

[18] The author of OM1 used one of the four Middle English verse versions of the *Vision of St
Paul,* that in the same tail-rhyme stanza form as OM1, extant in Bodleian Library, MS. Laud
Misc. 108.

terminological separation between these two realms was not always secure even in the early fourteenth century; there are numerous occasions where (as here) a particular emphasis is laid on clarifying the separation.[19] Moreover, the 'infernalised' view of purgatory, which is found in St Patrick's Purgatory texts and which was widespread in popular eschatology, could blur the distinction between hell and purgatory if the reader or audience were inattentive. It is significant, therefore, that OM1 frequently disabuses the reader of any impression that the torments encountered by Owein may be in hell.[20] OM1 also omits the demons' speech about the pit being the 'false' hell, thereby obviating possible confusion.[21] In the section on the Earthly Paradise OM1 again clarifies some of the eschatological implications of the story. The delay in the Earthly Paradise before entry into heaven is spelt out by Owein's guides, who comment also on the relative speeds of transit through purgatory of the innocent newly born and the old sinner.

But doctrine is clearly subservient to another emphasis. OM1 may well have been translated in the London 'bookshop' where the Auchinleck manuscript was probably produced, and the poem has clearly been prepared for a secular audience with a penchant for romances as well as for religious tales. By a variety of additions and omissions, the author of this version makes the most of the narrative's romance potential: the adventures of a knight encountering the ultimate perils and delights of the otherworld.

The amplification in the first two parts of the tale, detailing the founding of the Purgatory by St Patrick and Owein's passage through the fields of torment, not only stresses the sins purged, but also aims at authenticating realism. Owein, we are told, visited the

---

[19] For example, *The Pricke of Conscience,* ed. R. Morris (Berlin, 1863), enumerates hell, purgatory, the limbo of infants and the limbo of the fathers, saying that all these four places men may call 'hell' (2816), and clarifies the potential confusion in the prayer for the dead:

Tharfor haly kyrke that for saulys prays,
Calles purgatory helle, that thus says:
Domine, Ihesu Criste libera animas omnium
defunctorum, de manu inferni!
That is to say, out [of] purgatory
That the saules er clensed parfytely.
Quia in inferno nulla est redempcio.

(2820-1, 2827-8)

[20] References are by stanza and line 42:6, 67:6, 72:6, 82:2, 160:6, 165:1, 166:2, 194:5.

[21] On the separation of purgatory from hell, see Jacques Le Goff, *The Birth of Purgatory,* translated by Arthur Goldhammer (London, 1984), and on his treatment of St Patrick's Purgatory, see Easting, 'Purgatory and the Earthly Paradise'.

otherworld in *flesche and fel* ('skin' 54:4) and went *Quic* ('living')
man into that place (139:6); there is nothing mystical in the St
Patrick's Purgatory tradition.[22] No mention is made of the
suggestion that instead of pursuing his penance he might adopt the
habit of a monk or canon; this version holds no brief for the
religious life, at least not until the end. Similarly omitted is the
passage about Owein donning the armour of God; Owein starts
out as a very worldly knight, an extravagant sinner and a fighter,
not a knight of Christ. Moreover, Owein is made an Englishman,
born in Northumberland; he is one of us, rather than an Irishman.
When he enters the 'cave' he is advised to keep north, a suitable
direction to find the domain of Lucifer, and the underground hall
he enters (we are twice told) is made of stone — the realm of the
dead is actual. No mention is made of God's help preventing him
from going mad with the demonic clatter, or of the power of his
prayer as the source of his feeling bolder when the first group of
fiends departs; Owein calls appropriately on Christ's five wounds
instead. No mention is made in advance of the possibility that
Owein will eventually reach the Earthly Paradise. The physicality
of the fields of purgatory and the pains is repeatedly emphasised
by further additions: there are no trees; the fire about the wheel
burns the souls to a fine powder; the mountain is as red as blood;
the river flows with the speed of a bolt from a cross-bow; the fiends
are as numerous as motes in a sun-beam; and Owein's clothes are
tattered and his body badly burnt.

The poem also makes more of the devils, who are notable for
their vicious irony. They grin at Owein with the faces on their
backsides; their leader falls on his knees before Owein in mock
reverence to welcome him; they promise him the 'joy of hell', and
threaten him with joining their dance and play, unless he allows
them to return to the entrance *with fine amour* (57:4), a nicely
incongruous expression. Owein, however, recognises their
treacherous testing of his heart and proceeds with determination.

A notable feature of OM1 is the presentation of the Earthly

---

[22] In the classification of visions proposed by Peter Dinzelbacher, Owein's story belongs very
much to Type I, the non-ecstatic, non-charismatic, non-allegorical: see *Vision und
Visionsliteratur des Mittelalters* (Stuttgart, 1981), pp. 229-33. For recent studies of such visions
in relation to modern research on near-death experience, see also Peter Dinzelbacher,
'Mittelalterliche Vision und moderne Sterbeforschung', in *Psychologie in der Mediävistik:
Gesammelte Beiträge des Steinheimer Symposions*, ed. Jürgen Kühnel *et al*, (Göppingen, 1985),
pp. 9-49, and Carol Zaleski, *Otherworld Journeys: accounts of near-death experience in
medieval and modern times* (New York and Oxford, 1987).

Paradise, which is more extended and elaborate than in any other St Patrick's Purgatory text. The additions include, for instance, an eleven-stanza section cataloguing the music, carols, birdsong, flowers, wells, and four rivers of Paradise, as well as the precious stones and the decorations of the gates; here the vocabulary is technically specific and suggests a desire to show that the artefacts in Paradise are the very best and à la mode. This is another aspect of the poem's appeal via romantic adventure to a secular audience.

Accordingly, the story concludes with an added lustre: Owein returns to the entrance amid a flame of light proving that he was now God's knight and a holy man. He goes on pilgrimage not only to Jerusalem but Bethlehem as well, and on returning to Ireland lives as a monk seven years before he dies. The poem leaves him if not enskied, then certainly imparadised, and almost sainted.[23]

It might be said that the verse in OM1 repeatedly aspires to the condition of poetry, despite the tail-rhyme stanza form (mocked by Chaucer in *Sir Thopas*); the metre of OM1 was later used by Robert Southey for his ballad written in 1798 based on the *Espurgatoire* of Marie de France. Jessie L. Weston, who herself translated the second half of OM1,[24] was rather too enthusiastic when quoting the poem as clinching proof of a link between 'pre-Christian initiations' and 'Medieval Romance',[25] but her susceptibility is also some tribute to this poem's undoubted attractiveness.

Over two centuries after the *Tractatus* was composed, we have the first brief account of an Englishman's visit to Lough Derg. Froissart reports a conversation which took place in 1395. This is valuable for its physical details of the Purgatory at that time, some two years before the visit of Ramon de Perellós. (I quote from the famous Tudor translation of Lord Berners.)

> Then on the Friday in the morning sir William Lisle and I rode together, and on the way I demanded of him if he had been with the king in the voyage to Ireland. He answered me, yes. Then I demanded of him the manner of the hole that is in Ireland, called Saint Patrick's purgatory, if it were true that was said of it or not. Then he said of a surety such a hole there was, and that he himself and another knight of England had been there, while the king lay at Dublin, and said how they entered into the hole and were closed in

---

[23] See the use of *seyn(t) Owain* at 94:1, 149:4, and 188:1.

[24] *The Chief Middle English Poets* (Boston, 1914), pp. 83-89.

[25] See *From Ritual to Romance* (Cambridge, 1920), pp. 173-4.

at the sun going down and abode there all night, and the next morning issued out again at the sun-rising. Then I demanded if he had any such strange sights or visions as were spoken of. Then he said how that when he and his fellow were entered and past the gate that was called the purgatory of Saint Patrick, and that they were descended and gone down three or four paces, descending down as into a cellar, a certain hot vapour rose against them and strake so into their heads, that they were fain to sit down on the stairs, which are of stone. And after they had sat there a season, they had great desire to sleep, and so fell asleep and slept there all night. Then I demanded that if in their sleep they knew where they were, or what visions they had. He answered me that in sleeping they entered into great imaginations and in marvellous dreams, otherwise than they were wont to have in their chambers, and in the morning they issued out and within a short season clean forgat their dreams and visions; wherefore he said he thought all that matter was but a fantasy. Then I left speaking any further of that matter . . . .[26]

Sir William Lisle may have had only extraordinary dreams, but some dozen or so years later another pilgrim was to claim more of the 'strange sights and visions' that Froissart was expecting to hear tell.

The Vision of William of Stranton is the sole major visionary account in English of a visit to St Patrick's Purgatory made by an Englishman, and as such forms the core of this chapter. It survives in two copies in the British Library, MS. Royal 17 B.xliii and MS. Additional 34193. The Royal manuscript (hereafter SR) dates William's visit to 1409, the Additional text (hereafter SA) to 1406. It is not possible to determine which, if indeed either, of these dates is correct, for Roman numerals are notoriously liable to mistranscription. The manuscripts are both later copies, probably at several removes from what may be assumed to have been an original text in northern dialect; the copies differ from each other considerably in verbal detail and have perhaps both been subject to scribal revision in the process of translation into the copyists' dialects: SR was copied in the mid-fifteenth century in Warwickshire, and SA a little later and further north in Nottinghamshire.

William's account tells us that he comes from the bishopric of Durham; Stranton is a parish south of Hartlepool, so I prefer the

[26] *The Chronicles of Froissart translated by John Bourchier, Lord Berners*, The Globe Edition, edited and reduced into one volume by G. C. Macauley (London, 1913), p. 425.

name William of Stranton as given in SA; SR reads 'William
Staunton'. Unfortunately, no description is given of William's
journey to Ireland or of the island location of the Purgatory. Both
texts agree on the time at which he was put into the Purgatory, the
eighth hour before noon, and both give a date, but here the
manuscripts again differ: SR specifies 'the Friday next after the
Feast of the Exaltation of the Cross', i.e. 20 September 1409; SA
says Easter Day, i.e. 14 April 1406. We are also told that William
was put into the Purgatory by Prior Matthew,

> keeper of the same Purgatory, with procession and devout prayers
> of the same prior and convent, the which taught me an orison to
> bless me with, and to write the first word in my forehead, which is
> this: *Jhesu, fili Dei, miserere mei.*[27] And the prior taught me to say
> this orison when any spirit good or evil appeared to me, or if I heard
> any noise that I should be affeared of, for if they were good spirits
> they should abide with me, and if they were evil they should void
> from me. And after, through the teaching of the prior, I came to a
> resting place of Saint Patrick, in the which he abode the revelation
> of God's angels when he would pass that way in his own time. And
> there I abode and somewhat I slumbered and slept. After that I was
> aware of more light coming to me, and me thought that I saw a man
> and a woman both clad in white, the man in habit of a canon and the
> woman in the same habit with a veil as a nun. And when I saw them
> first I was somewhat dread, and said my prayer and blessed my
> forehead. Then they laughed on me and bad, 'God speed'.[28]

By the simple connection *After that,* William neatly blurs the
issue of whether he believed he visited the otherworld in the flesh,
as Owein claimed, or in spirit, in a vision during sleep. The latter
seems more likely, however, for he carefully allies himself with St
Patrick who waited in the same resting place for the revelation of
God's angels. William's visit also differs from Owein's in the

[27] 'Jesu, son of God, have mercy upon me.' SR has the more authentic reading: *Jhesu
Christe, fili Dei viui, miserere michi peccatori,* 'Jesu Christ, son of the living God, have mercy
upon me, a sinner'. This is the same form as the prayer given to George Grissaphan and
Laurence Rathold.

[28] Quotations are from my own transcription of SA, unless otherwise indicated, and are
given in modern spelling with minimal translation. SA has not previously been printed. SR was
published by G. P. Krapp, *The Legend of Saint Patrick's Purgatory: its later literary history*
(Baltimore, 1900), pp. 58-77. Krapp prints only brief passages from SA in footnotes.
Modernized extracts from Krapp's text are given by Leslie, *Saint Patrick's Purgatory,* p. 28-33.
The texts of both manuscripts are presented in parallel with fuller discussion in my forthcoming
edition for the Early English Text Society.

appearance of the canon and the nun, who subsequently act as his guides and guardians; Owein first met a company like monks in a cloistral hall but thereafter he was dragged across the fields of torment in purgatory by various troops of demons.

The canon reassures William straightaway that though he has undertaken a great thing, yet ' " through the mercy of God thou shalt well do and well fare" '; William's progress is to be more a guided tour than a knightly quest like Owein's.[29] But he is not accompanied at the start or all the time.

The canon then warns William that he will first come to two paths, on the right and left; he is to avoid the fair left-hand path and take the right one, which is ' "narrow and somedeal foul in the beginning" '. William will meet evil spirits ' "like in shape and in colour to men of thy country which are yet living" '; they will try to stop William, but he must say, ' " 'Certainly, this way will I pass, through the help of God' " '. Also when he later sees ' "more grisly sights and more ugly there of evil spirits" ', he must think on our Lord's Passion and then they will do him no harm. Grateful for such advice, William requests to know who is giving it. The canon replies, ' "In your country they call me John of Bridlington, and so I am, and this woman is my sister, Saint Hilda of Whitby, that lived therein sometime." '

It is entirely appropriate that William of Stranton's guides are these two famous northern saints, one from closer to the time of Saint Patrick, the other William's near contemporary. Before she moved to Whitby in 657, St Hilda held the monastery at Hartlepool, less than two miles from the parish of Stranton, so she would have a special significance for William. St John of Bridlington was an Augustinian canon, and as the same order held the Saints' Island priory and Station Island, Lough Derg, his appearance here is doubly appropriate. He died in 1379 and was canonized in 1401; his relics were translated in 1404, only a few years before the supposed dates given for William's encounter with him in Saint Patrick's Purgatory. St John's splendid shrine attracted many pilgrims, and William was obviously a devotee, for the saint says, ' "Thou hast often come to me, where my body lies, and to my sister Saint Hilda. That more dis-eased thee than our coming does us." ' If we interpret *often* here to mean that William

[29] See also Carol Zaleski, 'St. Patrick's Purgatory: pilgrimage motifs in a medieval otherworld journey', *Journal of the History of Ideas*, xlvi (1985), 467-85, who stresses the correlation of physical and spiritual pilgrimage at Lough Derg.

was in the habit of making, say, an annual pilgrimage to Whitby
and Bridlington, then 1409 would be a more likely date than 1406
for his pilgrimage to Lough Derg.

At this point the saints leave William, who soon after finds the
men blocking the right-hand path. These claim to be his fleshly
friends, come to protect him from certain death, but when William
thinks of Christ's Passion and signs his forehead with the prayer he
was taught, the men fly away in the likeness of evil spirits, which is
what they really were.

William next encounters grisly looking spirits with four heads
and four faces on their heads and five or six horns, and faces also
on their elbows and knees. Such demonic deformity is not
uncommonly found in manuscript illustrations and wall-paintings
of the fourteenth and fifteenth centuries, and may well derive from
costumes used in dramatic representations such as *The Harrowing
of Hell* and the *Judgement*. The *Tractatus* gives no such visual
details, but similar descriptions are found, for instance, in OM1,
where, as mentioned, demons grin at Owein with faces on their
foul backsides.

The devils stick out their (multiple!) tongues at William and
shriek so hideously that he forgets his prayer; he is rescued only by
the intervention of St Hilda, who rebukes him sharply as ' "Mad
man" ', and tells him never to forget Christ's Passion. Once again,
when William prays, the fiends vanish from sight.

A mile further on an interesting personal incident occurs. 'I met
again Saint John and Saint Hilda, and a sister of mine own that was
dead (long before in a pestilence time (SR)), and another man that
I knew well loved my sister in her life.' Firstly, St John chastises
William for forgetting his prayer and for his lack of stedfastness;
William, he says, is too simple to undertake such a journey without
God's mercy. Then William's sister speaks to St John:

> "Hail, father, ye are here in God's stead, and I make my complaint
> unto you of my brother that here stands. That is to say, that he has
> sinned greatly against God, for this man that here stands loved me
> and I loved him, and either of us would have had other after the law
> of God, as Holy Church teaches, and he should have gotten and I
> borne three souls to God; and my brother let *(hindered)* us go
> together, for he said, if we did, there should neither of us have joy
> of other, and for that cause we left [it]."

St John sternly rebukes William for preventing the marriage:

". . . there is no man nor woman that hinders man and woman to go together in the law of God, though the man be a shepherd and all his ancestors and the woman be come of kings and emperors, or if the man be come of never so high kin (and the woman of never so low kin (SR)), if they love each other, he that hinders it sins deadly against God and cursed he is of the deed, whatsoever he be . . .".

St John instructs William to confess this sin to the prior of the Purgatory when he returns to the world, and to do the penance imposed. If he had been shriven previously but not completed the penance, then he would have had to do penance there and then in purgatory before proceeding.

This incident has the particularity of autobiographical truth, and is one of the rare moments when we catch a glimpse of William's personal past. The memory of his earlier family arguments with his sister must have weighed heavily on him, and in the otherworld her spirit stands and accuses him with an affecting simplicity and forthrightness.

William is thereafter led by St John to observe the torment of souls in nine different fires, each purging different sins, as the saint explains. In the first are those who indulged in 'a false pleasing of vain glory of pride and array', wearing gold and silver collars, fashionable slashed clothing decorated with bells and jingles, long sleeves and trains, and headdresses set with pearls and other precious stones. These ornaments and attire are cut, bitten, sucked and rent from them by adders, dragons, toads and other horrible beasts, and thrust burning upon their bodies and even into their mouths, noses and ears. The precious stones become burning nails of brass, hammered by fiends into the bodies of the sinners. St John laments:

"Alas, why would they be so mad as to love more the fiend their enemy, than God that is ever ready for us at our need, as our suffering friend? . . . better had they been to have left their sin and their foul pride [of] array by counsel of their ghostly fathers or of other good livers."

The remaining eight fires contain equally horrific scenes of demons variously torturing souls in ways which more or less befit their sins. Those who swear by God's body, arms, wounds, etc., are themselves hideously dismembered by fiends who then stick them back together with molten metal. Those who go to taverns and plays on holy days are shoved full of filth as one stuffs a wool-pack. Fiends shit dung mingled with sparks of fire in the faces of those who dishonour their parents. Robbers and false executors of wills are tormented by the goods they have stolen or purloined: horse and cattle thieves, for instance, are bitten in pieces by their booty. In a truly surreal passage, false witnesses, who had illegally acquired or accepted land, have great burning hills, rocks and woods falling on them. With keen swords fiends smite off the heads of murderers and mangle all their limbs.

> [The eighth fire] was hot out of measure and black as any pitch, and small sparkling lights of blue like unto brimstone came out thereof. In that fire were many souls, both of men and women, some hanging by their privy members with chains of iron burning, and some by the heart and some by their eyes, and fiends beating on them with burning hammers.

St John explains:

> "These are they that led their life in lechery, and for they sinned in deed they are hanged by the members, and they that sinned in willing and in desire are hanged by the heart, for the heart was in will for to do the deed, and they that kept not their eyes from vanities but with them looked on women and on their gay array and vanities of the world, and women that behold the stout array of other women, that turned their hearts to so great vanity that they covet passing their estate, even though their husbands and their children therefore were in great debt, and by that covetousness fell into more sin, therefore they are tormented in their eyes."

This passage is typical of the mixture of careful subdivision and breathless syntax in many of St John's tirades. In the last of these fires, men and women who failed to chastise their children are beaten by their offspring, even as these acknowledge ' "the tender deeds that you did for us" '. Such divine sanction for corporal punishment of the young was frequently voiced in homiletic material of the day.

But the catalogue of woe does not end here. William is next led to a rock overhanging all these fires, where souls enclosed by a wall lie stretched and bound, and gnawed by dragons, snakes and toads.

"William", [says St John,] "these are backbiters and [they] that
were busy with their shrewd tales to go from house to house,
speaking evil of their fellow christian, having rejoicing of their
neighbour's harm and sorriness of their welfare . . ."

So far William has been shown the penitential torment imposed
on the laity for venial and unshriven mortal sins, for the everyday
laxity and malice of domestic and social life. But the clergy fare no
better, and all the remaining scenes of purgatory are reserved for
ecclesiastics.

In two towers, one full of fire, the other of ice, bishops, prelates
and curates, who ' "should have preached the law of God to the
people and given them example of good living" ', are belaboured
with firebrands by the souls of their servants whom they allowed to
live in luxury and fine array. In another fire, ' "canons, monks,
friars, and others that should have lived in contemplation and
abstinence of their body" ' are alternately swollen up and then
punctured and consumed by noxious beasts that exude from their
fingers and toes. The souls of the poor cry out in accusation of
their superfluity and wastefulness.

Next William sees souls closed about with plates of iron which
have letters and words written on them, through which nails are
driven into the souls. One has his tongue and heart taken out and
shorn small and cast in his face; this is William's uncle, a parson
who died sixteen years previously. He is in the company of other
vicars and priests who failed to say the words of the divine service
every day.

". . . they have more false devotion and lust in hawking and hunting
and other lewd plays and idle occupations and worldly mirths than
in the service of God, and therefore they are thus tormented with
horrible pains. And if they had served God as they should have
done, by reason of their charge that they took, greatest bliss in
heaven might they have had. Alas! that such priests should be called
God's knights, that fight every day against their liege lord. And
therefore they shall be called by right of their false governance, the
Devil's knights and God's traitors, and for such are they now
tormented, and shall be while God's will is."

A great house, strong-walled and stinking, is full of naked souls;
their mouths are stopped by moths and worms emerging from
huge presses of clothes; doublets, fiends' shit and hailstones beat

upon them. These are parsons, vicars and priests who neglected their parishioners, dressed as though they were secular men, allowed hail, snow and rain to fall into their chancels and upon their altars by spending money for church maintenance on clothing, and who closed themselves ' "within their high houses when they should eat, for they would not hear the poor people cry." '

The last punishment in this section of the vision is that of a bishop, his clerks and officers. As they cross a great broad bridge above black water, yelling fiends mine and pull away the pillars; as the bishop and his company fall an angel takes the bishop's cross and mitre and vanishes. The bishop had performed a good deed — building a bridge ' "for easement of the common people" ' — but for the wrong reason — vainglory, ' "to have thank and praising of the people" '. Moreover the goods with which he built it were ill-gotten: bribes collected by his officers for turning a blind eye to lechery, and fees for deliberately protracted cases in the consistory courts. The angel's preservation of the bishop's cross and mitre signifies the sanctity of the office and its separation from the sins of the holder.

At this point SR reads *Fin[i]s reuelacionum penalium,* the end of the revelation of punishment. The reader reaches this with almost as much relief as William, whose reaction to these horrible pains is to ask St John if there is no remedy or mitigation for these souls. His guide assures him there is, principally the mercy of God and ' "the good deeds that their friends and other people living in the world may do for them" '. He lists the offices of the clergy, such as singing masses and saying psalms, and of the laity, such as saying the *Pater, Ave* and *Creed,* giving alms, going on pilgrimage, and fasting. These abate the suffering of the souls in purgatory just as the addition of cold water lessens the pain of scalding hot water.

St John then departs; he does not reappear in the rest of the vision. William is left alone by the deep and grisly water. 'And ever I looked after a bridge over that water, which I had heard speak of, that is to say, of the bridge full of spikes *(pykys)*. And when I saw none I was the more afraid.' In the *Tractatus* Owein passes from purgatory to the Earthly Paradise via a bridge which is slippery, narrow, and high, but it does not have spikes on it. It seems that William has heard about the spiked bridge across the otherworld river from some form of the *Visio Tnugdali* or *Vision of Tundale,* another enormously popular story of an otherworld journey experienced in a vision by another Irish soldier. It was translated into Middle English and survives in five manuscripts.[30]

But no bridge appears for William. Instead, he hears 'the greatest and the most hugest noise of fiends that ever I heard before'. As at the beginning, William is so terrified that his wits and spirit fail him and he forgets his prayer, and again St Hilda appears and calls him a madman (SR), and bids him remember Christ's Passion and his prayer. Thus saved, William proceeds.

And then I went forth on my right hand by the water side, and on that other side of the water I saw nothing but a huge rock. And so long I went by the water-side that I saw on the other side a high tower. And there I saw a great[er] light than I did in all the way before. And on the top I saw a fair woman standing and looking to me. And then I was glad, and set me down on my knees with good devotion, till I had said five *Pater nosters* and five *Ave Marias* in the worship of Our Lord's five wounds and of Our Lady's five joys. And then I blessed me with my prayer, and ere I rose up I looked to the tower, and there I saw a ladder from the top of the tower reaching to the ground where I kneeled. And for gladness I rose up and went to the ladder, and forsooth methought it was so right weak, that methought it would bear nothing that had any weight. And the first stile was so high that scarcely I might reach my finger thereto, and that was sharper than any razor, and for dread I took my hand away. And with that I heard a thousandfold more grisly noise come toward me than ever I heard before, and as fast as I blessed me with my prayer, quickly it vanished away. And then I looked to the ladder, and I saw a cord coming from the top of the tower to the foot of the ladder. And the woman bade me knit the rope to my middle, and so I did, and went then to the ladder again, and put my hand to the stile, and then I felt the stile of no sharpness. But then I heard a thousand more fold more grisly noise than I heard before, under me in the water and on the land, than ever I heard at any time in all my way. Then through the help of the mercy of Our Lord Jesu Christ and the woman that was above there on the tower, I was soon brought to the tower top, and then I was past all dread. Then I fell on knees and inclined before that fair woman and said, 'Jesu Christ, God's Son in heaven, quit *(reward)* you for your good deed and help, and your cord.' Then the fair woman said, 'William, this is the cord that thou gavest the chapman *(merchant)* for pity when he was robbed of thieves, when he asked thee some of thy good[s], for the love of God.'

[30] See the most recent edition by Rodney Mearns, *The Vision of Tundale*, Middle English Texts, 18 (Heidelberg, 1985), lines 609-10.

The fair woman is not identified, and we are not invited to equate her with St Hilda, whose last appearance was to admonish William to remember Christ's Passion and his prayer. The woman's appearance amid a great light on the top of the tower on the high rock beyond the water is a striking emblem of spiritual salvation, and after St John's guardianship in the fires of pain it is noteworthy that two women facilitate William's escape across the river and his entry into the Earthly Paradise. The ladder of salvation, a variation on the expected bridge, is also a powerful image with many antecedents in vision literature, and the sharpness of the first rung is a characteristic feature of otherworld bridges: in OM1, for instance, the same simile is used, though this is no basis for supposing that William knew that poem. The cord given to a merchant seems to be a specific personal reminiscence; its use as a kind of safety harness reflects the popular notion that the objects of good deeds in this life can be beneficial to the soul in the otherworld.

> Then the woman went from the tower and I followed after. And all the earth of the country was white and clear as cristal, and there was no grass growing, but the fairest tree that ever I saw grew there and sweeter of savour than all the spice shops of all the world. And many fair birds of diverse colours were in that tree, full merrily singing with many sweet noise and delectable, passing all the songs that ever I heard. And in that country I would fain have bidden *(remained)* for it was so passing merry in that country. I went right fast forth. Farthermore I went the better, and the farthermore, more mery and gladder I was. And truly, there came against me a fair company of monks and canons and priests, and all clad in white array, and they welcomed me and walked with me full goodly and gently, as I had been their born brother by father and mother.

The brief description of paradise here is striking for the lack of grass and the cristalline earth. The welcoming host of ecclesiastics is reminiscent of the company which greets Owein.

SR preserves or adds an interesting passage that has been omitted by SA.

> And that ever I did any good deed in this world, they thanked me therefore, insomuch that for a candle that I set sometime in a church before an image — not for the image, but in worship of that saint that the image betokened — I was thanked therefore.

Again a brief moment of William's devotion is caught, along with punctilious discrimination about the purpose of the offering.

A bishop then greets and blesses William; Owein was addressed by two men like archbishops, who explained to Owein the significance of all he had seen. When William asks if he can stay, ' "for truly here is merry abiding" ', the bishop replies,

> "No, William, thou may not abide here now, but look thou be a good man, and thou shalt come hither. And look thou ask nothing of God that may displease Him, for that is a great sin to thee to covet to abide here yet, for thee behoves needs to go again. And thou shalt see an examination of a prioress, for her soul is come hither now to have her judgement."

This individual judgement immediately *post mortem* takes place on a high hill in what is still presumably paradise, though it is never called that specifically. The soul of the prioress is there surrounded by fiends who have come to accuse her of the sins contained in 'a book of all evil deeds that she had done', borne by a monk who conducts the examination.

> . . . the fiends accused her and said that she came to religion all for pomp and pride, and for to have abundance of worldly ease and riches, and not for devotion nor meekness and lowness of heart, as religion asks to do, both of men and of women. And yet said the fiends that it is well known to God and all the angels of heaven and to men dwelling in that country where she dwelt, and to all the fiends of hell, that she against her order was of misgovernance, in wearing of fur and girdles of silver, and gold rings on her fingers, and silver buckles on her shoes, and lying on nights like a queen or an empress, nothing desiring but ease and rest, and not rising on nights to God's service; and with all delicate meats and drinks she was fed.

In her defence the prioress says she had shrift and full repentance of her misdeeds and wickedness; as she died before she had time to do penance, the bishop sentences her to pain till the Day of Doom. The bishop then laments how worldly men

> every day fight against [Jesu Christ] and against his commandments, and sin in the seven deadly sins, and in their five in-wits;[31] which

---

[31] I.e. will, reason, mind, imagination and thought.

unkind souls be called unwitty, for their wits turn them to folly, for God ordained them to get them heaven with them, and they purchase them hell.

The final few lines are again missing from SA.

Then the bishop said to me, 'William, pass thou home in the blessing of God and mine, and say as thou hast heard and seen to them that this belongeth to. And live rightfully and thou shalt come to everlasting joy. And dread thee not of thy way as thou passest homeward, for thou shalt see no evil sprites that shall dis-ease thee; thou shalt not fail of thy way.' And with that I took my leave. Anon I was at the door where I went first in.

Wherefore, all christian men that hear or read this, I beseech you for the love of God, that ye have me in your prayer, and ye shall be in mine.

William of Stranton's vision is an important witness to the cult of St Patrick's Purgatory. We may regret his silence about his journey, Lough Derg, and the purgatorial cavern, but there is no reason to doubt the authenticity of William's visit to Station Island. His mention of the procession and prayers, his naming of the prior, and details such as the door of the Purgatory, the time of his entry and the resting place of St Patrick all serve to confirm his first-hand experience. He also presents himself as a devoted pilgrim, prepared to travel long distances frequently. Unfortunately, he tells us only fleetingly or indirectly about himself, as in the incidents involving his sister, the cord, and the candle. He was clearly no knight like Owein or Sir William Lisle. We do not know if he was in orders or a pious layman; he may have been a priest as was his uncle. His repeated complaints against the idle and negligent rich place him close to the plight of the common people, a stance found frequently in sermon material of the period. Attacks on fashionable excesses are also found in the near contemporary visions at Lough Derg by Ramon de Perellós, Antonio Mannini and Laurence Rathold. In addition, all denominations of the ecclesiastical hierarchy from bishops to parsons are exposed by William's forbidding rectitude. Even in paradise he includes the judgement of the prioress. He is also confidently knowledgeable about all the means by which both laity and clergy can assist souls in purgatory.

William's account was probably more widely known in the

fifteenth century than the two surviving copies might suggest, and there must in any case have been at least two intermediate copies between the original text and SR and SA, for neither of these is dependent on the other nor do they derive from a common exemplar. Traces of the influence of William's *Vision* can definitely be seen in the *Vision of Edmund Leversedge,* seen at Frome in Somerset in May, 1465, and recorded by a different copyist in the same manuscript as SA, though it is possible that similarities here may be the result of scribal interference.[32]

The contents of the surviving manuscripts provide interesting contexts for William's *Vision,* suggestive of ways in which it may have been read or at least of the taste of a particular readership. The text has been copied at a late stage into the Additional manuscript for it occupies three different series of leaves originally left blank at the end of other complete or abandoned items. Additional opens with the *Pilgrimage of the Soul,* a lengthy allegorical otherworld journey in prose, translated from the French of Guillaume de Deguileville. This obviously set the tenor for the collection which also contains the *Vision of Edmund Leversedge,* as mentioned, and among further devotional material in English and Latin, *De spiritu Guidonis,* a tale from the thirteen-twenties, which relates how the dead Guy's spirit is released from purgatory to appear to his wife and appeal for her prayers. The Royal manuscript comprises three originally separate manuscripts which appear to have been bound together in the fifteenth century and re-bound in the eighteenth. The first is a copy of Mandeville's *Travels.* The second contains William's vision, preceded by the romance *Sir Gowther,* probably copied by the same scribe as copied SR. The third is a copy of the Middle English *Vision of Tundale. Tundale* and SR are both preceded by crude coloured drawings, seemingly by the same executant, the one representing Tundale's guardian angel and the other St John of Bridlington.[33] These two otherworld journeys are thus here read alongside travels which are scarcely less a matter of fantasy for being of this world, and a demonic romance involving lavish sin and saintly penance. It is not hard to see how William's text is at home in such company or to imagine the tastes for which such manuscripts catered.

[32] See E. M. Thompson, 'The Vision of Edmund Leversedge', *Notes and Queries for Somerset and Dorset,* ix (1904), 19-35.

[33] This illustration is reproduced in black and white by Leslie (1932), opposite p. 28.

The Vision of William of Stranton is the first and last extended account to be composed in English of a vision at Lough Derg following the pattern established by the *Tractatus*. Later notices are usually translations of earlier material, such as Holinshed's rehearsal of extracts from Gerald of Wales and Higden's *Polychronicon*.[34] Caxton is worth quoting, however, from his 1480 translation of the thirteenth-century French *Image du Monde*. (I retain his spelling, as it causes little difficulty.)

> Ther is also in Irlonde a place called seynt Patryks purgatorye, which place is perillous. Yf ony men goon therin and be not confessed and repentaunt of their synnes, they be anon rauysshed and loste in suche wyse that noman can telle where they be come. And yf they be confessyd and repentant, and that they haue don satisfaccion and penaunce for their synnes, without that alle be clensed and ful satisfyed, therafter shall they suffre payne and greef the tormentis in passing this crymynel passage. And whan he is retorned agayn fro this purgatorye, neuer shal no thyng in this world plese hym that he shal see, ner he shal neuer be Joyous ne glad, ne shal not be seen lawhe *(laugh)*, but shal be continuelly in wayllynges and wepinges for the synnes that he hath commysed *(committed)*.

Caxton then adds a passage of his own.

> Hit may wel be that of auncyent tyme it hath ben thus as a fore is wreton, as the storye of Tundale & other witnesse, but I haue spoken with dyuerse men that haue ben therin. And that one of them was an hye chanon of Waterford whiche told me that he had ben therin v or vi tymes. And he sawe ne suffred no suche thynges. He saith that with procession the Relygious men that ben there brynge hym in to the hool and shette the dore after hym; and than he walketh groping in to it, where, as he said, ben places and maner of cowches to reste on. And there he was alle the nyght in contemplacion & prayer, and also slepte there; and on the morn he cam out agayn. Other while in their s[l]epe somme men haue meruayllous dremes. & other thyng sawe he not. And in lyke wyse tolde to me a worshipful knyght of Bruggis named sir John de Banste that he had ben therin in lyke wyse and see *(saw)* none other thyng but as afore is sayd.[35]

[34] See the extracts in Leslie (1932), pp. 44-45.
[35] *Caxton's Mirror of the World,* ed. Oliver H. Prior, Early English Text Society, Extra Series 110 (1913, reprinted 1966), pp. 98-99. See also p. xviii; Sir John de Banste was three times burgomaster of Bruges, and died in 1485.

Caxton makes the mistake here of supposing that Tundale's vision of the otherworld took place at Lough Derg, a misapprehension he repeats in his translation of the *Golden Legend*, where he says of St Patrick's Purgatory,

> . . . certeynly such a place there is in yrelonde wherein many men haue been, and yet dayly goon in & come ageyn, & somme haue had there meruayllous vysions and seen grysly and horryble paynes, of whome there been bookes maad as of Tundale and other.[36]

The personal testimonies to lack of visions, that Caxton reports, are very close to Sir William Lisle's experience. Despite the continued copying and translating of the *Tractatus* in the fifteenth century, and despite the example of William of Stranton, the great age of such visions seemed to Caxton to be far gone, of *auncyent tyme*.

At the end of the period covered by this book post-Reformation authors in England wrote off Lough Derg and 'all that matter' as 'but a fantasy', as Sir William Lisle had said. Robert Burton, for instance, mentions the visions of Owein at St Patrick's Purgatory alongside other visionaries' experiences as the effect of 'much solitariness, fasting, or long sickness, when their brains were addle, and their bellies as empty of meat as their heads of wit'.[37] In his fancy, Burton ranks Lough Derg first among European otherworld entrances:

> I would have a convenient place to go down with Orpheus, Ulysses, Hercules, Lucian's Menippus, at St. Patrick's Purgatory, at Trophonius' den, Hecla in Iceland, Ætna in Sicily, to descend and see what is done in the bowels of the earth . . .[38]

When in Ireland in 1586 Sir John Harington enquired after St Patrick's Purgatory and later he wrote, 'I found neither any that affirmed it or beleeved it'.[39] Belief is not the same as knowledge,

---

[36] Jacobus de Voragine, *The Golden Legend*, translated by William Caxton, Kelmscott Press (3 vols., London, 1892), i. 420.

[37] Robert Burton, *The Anatomy of Melancholy*, Pt. 3, Sec. 4, Mem. 1, Subs. 2 ('Causes of Religious Melancholy'), edited with an introduction by Holbrook Jackson (London, 1932), p. 345.

[38] *The Anatomy of Melancholy*, Pt. 2, Sec. 2, Mem. 3, p. 40.

[39] See *Ludovico Ariosto's* Orlando Furioso *translated into English heroical verse by Sir John Harington (1591)*, ed. with an introduction by Robert McNulty (Oxford, 1972), p. 122, and see Book X stanzas 77-78.

however. Though we might expect one as learned as Burton to be familiar with our subject, St Patrick's Purgatory was still widely, or as Holinshed puts it, 'most notoriously known' in Protestant England at the end of the sixteenth century, and not always as the object of anti-Catholic polemic. Perhaps the most telling evidence of Lough Derg's continued fame is the glancing reference in *Hamlet*.

> *Horatio:* There's no offense, my Lord.
> *Hamlet:* Yes, by Saint Patrick, but there is, Horatio,
>   And much offense too. Touching this vision here,
>   It is an honest ghost, that let me tell you.[40]

This suggests that Shakespeare could assume his audience's ready recognition of the link between St Patrick and purgatory. Shortly before this, Hamlet heard his father's spirit, like Guy's temporarily released from purgatory, recount his death:

> Cut off even in the blossoms of my sin,
> Unhouseled, disappointed, unaneled,
> No reck'ning made, but sent to my account
> With all my imperfections on my head.

Some visitors may have entered St Patrick's Purgatory in order to prove the existence of the otherworld *by assay,* as Caesarius of Heisterbach had advised.[41] Some may have seen visions or dreamed dreams. But notwithstanding Trevisa's tart remark that the truly penitent would be saved whether they had heard of the place or not,[42] it was to avoid meeting death thus *disappointed* or 'unprepared' that generations of pilgrims from the twelfth to sixteenth centuries journeyed to Lough Derg.

ROBERT EASTING

[40] *Hamlet*, I. v. 135-8.

[41] 'Let anyone who doubts the existence of purgatory go to Ireland and enter the Purgatory of Patrick and he will have no further doubts about the punishments of purgatory.' *Dialogus Miraculorum*, xii. 38.

[42] '. . . euery man that is verray repentaunt at his lifes ende of al his mysdedes, he schal be sikerliche i-saued and haue the blisse of heuene, they *(though)* he neuere hire speke of Patrik his purgatorie.' John Trevisa's addition to his translation (1387) of Ranulf Higden's *Polychronicon*, Rolls Series, 41 (9 vols., London, 1865-86), Book I, chapter xxxv, i. 362.

IV. The French Accounts

In the eighteenth century an unknown person wrote in French, on the flyleaf of a copy of a popular book on the legend of Lough Derg, that it was 'as good as a novel of chivalry for the Catholic Irish'.[1] The remark showed little acquaintance with Ireland, but it usefully reveals that in its day the legend of the Purgatory was still flourishing on the continent, and notably in France. This interest was of long standing, for it was most of all through French culture, and from the very twelfth century in which the Saltrey treatise was composed, that knowledge of the pilgrimage was transmitted to the rest of Europe, just as those novels of chivalry, many of ultimately Celtic inspiration, were promoted in a French environment from that same period. Great popularizers already, the French quickly possessed themselves of this newly published vision and gave it many literary forms, through which potential pilgrims could first learn of the remote but firmly located site and the less firmly attested beliefs surrounding it. This chapter will outline the French literary promotion of the legend — a matter of European interest — before going on to summarize what we know of medieval pilgrims that set out to visit Lough Derg from France or that are mentioned in French documents.

Right away we have to remark that the well-known literary form of the legend, the Latin treatise, was in significant ways itself a promotion of French culture. Its early history unwinds in various Cistercian houses of England, Wales and Ireland: communities, in other words, of an order of French origin which had been actively colonizing since it was founded earlier in the century. Whatever may have been the name of its reputed author 'H', said to be 'of Saltrey', we know that his informant, who was Owein's confidant, was called Gilbert: a name befitting an environment — Louth Abbey, Lincolnshire — which must have been at that time more French than Anglo-Saxon. In fact, it was in the French-speaking society of England that re-tellings of the legend first began to appear in any vernacular language. By that time the Normans were in possession of parts of Ireland, not to speak of Britain, and for

[1] '. . . tient lieu de roman de chevalerie à tous les Irlandais catholiques', copy of F. Bouillon, *Histoire de la vie et du Purgatoire de S. Patrice* (Paris, 1676) for sale c. 1965 in a Dublin bookshop. Cf. n. 23.

some decades the royal court had already been a focus of
attraction for exotic facts and fictions of British and Irish history.
One of the re-tellings of the Latin legend was the lively poem
attributed to Marie de France, the first such adaption to be made,
very soon after the Latin had appeared.

Revealing no more than her common Christian name, 'Marie'
states the purpose of her poem as she finishes it:

> Jo, Marie, ai mis en memoire
> Le livre de l'Espurgatoire
> En romanz, qu'il seit entendables
> A laie gent e covenables . . .[2]

> *I, by name Mary, have made a record*
> *of the book of the Purgatory*
> *in the French language that it be*
> *properly intelligible to lay people.*

Written in a vernacular and in verse it could hardly have been
otherwise. This medium had everything to commend it; it was
intended for oral recitation and the poetic form Marie used had a
rising vogue; the story was unfamiliar and the concept of what she
called an 'Espurgatoire' was relatively new. The audience, it must
be said, was more courtly than common in class; but so the non-Irish
public of the Purgatory legend would remain in so far as literacy was
a prerequisite of its dissemination. And little, unfortunately, is
known about the kind of popularity that was able to dispense with
literacy: that of the oral circulation, in the form of folklore, of
knowledge of the legend and the pilgrimage.

Marie was literate and her poem was an elegant production in a
form well suited to its day. After her came others, and it may
surprise that before the thirteenth century ended, and even perhaps
in its early decades, no less than four French poems had in turn
adapted the Saltrey treatise in England alone.[3] Why, one might ask,
was one poem not sufficient, since in any case Marie's seems today

---

[2] The most recent published edition is by Warnke, *Das Buch vom Espurgatoire S. Patrice*. See
Owen, *The Vision of Hell*, pp. 64-6; Y. de Farcy de Pontfarcy, *L'Espurgatoire seint Patriz de
Marie de France* (Univ. Rennes, 1971, unpubl. thesis).

[3] Three of the poems have been published: *Le Purgatoire de S. Patrice par Berol*, ed. M.
Mörner (Lund, 1917); *Le Purgatoire de S. Patrice des mss. Harl 273 et fonds fr. 2198*, ed. J. Vising
(Göteborg, 1916); C. M. Van der Zanden, *Etude sur le Purgatoire de S. Patrice accompagnée du
texte latin et du texte anglo-normand de Cambridge* (Amsterdam, 1927). One is unpublished: B.L.
Cotton Domit. A 4, fos. 257-67. They are described by Owen, *The Vision of Hell*, pp. 66-75.

the best of the five? The situation reflects medieval society well: its lack of means of multiplying books by print or of advertising their existence through the accessories of many media. People were fewer, and few could read; readers learned of new writings, inevitably somewhat randomly, from their friends.

Each of these poems used a text of the Latin legend, which, of course, had itself been written in England. We may guess that such texts were less available in continental France down to about the second quarter of the thirteenth century, when versions in the French of France began to be made there. In contrast with the situation in French-speaking England, these include only one independent poem based directly on the Latin treatise, and that a poor thing dating from the end of the century.[4] A new vogue had sprung up for writing French as prose, which was a medium previously thought suitable in general only for Latin and for learning. Soon French prose translations of the Latin treatise began to appear: two of them little known while a third — actually the earliest, dating from about the 1230s — was copied in an abundance of manuscripts.[5]

These three versions belong to a period of energetic and diverse literary productivity in French. Useful compilations came into being in which the legend of the Purgatory deserved to be mentioned. Some time before 1243 a certain Geoffroi de Paris, wishing to make a full-length text from the Latin legend for inclusion in one of these, followed an easy method he had used already: without referring to the Latin he simply versified the oldest French prose version of it in the metre of the work it was to be included in, his *Bible des set estaz dou monde* 'Bible of the Seven Ages of the World'.[6] Geoffroi had not yet adopted the new fashion of writing prose. At about the same time Gossouin de Metz produced a kind of encyclopedia of geography, science, theology etc. which he entitled *L'Image dou monde* 'World Picture' and provided with a brief entry on the Purgatory. This began and ended with reference to a perpetually burning fire somewhat suggesting

---

[4] *Le Purgatoire de S. Patrice du ms. de la Bibl. nat., fonds fr. 25545*, ed. M. Mörner (Lund and Leipzig, 1920). See Owen, *The Vision of Hell*, pp. 125-7.

[5] Owen, *The Vision of Hell*, pp. 127-30, describes the three prose versions but has not noticed that MSS Dublin, Trinity College 951 and Bibl. nat. fr. 15210 contain texts of the same translation. See H. Shields, 'Légendes religieuses en ancien français. Ms. 951 de la Bibl. de Trinity College à Dublin', *Scriptorium*, xxxiv, 1 (1980), 59-71, esp. p. 70; idem 'An Old French Book of Legends', pp. 356-60, text 428-58.

[6] Owen, *The Vision of Hell*, pp. 127, 89-90.

the influence of another Irish legend, *St Brendan's Voyage,* chapter 24 of which describes a kind of volcanic Hell.[7] But the chief source of the short entry seems to be a near contemporary French work in Latin, Jacques de Vitry's *Historia orientalis.* Both accounts strongly emphasise the inability of pilgrims who have emerged from the Purgatory ever to take pleasure in earthly life again:

> Whosoever enters, except he be truly penitent and contrite in heart, is snatched away by devils and never returns. But he that with true contrition confesseth his sins, and goes in there, tho' the devils vex and torment him, by fire and water and many other torments, yet is he purged of all his sins. Now they that are thus purged and return are never more seen to laugh or play or to take pleasure in any thing in this world, but constantly weeping and sighing forget the things that are behind and stretch forward to the things that are before them.

Jacques de Vitry is here quoted from an early translation of the seventeenth-century Irish writer of Latin Thomas Messingham,[8] who, somewhat amusingly, goes on to take issue with this stern view of his medieval author. Other French compilations written in Latin in this period include references to the Purgatory, among them the frequently copied and subsequently translated *Speculum historiale* 'Mirror of History' of Vincent de Beauvais.[9] A moral treatise by Etienne de Bourbon, *De septem donis spiritus sancti* 'The Seven Gifts of the Holy Ghost', was substantially based on the Purgatory legend.[10]

The cultural significance of these run-of-the-mill writings in French or in France, including the straight prose translations of the Saltrey treatise, deserves not to be overlooked. They were a contribution to a popular synthesis of knowledge through literature that was to serve until many of its assumptions began to be called into question in the epoch of reform and scientific discovery. After the thirteenth century, further French versions of the Purgatory legend stopped being made (one exception printed at Lyon in 1506

[7] *Navigatio sancti Brendani abbatis,* ed. C. Selmer (Univ. Notre Dame, Indiana, 1959), pp. 64-5.

[8] From an English translation of Messingham's *Florilegium insulae sanctorum* (1624): *A Brief History of St Patrick's Purgatory and its Pilgrimage* (Paris, 1718), pp. 9-10. For the original: *Jacobi de Vitriaco libri duo quorum prior Orientalis sive Hierosolymitanae, alter Occidentalis Historiae nomine inscribitur,* ed. F. Moschus (Douai, 1597), pp. 216-17.

[9] See Owen, *The Vision of Hell,* pp. 15-18 and passim.

[10] See L. Frati, 'Il Purgatorio di S. Patrizio secondo Stefano di Bourbon e Umberto da Romans', *Giornale storico della letteratura italiana,* vii (1886), 140-79.

is discussed below). The usual view seems to have been that old copies were good enough, and particularly good the oldest of the prose translations. Collections of saints' lives in French prose, often illuminated, were a new feature of book production from the thirteenth century; the Saltrey treatise was by no means a saint's life yet its interest qualified it for admission — in the form of its popular translation — to the cycles of transcription of these 'légendiers' (19).[11] Other kinds of manuscript also welcomed the same version, ranging from miscellanies (17) to purposeful compilations. Among the latter there are French texts of the *Golden Legend*, into which a fourteenth-century French manipulator, unsatisfied with the brief account of the Purgatory already in the original, inserted the existing translation in full (3). Unlike the *Golden Legend*, a work by a certain 'Robert' which he called *Tresor de l'ame* (Soul's Treasure) is hardly known today, yet it had good success in fifteenth-century manuscripts (5+) and was finally — and sumptuously — printed about the year 1497 for Antoine Vérard: at least one copy is printed on vellum. All the texts of this *Tresor* contain the popular translation of the Saltrey treatise. Again this translation appears, this time as a separate work, in one, two and probably several sixteenth-century printed editions.[12]

Who were the readers of so many copies? We need not expect to find the answer in the margins of the manuscripts. From time to time scribes or translators — not usually a communicative breed — relieved the tedium of their task by some intercalated comment. A couplet indicating its function is added to the end of one text of the most popular translation:

Cy est le chemin et la voie   *This is the road and this the way*
Qui l'ame en paradis avoie.[13]   *that guides the soul to paradise.*

Another translator, after the refusal of the pagan Irish to believe St Patrick's description of the joys and pains of the otherworld unless they could *see* them, inserts a blunt rhyming proverb:

[11] In brackets in this paragraph are given the numbers of MS and printed texts of this translation which I identified and listed in each category. More doubtless exist; in the case of the *Tresor de l'ame*, '+' means that I noted references in print to texts of this work which I did not have opportunity to read. See Shields, 'An Old French Book of Legends', pp. 349-60.

[12] I have read the text, which is of this translation, in the edition by Jean Trepperel, Bibl. nat., Rés. p.Y²49; it is said to be the same translation as contained in an edition by Jean Bonfons, see Veinant and Giraud, *Le Voyage du Puys sainct Patrix* (Paris, 1839), page following the facsimile.

[13] Bibl. nat. fr.25549, fo.108ᵛ.

Ce creés que vous veés
Non ce que vous oés.[14]

Believe what you see
not what you hear.

The Saltrey treatise was critical of this demand, its purpose being to deal centrally with Owein's more estimable motive: the achievement of personal salvation. But we must admit that many a historical pilgrim mixed a strong dose of curiosity with piety in setting forth for Lough Derg. None did so more than the individual who gives us actual evidence that he had read one of the works we have discussed, in fact, the most popular French translation, read it and used it shamelessly in his own 'account', apparently also made it accessible to others in his circle. This was the colourful Ramon de Perellós, who is described in chapter V and who mixed literature with experience as it was becoming increasingly common to do in the later Middle Ages. Mention of him brings us to the second part of our French survey which is mainly concerned with the pilgrimage and with actual pilgrims from France.

It is not simply by accident that the phase of proliferating literary versions of the legend preceded the reports of pilgrims chronologically. It could, of course, be conjectured that the pilgrims necessarily came after because they learned what they knew of their voyage and objective from the literature, as the Catalan Ramon so gratefully did. Indeed the literary legend evidently was known to at least several of the pilgrims, though none of them 'plagiarized' it so freely as Ramon or so literally that it can be confidently stated, as in his case, that a French version was what they knew. Generally it is difficult to refer their statements to anything more specific than the Saltrey Latin text. And since they have other things to say which are partly original we must be content to note the substantial influence of the literary legend on the pilgrims without concluding that it was the only significant influence on them. We do not know how many medieval Europeans visited Lough Derg without leaving any documentary trace of their visit, or how many first heard of it without a written document being the source of what they heard. Though the contribution of medieval oral tradition in this regard is so regrettably imponderable today, it would be foolish to suppose that it was therefore negligible.

The later medieval documents are an assortment of reports on things seen, traditional beliefs and personal invention. By the end of the fourteenth century it is evident that the Purgatory is a

---

[14] Dublin, Trinity College 951, fo.90ʳ.

geographical and spiritual landmark which may figure in all kinds of
writings, certain of which concern actual journeys. It is in that
century that the known pilgrimages begin, if we discount vague
references to unsubstantiated visits, only one of which has any link
with France, and that an illusory one. A certain 'Vesion de Godalh'
seen in 1248 was explained from an unpublished manuscript as a
descent into St Patrick's Purgatory.[15] Unfortunately the manuscript
in which it was written, in langue d'oc, was destroyed by fire in 1906.
But a transcribed extract of the text survives which is enough to
show that the mysterious 'Godalh' is actually the well-known
Irishman Tundal (or Tnugdal) who was traditionally supposed to
have seen a vision unrelated to the Purgatory in the year 1148. His
name recurs in similar form, 'Gaudal', in a Catalan version of that
vision which does survive and also bears the date 1248[16]: allowing us
to reject definitively this phantom candidate for the pilgrimage of
Lough Derg.

So it is that the first proper reference we find to pilgrims from
France is in a few lines of the Chronicle of the First Four Valois
Kings under the year 1352 in which the nobleman who is described
died in battle. Among the remarkable features of his life is briefly
mentioned a visit to St Patrick's Purgatory. The Sire de Beaugeu
went there accompanied by his squire Heronnet, who seems to have
provided all the information the chronicler, some decades later, had
at his disposal:

> Milord of Beaugeu was descended from the counts of Flanders and of
> the blood royal of France. When he was made a knight he vowed that
> he would never flee in any mortal danger. He was in Scotland at the
> battle of milord William Duglas and he raised the siege of Berwick
> when milord Lyon de Gant, son of king Edward of England, had
> besieged it. There he acquitted himself so bravely that the English
> were dislodged. Milord of Beaugeu, a most valiant man, visited the
> Purgatory of St Patrick and in it he saw the torments of Hell as related
> by his squire Heronnet who spoke of great wonders in that place.
> Heronnet says that he saw Burgibus the gatekeeper of Hell turning a
> wheel a hundred times a hundred thousand turns in a single day, and
> on it there were a hundred thousand souls. He saw the bridge that
> must be crossed that is as sharp as a razor where you enter upon it. He

[15] H. Delehaye, 'Le Pèlerinage', pp. 35-60, see p. 36.

[16] R. Miquel y Planas, *Llegendes de l'altra vida: viatges del Cavaller Owein y de Ramon de
Perellós al Purgatori de Sant Patrici* (Barcelona, 1914), pp. 71-94; N. Mac Tréinfhir, 'The Todi
Fresco and St Patrick's Purgatory, Lough Derg', *Clogher Record*, xii, 2 (1986), 141-61, see 149
n.40.

saw souls lying in beds of fire and recognized some of them. He saw the gallows of Hell. He saw the pit of Hell. He saw the abyss of Hell. After that they came into the earthly Paradise.[17]

It is not clear, but probably unimportant anyway, whether Heronnet is speaking for himself or for his master. For the visiting mortal, in either case, the emphasis is all on simple vision and none on testing pain. Nothing absolutely confirms that this visit actually took place, least of all the saucy style. But the style is of interest since it looks attributable to a low-born person without education who is remembering — and misrepresenting — features of the Latin legend. Should this be so, these few lines are the only survival of impressions of the Purgatory in the words of a medieval person of no eminence, and as such well worth having.

Stretching chronology a little for the sake of contrast, let us see next what the chronicler Jean Froissart learned of the subject. His report is of a visit to the Purgatory in 1394-5, just before that of Ramon de Perellós, with which it makes perhaps an even better contrast than with Heronnet's.[18] A native of northern France, Froissart travelled in Britain and wrote much from personal interviews, especially when seeking information about things unknown and places unvisited. When we read his dry report of the Purgatory (see chapter III), obtained from a 'knight of England' of king Richard II's court, we cannot help wondering how Froissart would have handled Heronnet's blandly offered marvels. He does not seem to have been a man eager for sensation, and was probably not displeased by the answer his informant gave him when he asked whether he had seen any strange sights in the place called the Purgatory or 'Hole' of St Patrick. Though the report mentions 'great imaginings' and 'extraordinary dreams' we get the impression that these could be attributed to physical discomfort and the natural apprehension caused by acquaintance with the legend. The knight and his companion had, moreover, slept most of the time. There is little doubt that this was a real visit for it would scarcely have been worth the recounting otherwise. Froissart's Chronicles were frequently copied and in due course printed, in English as well as in French, and their negative account of the Purgatory would not have gone unread.

[17] *Chronique des quatre premiers Valois (1327-1393)*, ed. S. Luce (Paris, 1862), p. 22. Text in French.
[18] *Chroniques de Froissart*, ed. Kervyn de Lettenhoeve (Brussels, 1871), xv. 145-6. Text in French.

Reverting briefly to mid-century we find documentation of a number of pilgrims apparently from Italy who present puzzling relationships with one another. The reason for an Italian excursion in this chapter is that it appears that in one case the author of a reported pilgrimage starting in Italy lived in France (and to him we will return), while in another the pilgrim himself was a Frenchman. This pilgrim is variously described in a number of texts evidently all referring to the same person who visited Lough Derg in 1358. In Latin he is named 'Ludovicus natione franchus de civitate Ansidiorensi' or 'Ludovicus de Sur (?)', and in Italian 'Lodovico de Franza de la cita de Anchisodia': he was then a native of France, an otherwise unknown Louis d'Auxerre (Burgundy). Though his report is written in the first person it gives less impression of being written by himself than the brisk narrative of Ramon de Perellós. The original text was probably written in Latin and translated into Italian — as well as Catalan, for a fragmentary text was unexpectedly discovered in that language — but no French version is known. The Catalan, as far as it goes, seems to represent the original quite well. A sample of it will illustrate the thoroughly fabulous quality of this Louis's vision, in which the most disconcerting feature is that the devils who tried to tempt Owein to turn back with offers of safe-conduct have been systematically replaced by women who try to seduce Louis!

> Encontinent algunes dones vengueren ves mi, ballant e cantant, la belea de les quals era tant gran que apenes la poria om dir ne altre creure. Car vestides eren com a regines e portaven en lur cap corones d'aur maravelloses ab moltes pedres presioses; lus crans avien pus blanques que let, la qual blanquor era mesqulada, la hon feya mester, ab color vermela fresca com a rosa . . .

> *At once some ladies came towards me, dancing and singing, and their beauty was so great that a man could scarcely describe it nor another man believe him. For they were dressed like queens and on their heads they wore fine gold crowns with many precious stones; their skin was whiter than milk, of a whiteness mingling as it should with the freshness of the red rose . . .*

This vision of the Purgatory is described more fully in chapter VII; eccentric as it is we cannot help wondering if Louis visited Lough Derg at all. And we wonder the more when his Italian text situates it in Brittany. But this term was evidently intended to indicate insular

Britain and to include Ireland. And Louis is said to have seen at Lough Derg, on awaking from his vision, the Italian Malatesta 'cum familia magna', whose visit in 1358 is firmly documented. The Italian text, moreover, is accompanied by illustrative drawings which include a reasonably plausible view of Louis's arrival by water.[19]

Despite functional resemblances of the devils and the 'queens', the introduction of women obviously changes the complexion of the Purgatory narrative. This change was adumbrated in the report of the Hungarian George Grissaphan, who had made the pilgrimage in 1353, and Louis's 'reporter' was doubtless influenced by him. But in its systematic presentation of temptresses, Louis's vision notably suggests comparison with the Appennine legend of the 'Monte della Sibilla', the Sibyl's Mountain: a site which, like the Purgatory, has its exact topographical location and was believed to give access to the otherworld. Though called a 'Paradise' the Sibyl's cave is described in literature as really a kind of Christian Hell, in which respect its influence on Louis's description of the Purgatory would have been quite conceivable. We have thus another reason to think that Louis lived in Italy, as the Hungarian George seems also to have done at the period of his pilgrimage. George himself has a French association, in that the compiler of his account is thought to have been a Provençal.[20]

Another Frenchman who travelled in Italy described the Monte della Sibilla in terms revealing his familiarity with the legend, though not the site, of the Purgatory (which like Heronnet above he calls a *puis* 'well'). This was the Provençal Antoine de la Sale, who wrote his *Paradis de la reine Sibylle* reporting experiences he had in the year 1420.[21] Antoine gave a detached account of the sibylline site and what was supposed to have happened there, leaving the reader to judge of the reliability of the reports himself. The legend is

[19] See K. Strecker, 'Literarische Nachfolge des "Georg von Ungarn" . . . "Visio Ludovici de Francia" ', in M. Voigt, *Beiträge zur Geschichte der Visionenliteratur im Mittelalter*, i (Leipzig, 1924), 219-45; L. Frati, 'Tradizioni storiche del purgatorio di S. Patrizio', *Giornale storico della letteratura italiana*, xvii (1891), 46-79; L. L. Hammerich, 'Le Pèlerinage de Louis d'Auxerre au Purgatoire de S. Patrice', *Romania*, lv (1929), 118-24; Miquel y Planas, *Llegendes de l'altra vida*, pp. 241-52.

[20] See below, p. 127.

[21] Ed. under this title by F. Desonay (Paris, 1930); for the passage quoted below, p. 19. The Sibyl's cave had already figured in the 1390s in Andrea da Barberino's Italian novel *Guerino Meschino* and later in its French translation (a copy of an Italian ed. of 1473 is in Trinity College, Dublin, Quin 8), in which the hero's penance for visiting it is a pilgrimage to St Patrick's Purgatory!

essentially the story of the German knight Tannhäuser, who visits temporarily the Sibyl's cave — a place of erotic pleasures — and finally, refused absolution by the Pope, returns to remain there for ever. In Antoine's account, what reminds us most of the Purgatory legend is the description of the dangerous bridge which must be crossed to reach 'Queen Sibyl's Paradise':

> There the traveller finds a bridge made of material which he cannot recognize, but not a foot wide, as it seems to him, and yet extraordinarily long. Below this bridge is a deep and hideous abyss at the bottom of which can be heard a river in full flood making such a roar that he fully believes, as he looks upon it horrified, that bridge and all are ready to be swept away. Yet *no sooner has he set his two feet on the bridge than it widens before him, and as he advances widens more and grows less treacherous* . . .

As the sentence in italics reveals, this is the bridge by which H. of Saltrey told us Owein reached earthly paradise, on which after invoking Christ's name 'he felt nothing slippery under his feet . . . and the higher he climbed, the wider he found the bridge'.

In these late medieval attitudes to the otherworld we perceive something less than whole-hearted acceptance of its physicality such as the Saltrey treatise had expressed. Some writers give a matter-of-fact account of physical conditions as they experienced them, with no strange happenings. Others fictionalize traditional beliefs, either by blandly accepting the incredible and even giving themselves a part to play in it, or by attributing to others the stories told and so putting the extravagance of these stories at a distance. One more example of the matter-of-fact pilgrim writing his reminiscences in French is to be found in the fifteenth century. Ghillebert de Lannoy, from what is now French-speaking Belgium, was, like Antoine de la Sale, something of a professional traveller: but one who did actually visit the Purgatory.[22] Arriving from Scotland in late May 1430 he describes his journey from Drogheda, making generally unfavourable comments on the towns he passed through, the inconvenient terrain, the 'ancient little churches and abbeys' of Lough Erne, shows indeed little of the spirit of pilgrimage even though eventually shut up in the 'hole' for two or three hours. He is aware that 'a mouth of Hell' *(sic)* is said to be at the end of it, but states that St Patrick stopped it with a stone which

---

[22] Leslie, *St Patrick's Purgatory*, p. 39, translation. *Oeuvres de Ghillebert de Lannoy*, ed. C. Potvin (Louvain, 1878).

is still in place. Truly untouched by the spiritual side of his undertaking, his best contribution is to have left some detailed measurements of the features of Station Island.

At this stage we must again remind ourselves of the generally high status of those who have left reports on the Purgatory, and recognize that popular belief in its supernatural attributes must have persisted better — insofar as there was knowledge of the site and its attributes — at a lower level in society. After all, it still persisted in eighteenth-century France, when the comment noted at the beginning of this chapter was written on the flyleaf of a much reprinted account of the legend. This was François Bouillon's French adaptation[23] of an imaginative Spanish account that relied in turn on the fourteenth-century Ramon de Perellós and he, as we noted, on the popular thirteenth-century French translation of the twelfth-century legend. This oddly diverse tradition of writing and printing, which begins with Cistercians of Saltrey and seems to get more popular in quality as it develops, did not end with Bouillon. The thread unwinds to a mystery play on the subject in Breton,[24] inspired by the reading of Bouillon and written to form part of a tradition of popular religious drama still flourishing in Brittany in the early nineteenth century. These late developments do not altogether lie outside our scope, for they may be taken to reflect, however imperfectly, something of the character of such a popular tradition on the Purgatory as there was in France at the end of the Middle Ages.

One text is of interest to the question of popular medieval usage of the legend, though its burlesque quality makes it difficult to judge. The French profane drama of the fifteenth century generated an abundance of farces and with them 'sotties' or fools' plays similar in tone. One of the latter, *La Sottie du gaudisseur qui se vante de ses faits et du sot* 'Fools' play of the Jolly Fellow boasting of his deeds and the Fool' is a simple exercise in the deflation of self-importance, in which the first character describes his travels and the second interrupts him constantly with facetious interpretations of them:

> GAUDISSEUR I rode upon the great red sea
> and went to St Patrick's Hole.

[23] See n.1. The first ed. was dated 1642, the latest I have noted is dated 1752. Another French version of the Spanish source (which was by Pérez de Montalván, 1627) had previously been made by 'F.A.S., Chartreux', *La Vie admirable du grand S. Patrice d'Hibernie* (Brussels, 1637).

[24] *Louis Eunius ou le Purgatoire de S. Patrice*, ed. G. Dottin (Paris, 1911).

> SOT   And there he got a slut with child
>   that went by the name of Lady Beatrice.
>
> GAUDISSEUR   You may guess I was frightened
>   when I went down into the opening . . .
>   Down I went step by step,
>   saw neither sun nor moon.
>
> SOT   He couldn't see for weeping
>   he had been tippling so much.
>
> GAUDISSEUR   And there I was in this plain
>   suffering pain in abundance
>   at the hands of his lordship Grimoire.
>
> SOT   Faith, the night was coming on
>   and he looking for oats
>   to feed his old nag.
>
> GAUDISSEUR   Up came a worthy man
>   and says he to me, asks me
>   how did I get into the place.
>
> SOT   By the true St Peter in Rome
>   it was a woman asked him
>   and she begging for money.
>
> GAUDISSEUR   Says I, a shade roughly,
>   'Avaunt thee, villain!'
>
> SOT   As true as goodness the rogue's a liar,
>   she let him have it twice with her fist.[25]

The lack of consequence in this rigmarole is typical of the genre. But perhaps we could reasonably identify in the Gaudisseur's words: the entrance to the actual cave in Lough Derg, with bawdy innuendo; purgatory as a place of darkness, a plain, a place of punishment by devils; one of the 'archbishops' whom Owein meets in the Saltrey treatise. Can we even recognize in 'la grant mer rouge' in the first line the name 'Loch Dearg' in translation? The text of a sottie does not have to be meaningful to that extent, but the interpretation fits well. The visit ends with the Gaudisseur taking to his heels in the direction of Santiago de Compostela.

Lough Derg was certainly much less visited than Santiago in the Middle Ages, but they are often mentioned together. No doubt the legend of the Purgatory owes much of its literary success to the

[25] *Le Recueil Trepperel*, ed. E. Droz, i (Paris, 1935), 9-10.

medieval love of fully developed physical images of the spiritual world and the expectation that nature should explain the supernatural. This uncertainly dated play (1450?) shows that these attitudes were pervasive, while indicating that there was a range of 'general knowledge' on the features of the Irish pilgrimage.

A less usual association of two places of pilgrimage, in documents concerning European visitors, is that of Croagh Patrick with Lough Derg. A record of three pilgrims — two men and a boy — nevertheless certifies that they visited both places in the year 1485.[26] Johannes Garhi and Franciscus Proly, said to be priests of the city of Lyon, with their servant Johannes Burges, are known to us only from the Latin letter of the Archbishop of Armagh stating that they had fulfilled the proper penitential exercises in the places they had visited, without further details of their circumstances. An early visitor to Lough Derg known to have ignored — or been ignorant of — the closure of 1497 was also French, though it is uncertain whether pilgrimage was his main concern. This unnamed *ridere Frangcach* 'French knight' is briefly described with little variation by various annals which state simply that he visited the Purgatory *d'á ailithri* 'on his pilgrimage', and then go on to enlarge significantly on Ó Domhnaill's hospitality and gifts to him. For his part the knight later sent Ó Domhnaill a ship enabling him to capture the castle and town of Sligo, which he had long wished to do.[27] Perhaps it is significant — even if something of an accident — that this first association of the Purgatory with politics that we have met falls in a century when the public perception of such legends as that of Lough Derg will be drastically changed.

On the other hand, we already noticed the persistence of traditional attitudes to the Purgatory in post-medieval popular culture. In France the legend continued to be evoked from time to time even in 'learned' contexts. Etienne Forcatel's eccentric account made unexpected associations: King Arthur visits the cave, in which his squire Gawain dissuades him from remaining; and Merlin tells him it was hollowed out by Ulysses when he visited Ulster and gave his name to that province.[28] More traditional is the window depicting St Patrick in the church dedicated to him at

[26] Delehaye, 'Le Pèlerinage', p. 39, translated by Leslie, *St Patrick's Purgatory*, p. 61.

[27] See *Annala Uladh. Annals of Ulster*, ed. B. MacCarthy, iii (Dublin, 1895), pp. 520-1; similar entries are in the annals of Loch Cé, the Four Masters, and Connaught.

[28] Stephanus Forcatulus, *De Gallorum imperio et philosophia libri VII* (Paris, 1580), fos. 462ᵛ-3ᵛ.

Rouen, dating from the sixteenth century, with a panel representing the Purgatory.[29] More popular in style than either is the chapbook version of the Saltrey treatise printed by Claude Nourry at Lyon in 1506, when it was apparently newly composed.[30] It is not so literal as the older prose versions, and more imbued with feeling. The French seems to have been translated into Italian,[31] but somehow it did not become the classic chapbook version of later centuries that might have been expected. Whether as a closing example of the medieval sensibility that we often call 'naive' today, or as a reminder of the excellent job that French was doing from early times to hasten the dissemination of whatever it expressed, let the chapbook's description of the dangerous and narrow bridge — last rite of passage into the Earthly Paradise — provide the concluding lines of this chapter:

Suddenly out of the pit came other devils in other shapes, and greeted the knight , telling him what was happening to him. 'Our companions told you that this is Hell, but they were lying. For it is our custom to lie in order to deceive anyone whom we cannot catch by telling the truth. So this, you see, is not Hell, but we will take you to where it is.'

Then the devils lifted up the knight crying loudly and carried him to a great river of dreadful appearance, very like a lake. This river was full of fiery flame that stank horribly, and on the flame there were several devils, and over the lake a bridge so narrow that a bird (?) could scarcely perch on it. The devils said to the knight; 'Now you must try and cross this bridge, and we will hold you under the arms to stop you falling into Hell, for if you fall our companions will never let you go.'

Then the knight took the devils' advice and placed himself between them. One took one of his hands and the other took the other and they began walking along the bridge. As soon as the knight put his foot on the bridge it began to give way so much that he thought he was going to fall into the lake. But the devils held him up and said: 'If you take our advice we'll bring you back safe and sound and you'll have no more bother with this bridge on which the only thing that can

[29] P. Baudry, *L'Eglise paroissiale de S. Patrice . . . Description des vitraux* (Rouen, 1850), offprint from *Revue de Rouen et de Normandie*, Aug. 1849, Jan.-Feb. 1850, p. 18. The panel has the inscription *Luy priant la terre s'ouvre que l'on appelle le Purgatoire de Sainct Patrice:* 'As he prays the earth opens at what is called "St. Patrick's Purgatory" '.

[30] Single copy in the Bibliothèque nationale. Ed. Veinant and Giraud, see n.12, and by 'Philomneste junior' (P.-G. Brunet; Geneva, 1867). See Shields 'An Old French Book of Legends', pp. 361-2 (but the Trinity College Dublin text I referred to there as the original is actually the Veinant and Giraud facsimile.)

[31] 'Philomneste junior', p. 51, notes a *Viaggio del Pozzo di S. Patrizio* which I have not seen.

happen to you is that you will fall down to Hell. And if you would really rather turn back, we can easily take you back to your own country without risk or harm, and we swear that whatever you ask for will be granted you.'

The knight thought on the name of his master and said: 'Good sweet Jesus son of Mary, I put my body and soul in your safe keeping: do not let me be damned with these devils in Hell.' Saying this, he made the sign of the Cross before him and put his foot on the bridge and it felt firm. So he put both feet on it and then, by God's will, it became so wide that two carts could have passed one another on it. The devils ran to and fro around him expecting him to fall off the bridge into Hell. When he reached the middle he saw a great cloud of devils rise and fly over the bridge in order to make him fall. But he thought often on his Master's name and they were unable to do him harm. When he came near the end of the bridge he felt more frightened than ever he had been in his whole journey for the devils started to make such fearsome cries, with thunderbolts and tempests, that he believed he was lost. But he called out the name of Jesus and escaped all danger. The devils, seeing that he had escaped and that they could go no further, returned to Hell shouting and howling as if mad with rage because they had not been able to catch the knight.[32]

HUGH SHIELDS

---

[32] idem, p. 26.

V. The Pilgrim from Catalonia/Aragon: Ramon de Perellós, 1397

By the end of the fourteenth century, the kingdom of Aragon which, early in the same century had controlled much of the Mediterranean coastline from Catalonia to Greece, was in decline. King John I (1350-96), more interested in the arts than in warfare, neglected his state and even sold strategically important border castles to raise funds for life at court. Music, literature, hunting and astrology were among the king's passions and the court over which he presided was so extravagant and luxurious that the thrifty citizens who made up the parliament or Cortes wisely refused to finance it. Undeterred, the king used the royal patrimony and, when there was nothing left to sell, became heavily involved with moneylenders.[1]

By 1396, many of John's courtiers were suspected of corruption and even the king (whose nicknames included 'the huntsman', 'the musician', 'the lover of courtesy' and 'the negligent') was not above suspicion. Suddenly, on 19 May 1396, the king was dead, frightened to death, it was said, by the sight of an enormous she-wolf when he was out hunting alone. Though few believed this unlikely story, there was widespread concern at the manner of the king's death: he had died without confession or the benefit of the church and he might be in hell. His close friend and loyal servant, Ramon, Viscount of Perellós and of Roda, who had obtained a copy of Saltrey's *Tractatus* for the king some years earlier, now set out from Avignon to visit St Patrick's Purgatory himself in an attempt to establish whether his lord was there and, incidentally, to atone for his own sins.

Fortunately, Perellós left an extended account of his journey from Avignon to Lough Derg, an account which is not only of great interest in itself but is also one of the fullest surviving descriptions of medieval Ireland from the point of view of a continental visitor.[2]

Ramon, first viscount of Perellós and second viscount of Roda,

---

[1] The best accounts of the life and times of John I are R. Tasis, *Pere el Ceremoniós i els seus fills* (Barcelona, 1957) and R. Tasis, *Joan I: el rei caçador i músic* (Barcelona, 1959).

[2] The fullest published account of the Perellós text is M. de Riquer, *Història de la Literatura Catalana* (revised edition, 3 vols, Barcelona, 1980), ii, 309-33 and 389-404.

was a diplomat and soldier who came of a noble Roussillon family. His date of birth is unknown and his death occurred around 1419.[3] As he tells us himself in the text of his account of his journey to Ireland, known as the *Viatge al Purgatori de Sant Patrici*, he was brought up at the French court and was a page of Charles V. He remained there until the death of that king in 1380 when he returned to Aragon and entered the service of Peter the Ceremonious (King of Aragon from 1336 to 1387), and his son, John I. He was to become governor of Roussillon (1390) and Captain-General of Avignon (1403).

The years spent at the French court deeply influenced Perellós, however. There he grew to love not only the arts, but travel and adventure. The tales told at the court by foreign knights and visitors seem to have awoken in him an insatiable curiosity regarding the marvels of the world and, in the course of an eventful life, he underwent all sorts of hardships, both on land and sea, in search of adventure. In 1374, for instance, he was taken prisoner in the Moorish kingdom of Granada and had to be ransomed by Peter the Ceremonious.

On his return to Aragon, Perellós soon became a favourite of the young prince John, later to be John I; the two men shared a great interest in literature and the arts. In 1378, John wrote to Perellós who was in Cyprus at the time, to ask him for a book called *De Mirabilibus Terrae Sanctae (On the marvels of the Holy Land);*[4] again, in 1379, he wrote to Perellós, after a visit to the latter's house in Perpignan, telling him that he had found there a copy of the romance of Lancelot which was so beautiful that he had decided to take it. On 13 August 1386, John wrote again to Perellós, who was this time in Paris, to ask him to send him the story of that knight who had entered St Patrick's Purgatory, for he had a great desire to know more about it.

> We beg you to send us, in writing, by means of a reliable person, the whole story of that knight who you said went into St. Patrick's Purgatory, and what he saw and what happened to him in that Purgatory; for we earnestly wish to know of it . . .[5]

---

[3] See Dorothy Molloy Carpenter, 'The Journey of Ramon de Perellós to Saint Patrick's Purgatory: the Auch Manuscript', (unpublished M.Phil thesis, National University of Ireland, University College Dublin 1984), chapter I; also S. Costello, 'The Life of Ramon de Perellós, Viscount of Roda and Perellós' (unpublished M.A. thesis, Queen's University, Belfast, 1930).

[4] Riquer, *Història*, ii, 310.

[5] R. Miquel y Planas, *Llegendes de l'altre vida*, pp. 295-96.

The text referred to may have been Saltrey's Latin *Tractatus* or possibly a French prose version of it.[6]

John ascended the throne in 1387 and chose Perellós as his chamberlain; he relied heavily on his advice and sent him abroad on a number of foreign missions. In 1390, he was in France as ambassador from the court of Aragon and in 1394 he was sent to Cyprus to arrange a marriage between the sister of John I and the son of the king of Cyprus. In May 1396, Perellós was once again engaged in matters of importance to the state and was sent to Avignon to confer with Pope Benedict XIII, the anti-pope, an Aragonese who was warmly supported by John I and Perellós, as well as by the charismatic Dominican preacher, St Vincent Ferrer. His task there was to try and divert French troops, poised to invade Catalonia, towards Italy; but the news of the mysterious death of King John cut short his discussions with Benedict, and Perellós returned to Aragon.

The immediate outcome of the death of the king was confusion; several of his officials and courtiers were put on trial, accused, rightly or wrongly, of a variety of crimes ranging from bribery and immorality to high treason.[7] One of those called to account was Perellós himself who was accused of having made potentially treasonable contacts with the Count of Foix. The charge was never pressed and Perellós was never seriously out of favour but at least one reason why he undertook the hazardous journey from Avignon to Lough Derg may have been to try and clear his name by seeming to make contact with the dead king.[8]

But whatever his reasons, Perellós left Avignon for St Patrick's Purgatory on 8 September 1397[9] and was back in France, present at the celebrations in Rheims given in honour of the Emperor Wenceslas at the end of March 1398; what happened in between is the subject of the *Viatge*. After his return from Lough Derg,

[6] See H. E. Shields, 'An old French book of legends'. Also Molloy Carpenter, 'The Journey of Ramon de Perellós', Appendix E.

[7] See Riquer, *Història*, ii, 313-14: also M. Mitjà, 'Procés contra els consellers domèstics i curials de Joan I . . .', *Boletín de la Real Academia de Buenas Letras de Barcelona,* xxvii (1957-58), 375-417.

[8] Another reason may have been the belief that, if the king (a supporter of the anti-pope) was in purgatory rather than hell, this would imply that the anti-pope was the true pope. See Molloy Carpenter, 'The Journey of Ramon de Perellós', p. 8.

[9] The date 1398, given in all the early texts, is an error. Perellós received a safe-conduct from Richard II of England which is dated 6 September 1397: moreover, he was present, on his return, at the celebrations in honour of the Emperor Wenzel or Wenceslas in Rheims at the end of March 1398.

Perellós remained in Avignon for several years in the service of Pope Benedict XIII with whom, while the pope was still a cardinal, he had become very friendly. He also played a major part in military and diplomatic affairs in Aragon and France; the last mention of him is as a deputy in the Generalitat de Catalunya 1416-19. There is no record of him after 1419 and it must be concluded that he died on or around that date.

There are two distinct parts to Perellós's *Viatge:* the first consists of his account of his journey from Avignon to Lough Derg and back again. His itinerary is given in full and it is important to note that in many details of persons, places and dates, this part of the work seems accurate and convincing. Though some scholars have cast doubt on the veracity of even this part of Perellós's account, my own opinion is that he did carry out the pilgrimage and that he did visit Lough Derg.[10] I believe his observations on Ireland and his accounts of the journey are as accurate and truthful as he was able to make them.

The second part of the *Viatge* is the account of Perellós's experiences in St Patrick's Purgatory. Much here is borrowed from Saltrey; but the section in which Perellós recounts meeting King John and other friends from Aragon — some of whom had been still alive when he left Avignon and whom he did not know to be dead — is original.

Historians have long recognised the importance of Perellós's account of his visit to Ireland. It is one of the fullest surviving descriptions of a journey through medieval Ireland and is particularly valuable for its account of the court of Niall O'Neill. Some nineteenth and early twentieth century commentators doubted Perellós's accuracy as the details he recounted seemed bizarre; however modern historians, who have found corroborative evidence for these details elsewhere, consider Perellós a reliable witness.[11]

Dr Art Cosgrove, for example, while admitting that Perellós's claim to have seen John I of Aragon and others known to him in purgatory does not 'enhance confidence in the credibility of the Spanish knight', concedes that 'in dealing with more mundane matters, like the customs prevalent among the Gaelic Irish of Ulster, his observations find support from other sources.'

[10] See Molloy Carpenter, 'The Journey of Ramon de Perellós', chapter II.
[11] See particularly A. Cosgrove, *Late Medieval Ireland, 1370-1541* (Dublin, 1981), pp. 73-4.

Perelhos noted the predominantly pastoral nature of Gaelic society in the north of Ireland, with its concentration on cattle as a source of wealth and the tendency of those looking after the herds to move with the cattle from one pasture to another. His view that the Gaelic Irish did not grow any corn and, therefore, had no bread is contradicted by other evidence and is probably a reflection of the fact that 1397 was a year of widespread failure of crops. Hence it was as a special favour to Perelhos that O'Neill sent him two thin oaten cakes which, despite their unattractive appearance, the traveller found very appetising. Nevertheless, Perelhos was correct in his stress on the predominant place of milk and butter in the general diet of the people, with beef as a food for special occasions; for, at Christmas, O'Neill gave alms of oxflesh to the many poor people who had come to his court for the celebration of the festival.[12]

There are, in fact, good reasons to consider that, despite the fact that over half the *Viatge* is borrowed from Saltrey's *Tractatus,* the remainder of Perellós's text is authentic.

Interesting as its content may be, it is not only this which concerns scholars today. Those studying the development of the vernaculars in Europe, especially Catalan and *Occitan,* find much of interest in the Perellós texts as early versions evist in Catalan and in two dialects of *Occitan* current in the Pyrenean region at the time. The linguistic aspect of these texts, according to Professor Germà Colon of Basel University, is especially valuable for the study of the consolidation and identification of Catalan as a language distinct from *Occitan.*[13] The relationship between the early texts is, however, very complicated. Though the original was probably in Catalan, the earliest extant version, which is the text from which the present translation has been made, is an *Occitan* manuscript now deposited in the Archives Départementales du Gers, Auch. It can be dated to 1441 or earlier, copied, in fact, barely forty years after its composition.

Ramon de Perellós's account of his journey to St Patrick's Purgatory (translated from Auch Ms. I-4066)

[Only those parts of Perellós's account which are his original work are here translated and the text from which they come is the earliest surviving

---

[12] Cosgrove, *Late Medieval Ireland,* p. 73.
[13] G. Colon, *El léxico catalán en la Romania* (Madrid, 1976), pp. 218-19; also G. Colon, 'Occità i català: necessitat de llur estudi recíproc' in G. Colon *La llengua catalana en els seus textos* (2 vols, Barcelona, 1978), i [101-39], 101.

manuscript of his account. However, folio xxix is missing from the manuscript and the corresponding portion of text has been translated from Miquel y Planas's edition of the earliest Catalan text (Barcelona, 1914).[14]

Unfortunately, Perellós was not a great stylist. His prose is stilted and pedestrian and the text is sometimes garbled. In the interests of the clarity of the narrative, therefore, I have aimed at a fluid and readable translation rather than a literal one which would, in places, be hard to follow.]

[Prologue]

JHS

In [nomine] sancte et individue Trinitatis. Amen. In the year of Our Lord 1398[15] on the afternoon of [the feast of] Holy Mary, in September, having obtained the blessing of Pope Benedict XIII,[16] I left the city of Avignon — I, Raymond, by God's grace viscount of Perellós and of Roda,[17] lord of the Barony of Céret[18] — to go to St Patrick's Purgatory. It is a fact that everyone desires to learn about things which are strange and wonderful and that, naturally, those things are more pleasing when one can see them for oneself rather than learn of them by hearsay alone. For this reason, I, brought up in my youth by King Charles of France,[19] in whose care my father, who was his admiral and chamberlain left me, in his Court — with all the knights and squires of his kingdom and of other Christian kingdoms — was eager to know and learn about the wonderful, diverse and strange things which exist in the world: and my heart was set on seeing those things rather than merely hearing about them from many and divers knights. I set off immediately in search of adventure in this world, throughout all the lands of Christians,

[14] The missing leaf, which contains a reference to the anti-pope, Benedict XIII, corresponds to lines 179-264 of the Catalan text in Miquel y Planas's 1914 edition. The leaf which must have contained the same reference is also torn from the other early *Occitan* translation, Bibliothèque Municipale de Toulouse, ms. 894. Clovis Brunel made the following comment in his article 'Sur la version provençale de la relation du voyage de Raimon de Perillos au Purgatoire de Saint Patrice' in *Estudios Dedicados a Menéndez Pidal,* vi (Madrid, 1956), [1-21] 14, 'It is remarkable that the leaf containing the same passage is also torn out of the Toulouse ms., leaving not a shred. The coincidence of these two mutilations is doubtless not accidental. One may suspect that one wished to get rid of a mark of attachment to the schismatic Pope Benedict XIII.'

[15] Perellós actually began his journey in September 1397; see above.

[16] The name taken by Pero Martines de Luna when he became Pope in 1394. He was born in Illueca, Aragon, *c.*1328 and died in Peñíscola in 1417.

[17] The viscountcy of Perellós was granted to Ramon de Perellós in 1391. It is always linked with the viscountcy of Rueda, or Roda, as it is spelt in Catalan.

[18] Céret belongs to the department of Pyrénées-Orientales, formerly Roussillon.

[19] Charles V ('le sage') king of France 1364-80.

infidels and Saracens, and the other various sects which exist on earth — wherever a man can travel within reason. And so, by God's grace, I have seen most of the strange and wonderful things I had heard talked of and described, both on land and sea, and I can testify to those things because I have seen them myself. I have endured great danger and hardship and [incurred] much expense both on land and sea and I have been imprisoned by Christian and Saracen alike. I will say little about these things, for I do not care to, unless I find it necessary with regard to the subject I wish to pursue. I only want to tell of the journey of St Patrick and this I will relate and describe in four ways: firstly, why St Patrick established the Purgatory; secondly, where it is to be found; thirdly, why I set my heart on entering it; fourthly, the things I saw there — those which can and ought to be revealed; for there are some things which God does not wish me to make known, as this would be inadvisable and not pleasing to Him on account of the irreparable harm which would befall me or those to whom they were revealed.

[Perellós here gives an account of the life of St Patrick and the conditions of entry to the Purgatory derived from Saltrey.]

[Autobiography][20]

When King Charles of France, died, I had been in his service for a long time. I then entered the service of King John of Aragon, whose principal knight I was, and he was my natural lord. For a long time I was his favourite and I was loved by him as much as any servant could be by his lord. I was aware that he felt great love for me and because of this I loved him as much as any servant could love his lord — so much that there was nothing in the world that I would not do for him. I left this lord, with his permission, and setting out from the Kingdom of Valencia, I came to a place called Millas,[21] which belonged to my patrimony in the viscountcy of Perellós. The death occurred of Pope Clement,[22] who was of the same family as the Count of Guyaynna. Several days later Cardinal de Luna[23] was

---

[20] As noted above, a portion of the Auch manuscript was torn out at an early date; the missing portion of text is here supplied in a translation made from the corresponding portion of the early Catalan printed text.

[21] Probably the town of Millars in Roussillon.

[22] Clement VII: Robert of Geneva. Elected by the French cardinals in 1378 to succeed Gregory XI, he returned to Avignon and was the first 'anti-pope' of the Great Schism. He died in 1394.

[23] See note 16 above.

elected Pope by the cardinals and was called Benedict XIII. When I was away on a voyage in the neighbourhood of Italy with three well-armed galleys on the high seas, they [the Cardinals] happened to go into the service of Pope Clement and his College. I got to know his cardinals very well. They left Italy in my galleys and in two others galleys belonging to the seneschal of Provence, who was called Folcaut d'Aguolt.[24] They came to me in the first year of the schism which has lasted so long but the bishop of Bar[25] remained in Rome with Pope Urban.[26] I got to know the cardinals very well, especially Cardinal de Luna, who had been newly elected [as Pope], and this Pope, Benedict, sent me a messenger, ordering me to go and serve him. This I did, serving him with the permission of my lord the king. I happened to be with this Pope when my lord the king died. Because of his death I was, contrary to God's will, as sorrowful and sad as any servant could be at the death of his lord. I set my heart at that moment on going to St Patrick's Purgatory in order to find out, if it were possible, whether my lord was in purgatory and the torments he was suffering. These ideas stirred my imagination because of what I had heard about that place and several days later I decided that I must go and enter it myself. I spoke about it in confession to the Pope, telling him of all my intentions. He strongly advised me against it and he frightened me greatly, warning me that I should not do it for any reason whatsoever. Besides what he himself said to me, he had some of the cardinals closest to him speak to me, especially two of them: one called Tarasçona, who was of the Galniello family,[27] the other called Jofre de Sancta Lena.[28] A brother of mine, called Mossen Pons de Perellós,[29] was also there. The Pope advised me strongly against going and they restrained me with such force that I was barely able to get away from them. A few days later I tried even harder to persuade the Pope, telling him that I would not give up this journey for anything in the world. Having [succeeded in] obtaining his blessing, I left him on Our Lady's Day in September of

[24] See Papon's *Histoire Générale de Provence* (Paris, 1784), iii, 237.

[25] The text may be corrupt here; Pope Urban VI was previously archbishop of Bari.

[26] Urban VI; 'Roman pope', 1378-89.

[27] According to Jeanroy and Vignaux, who equate Galnielho with Calvillo, this was Fernando Pérez Calvillo, bishop of Tarascon and later a cardinal.

[28] Untraced.

[29] The titles *Mossen* and *Mossenhor* (roughly equivalent to the title 'my lord') distinguished those of noble birth. Ponç de Perellós was a brother of Ramon. His date of birth is unknown but he died in Millars in 1416. He was majordomo to John I of Aragon and chamberlain to John's wife Violante.

the above-mentioned year. And I made my way through France to
the court of the king — whose servant I had been — in Paris. The
king's father, whose name was Charles [also], had brought me up
from a very tender age and he had made me his chamberlain. From
the king of France and from his uncles, the duke of Berry[30] and the
duke of Burgundy,[31] who are brothers, I obtained letters of
recommendation to the king of England,[32] who was [the French
king's] son-in-law, and to other English lords. [The two kings] had
made a thirty-year truce from the date of the marriage. I left Paris
and a few days later I arrived in Calais where I took to the sea to
cross over to England.

[Journey to Ireland]

I left that place on All Saints' Day and made my way to London
passing by [the church of] St Thomas of Canterbury. In London I
was told that the king of England was in a great enclosed park, like
the Bois de Vincennes near Paris, called Got — some eight miles
away from Oxford, where there is a great university — which the
English call Estanefort.[33] This park is very beautiful and the king
has a very fine residence there with great houses in it. Because of the
letters I brought him from the king of France, I was well received
and they treated me with great honour, for love of the king. He
arranged for me to be guided and brought safely across his
kingdom, the whole of which I traversed without delay, although it
is true that I stayed with the king for ten days. Upon leaving his
court, I spent several days in a district called Setrexier[34] where I
chartered a ship so as to cross over to Ireland. I went on board and
we kept to the Welsh coast till we reached a place called Holyhead.
Setting out from there, I crossed the gulf with a fair wind till we were
on course for Ireland. I landed in the Isle of Man which, in King
Arthur's time, had belonged to the king of the hundred knights.
Today it is well populated and now belongs to the king of England. I
crossed over [the sea] from there and had good weather all the way,

[30] Jean, count of Poitiers and duke of Berry (1340-1416).

[31] Philippe le Hardi, duke of Burgundy (1341-1404).

[32] Richard II, king of England 1377-99.

[33] There is some disagreement over the identification of 'Got' and 'Estanefort'. James
Hamilton Wylie, *The Reign of Henry the Fifth, I, (1413-15)* (Cambridge, 1914), maintained that
'Got' was Woodstock Manor, eight miles north of Oxford; Jeanroy and Vignaux, however,
identified it as 'Godstow, a royal residence west of Oxford on the river Thames'. Brunel believes
that 'Estanefort' is 'the Anglo-Saxon translation of Ocsonia, in the middle ages, Oxenford.'

[34] Cheshire.

thank God. Then I reached Ireland and a few days later I landed in Dublin which is quite a big city. There I met the earl of March,[35] who was a first cousin of King Richard of England. He received me very well because of the letters of recommendation from that king, for the government of that island was in his charge. I told him of the journey I intended to make. This lord advised me strongly against it, telling me that there were two reasons why I should not do so. The first was that I would have to travel a great distance and go through the lands of savage, ungoverned people whom no man should trust. The other reason was that entering the Purgatory was a very dangerous thing and many a good knight had been lost there never to return. So, on no account should I wish to tempt God or deceive myself. The earl of March objected, in the strongest possible way, to my going. When he saw that I was still that way inclined, he gave me horses and jewels and also two squires. One was called John Devry.[36] He guided [me] through the land which the king of England had in Ireland and while we were riding he did not let me spend anything, but paid our expenses, much to my displeasure. The other was called John Talbot.[37] He knew the language of Ireland and was my interpreter. These two men had been ordered to conduct me to the archbishop of Armagh,[38] which they did. He was the primate of the island and the Irish consider him as Pope. I met him in the town of Durdan[39] which is as big as Puigcerdà or Tarragona.[40] The two squires presented me to the archbishop and I gave him the letters from the king and queen of England and from the earl of March. The archbishop received me very well and he treated me with great honour. After he learned of my intention, he strongly advised me against such a journey. He warned me not to go there, telling me that over and above the danger involved in entering the Purgatory itself, neither he nor anyone else could ensure my safety in the lands of King O'Neill[41] or [in that] of [the] other lords whose territory I would have to cross before I reached the Purgatory. Unless I deliberately wished to lose my life, I should on no account attempt to go there. He then had me go into the

---

[35] Roger Mortimer, earl of March, cousin of Richard II (1374-98).

[36] Brunel confidently, but without giving any reasons, asserts that John Devry was a member of the d'Ivry family from near Evreux.

[37] Possibly John Talbot, first earl of Shrewsbury.

[38] John Colton, archbishop of Armagh 1361-1404.

[39] This is almost certainly Drogheda.

[40] Spanish cities.

[41] Niall Mór O Neill of Tyrone, 1364-98.

sacristy of the church where he admonished me very strongly. He begged me not to enter the Purgatory for any reason at all and he told me of the many perils and horrible things which had befallen several [other] men who were lost there. Moreover, he told me of all the dangers which could be encountered there, to which I replied as God directed me, affirming that I would never abandon my purpose. When he saw that he could not change my mind, he gave me all the directions he could. He gave me permission to go ahead and he was full of good will [and] love towards me. He heard my confession and in great secrecy I received Our Lord from his hand. He told me that for the whole of that week he would be in a town called Dondale.[42] Indeed, just as he told me, he did go to Dondale and I went to [see] him there. He sent a message to King O'Neill, who was in the city of Armagh. The latter immediately sent me a [letter of] safe-conduct with one of his knights and a messenger to guide me. When the archbishop came on the day he had promised, he brought with him a hundred men, armed in their manner, to accompany me, and he gave me another interpreter, [who was] a first cousin of John Talbot. With the hundred armed men I went into the land of the savage Irish where King O'Neill reigned supreme. When I had ridden some five leagues, the hundred armed men did not dare to proceed any further, for they were all great enemies. So they remained on a hill and I took my leave of them and continued on [myself]. When I had ridden a further half league or so, I met King O'Neill's constable with a hundred men on horseback, armed also in their manner, and I conversed with this constable. I left him then and I went to the king, who received me well, according to their custom, and he sent me a present of food, in the form of ox-meat, for they do not eat bread, nor do they drink wine, for in that country there is none. However, the great lords drink milk as a sign of their nobility and some drink meat-broth. The common people eat meat and drink water. Because their customs are very strange, I will tell you as briefly as I can something about their [living]-conditions and ways and also about what I saw [when I was] with King O'Neill with whom, on my return, I spent the feast of Christmas — in spite of the fact that when I was there en route to the Purgatory I had seen enough of their ways.

[The customs of the Irish]

It is true that the kingship is passed on by succession and there are

42 Almost certainly Dundalk.

several kings on that island, which is nearly as big as the island of
England. But he [O'Neill] is the greatest king and he has forty
horsemen. They ride without a saddle on a cushion and each one
wears a cloak according to his rank. They are armed with coats of
mail and round iron helmets like the Moors and Saracens. Some of
them are like the Bernese. They have swords and very long knives
and long lances, like those of that ancient country which were two
fathoms in length. Their swords are like those of the Saracens, the
kind we call Genoese. The pommel and the hilt are different; the
pommel is almost [as big] as a man's hand, the knives are long,
narrow and thin as one's little finger, and they are very sharp. This is
how they are armed, and some use bows which are not long — only
half the size of English bows, but their range is just as good. They
are very courageous. They are still at war with the English and have
been for a long time. The king of England is unable to put an end to
it, for they have had many great battles. Their way of fighting is like
that of the Saracens who shout in the same manner. The great lords
wear tunics without a lining, reaching to the knee. [They wear them]
cut very low at the neck, almost in the style of women, and they
wear great hoods which hang down to the waist, the point of which is
narrow as a finger. They wear neither hose nor shoes, nor do they
wear breeches, and they wear their spurs on their bare heels. The
king was dressed like that on Christmas Day and so were all the
clerks and knights and even the bishops and abbots and the great
lords. The common people clothe themselves in whatever way they
can — [they are] badly dressed. However, all the principal ones
[among them] wear frieze cloaks and both the women and the men
show their shameful parts without any shame. The poor people go
totally naked, although the majority wear those cloaks, [whether
they be in] good or bad [condition]. Thus were the ladies dressed.
The queen, her daughter and her sister were dressed and girded, but
the queen was barefoot and her handmaidens, twenty in number,
were dressed as I have told you above, with their shameful parts
showing. And you should know that all those people were no more
ashamed of this than of showing their faces. The king had then three
thousand horses or more. There was a great number of poor people
following him and I saw the king giving them great alms [in the
form] of ox-meat. They are among the most beautiful men and
women that I have ever seen anywhere in the world. They do not
sow corn nor have they any wine. Their only meat is ox-meat. The
great lords drink milk and the others meat-broth, and the common

people drink water, as I said before. But they have plenty of butter, for oxen and cows provide all their meat. In that country there are very good horses. On Christmas Day, as my interpreters and others who could speak Latin told me, the king held a great court. Nevertheless, his table was [made] of rushes spread out on the ground while nearby they placed delicate grass for him to wipe his mouth. They used to carry the meat to him on poles, in the same way as they carry *semals*,[43] in this country, and as you can imagine, the squires bearing this were badly dressed. The animals eat only grass. Instead of oats they eat holly leaves which are roasted over the fire so that the thorns of the leaves do not harm the animals' mouths. I will say no more about their customs for the moment, but I will return to the purpose of my journey, *Deo gratias*. The king received me very well and he sent me an ox and his cook to prepare it. In all his court there was no milk to drink nor bread nor wine, but as a great gift he sent me two cakes as thin as wafers and as pliable as raw dough. They were made of oats and of earth and they were black as coal, but very tasty. The king gave me [a letter of] safe-conduct to travel through his land and his people on foot or on horseback. Then he spoke to me at length, asking me about the Christian kings, especially the kings of France, Aragon and Castile[44] and about their customs and the way they lived. It appeared to me from his words that they consider their own customs to be better than ours and more advantageous than any others in the whole world. Their dwellings are communal and most of them are set up near the oxen, for that is where they make their homes in the space of a single day and they move on through the pastures, like the swarms of Barbary in the land of the Sultan. Thus in a short space of time their towns can be moved and they travel together always.

[Arrival and preparations]

I left the court of that king and continued on my way for several days — as the journey is very long — till [I reached] one of their towns called La Pross[es]iho.[45] It is so called because in that town no one has ever harmed any of the pilgrims. They also have great

---

[43] Tubs or receptacles for carrying grapes; the word comes from Languedoc.

[44] Charles VI, John I and Henry III.

[45] There has been some discussion about the identity of this place; it is probably Termon Magrath. The Magrath family were 'coarbs' of the Augustinian canonry on Saints' Island in Lough Derg from the thirteenth to the sixteenth centuries. (See Aubrey Gwynn and R. N. Hadcock, *Medieval Religious Houses — Ireland* (London, 1970), p. 193).

devotion to St Patrick. Because this place is [situated in an area]
between the various kingdoms, they want to keep that way safe.
[When] all the kings of that island and the pilgrims go there, they are
obliged to leave their animals in that place, for horses and other
beasts would not be able to get across the mountains or the waters.
So I went on foot to the town where the priory is. The Purgatory is
inside the gate of the town. There is a great lake there with several
other islands in it. There is so much water everywhere that a man
can barely cross over even the highest mountains without sinking to
his waist. The ground is so boggy, and also the paths along which he
has to travel, that he is barely able to keep going and would never be
able to do so on horseback. I then set out from the town called La
Prossesiho. The lord of that place, who was a great lord, and his
brother, who had very great devotion to St Patrick, used to help the
pilgrims considerably [by giving them] directions. He wanted to go
with me and he accompanied me to the monastery where I was very
well received. I went across the lake in a boat made of hollowed-out
wood, for there were no other boats. The lord of La Prossesiho and
the prior, who was also there, were arguing with another man. As
soon as he saw me, I went [to speak] to him in the monastery. They
asked me if I wanted to go into the Purgatory and I said that I did.
Then they urged me strongly not to go in there for any reason
whatsoever and not to tempt God, for not only the body, but also
the soul which is worth more, would be imperilled and they told me
how very great were the dangers experienced by those who had
entered and who had died in that pit. When they saw how very
determined I was, they — and especially the prior — told me that I
must follow the rules of the monastery, as laid down by St Patrick
and his successors, and as described in the chapter dealing with St
Patrick. So I did as they commanded, everything that is done by
those who, because of illness or other dangers, are awaiting death. I
did all that accompanied by a great procession, for their custom is to
go to the church first with the person who wants to enter the
Purgatory. They urged me all the time not to go in for any reason
whatsoever, to renounce my intention of doing so and, in order to
purge my sins, to enter some religious order to serve the monks, or
else to become a monk myself and not run such a great risk of losing
body and soul. When all the requirements had been carried out in
the church, according — as I have already explained — to what St
Patrick had ordained, the prior and all the clerks who could be
convened from the whole district, along with all those who were

chaplains, sang a Requiem Mass early in the morning for the one who wanted to enter [the Purgatory]. They all did this for me because they did not wish to leave anything undone. When I was in the church I spoke to a nephew of mine, my sister's son, who was of the Sentelhas family.[46] He was a doctor and a good clerk. I spoke [also] with my two sons, the elder of whom was called Loys and the other Ramon,[47] and [also] with my servants. Together they were making arrangements for their return journey, in the event that God disposed of me according to His will. I made my will and gave it to my nephew Mossen Bernat de Sentelhas, sacristan of the church in Mallorca. When all that was done, the prior, the monks and the lord of the town called La Prossesiho asked me where I wanted to be buried if God did as He pleased with me. I replied that the earth was the sepulchre of the dead and that I would leave it up to them. They led me then in procession to the gate of the Purgatory. There I dubbed four knights, two of whom were my sons and the others were an Englishman called Mossen Thomas Agut[48] and Mossenhor Peyre Masco[49] from the kingdom of Valencia. After that we all sang the litanies and they gave me holy water. The prior then opened the gate of the Purgatory and he said these words to me in front of all those [present]: 'Here then is the place you wish to enter, but if you would listen to some good advice from me you would turn back and amend your life in some other way in this world, for many have gone in there never to return. They all perished in body and soul because they did not have strong [enough] faith in Jesus Christ and were unable to endure the torments which they experienced. Nevertheless, if you want to go in I will tell you what you will find there'. I then told him that without fail [and if it were] the will of God, I would go in so as to purge my sins. Then he said to me: 'I do not wish to tell you anything more about the pit, for you will soon find out about it yourself. But in certain places God will send you His messengers who will show you all you must do. As soon as they go away, you will be left alone, for that is what happened to everyone who went in there before you'. Then I took my leave of all those who were there, kissing them on the mouth, and,

---

[46] Bernat de Centelles, from Mallorca, a son of Perellós's sister, Brunissenda, and Eimeric III, Baron of Centelles.

[47] Perellós's sons died in 1437 and 1441/44 respectively.

[48] This is probably a mistranscription of the name Montague or Montacute. (Could this be Thomas de Montacute, fourth earl of Salisbury? See *D.N.B.*).

[49] This name appears as Pere de Massa in the Catalan text. Riquer (*Història,* ii, 321, n.2) describes him as 'well-known', but gives no further information.

commending myself to God, I went inside. A knight called Mossen William, lord of Corsy,[50] who was a Norman, came in after me. He was the chief [gentle]man and his wife the chief lady in the service of the Queen of England,[51] who was a daughter of the king of France. This knight did all that was required at the entrance to the pit, just as I had done myself. The monks advised us very strongly against speaking to each other as we went along inside the pit. But, from what had already been said and pointed out to me regarding the various torments suffered by those who had gone in — only to be lost and to perish there — my heart and mind were full of fear. Nevertheless, my great desire to know in what state my lord the king was, and also to purge my sins, made me forget all that could happen to me. So I commended myself to the prayers of the holy men and, arming myself as well as I could with faith and trust, I made the sign of the cross and commended myself to God. I then went into the Purgatory and my companion came in after me. The prior immediately closed the gate and he returned with the clerks to the church.

[Transition]

When I went into the pit I immediately came to the end of it, for it was only two *canas*[52] of Montpellier in length. The end of the pit, as one goes in, is a little crooked on the left-hand side. As soon as I got there I tried, with my hands, to find a hole or a place through which I could go further but there was none. It is true that as I went along I felt that the end of the pit was firm and it seemed that one could safely stand there. But then I felt that [something] was giving way under my feet and so I sat down as well as I could. I was in that state for well over an hour and I did not think there was anything else there. It is true that I was sweating and overcome with great anguish of heart, as if stricken with seasickness while sailing. After a while I almost lapsed into sleep because I had been feeling so ill. Then there

---

[50] There is some uncertainty about this William de Couci or Courcy; the most recent commentator, following Perellós himself, identifies him as the husband of Isabelle of Lorraine, lady-in-waiting to Isabelle of France, wife of Richard II. (This is an attractive supposition as this nobleman had previously been in the service of John I of Aragon.) Others consider this identification impossible since Isabelle of Lorraine's husband was called Enguerrand and had died in February 1397. (See Riquer and Castellane respectively.)

[51] Isabelle of France, daughter of Charles VI of France.

[52] A *cana* is an ancient measure of length which equals roughly thirty-three inches; it was used in Catalonia and in other places.

was a great thunderclap, greater than all those I had ever heard on earth combined. All the people who had come with me from the monastery — the canons as well as my companions — heard it. It seemed to them like one of those earthly thunderclaps which occur in summer. That is what they heard, although it was wintertime — the month of September *[sic]* — and the sky was clear, so that all those who were outside were filled with great wonder. As that very moment I fell in such a way that it seemed, in my opinion, that I was falling from the sky itself. Yet I did not fall more than about two *canas*. Because of the anxious time I had been through, however, I was very sleepy and I was somewhat stunned because of the great thunderclap which was so terrible it had almost deafened me. After a short time I revived and I said the following words which the prior had taught me: *"Christi filii dei vivi miserere mei"*. Then I saw the pit open [up]. I went along it a good way and I lost my companion whom I could no longer see nor did I know what had become of him . . .

[Perellós now entered purgatory and his account closely follows that of Saltrey. His description of the fourth plain, however, contains an important original insertion.]

[The fourth plain]

They [the devils] tried hard to harm and injure me. They led me from that plain into another which was full of fire. In that fire there were all kinds of people and torments. There were many grave and pitiful types of torture and countless numbers of people. Some were hanging by their feet from red-hot iron chains, others by their hands, others by their arms and others by their legs and they were hanging upside down, [so] that they were burning in sulphurous flames. [The devils] were roasting them on great grids of red-hot iron. Others were being roasted on great spits over the fire and they had drops of different kinds of molten metal — which the devils were melting over the souls — dripping onto their flesh. The devils were torturing them in so many different ways that it was impossible to describe them, and between one torment and the other there was no way that one could see them all, never mind imagine how bad they were. There I saw many of my companions and people that I knew, and many of my relatives, both male and female. And there I saw the king, Don John of Aragon, and I saw Brother Francis del

Pueh,[53] a Franciscan from the monastery of Gerona, and also my
niece, Na Aldolsa de Quaralt.[54] She was not dead when I left the
earth, nor did I know of her death. All those people were on the
road to salvation, but because of their sins they were in that painful
state. My niece had to undergo and suffer her greatest torment on
account of the paints she put on her face when she was alive on
earth. And Brother Francis, to whom I also spoke, suffered his
greatest torment because of a nun whom he abducted from a
convent. Were it not for the great contrition he had for his sin and
the penance he did while alive, he would have been damned
[forever]. There I spoke at great length to my lord the king who, by
God's grace, was on the road to salvation. I do not wish to say on
any account the reason he was suffering those torments. But I will
tell you that the great kings and princes who are in this world ought,
above all else, to avoid committing injustice in order to give
pleasure or favour to anyone, male or female, no matter how close
[they may be] to them, [even if they be] male or female relatives of
[their own] family. For I saw several women and men there of whom
I do not care to speak, but I thanked God that they were on the way
to salvation. May it please God, our Creator, that we may all be in
that number, if that is the best we can do. But if people on this earth
[only] knew how sins were punished in hell or in purgatory they
would rather let themselves be cut up into little pieces before they
would sin. No one could think up or ever imagine those evils, nor
could they ever count the cries and shrieks of the sinners on the one
hand [and] the devils on the other, nor the wicked things which they
do to them. For the devils, as they were tormenting the suffering
people, were all the while shouting and howling and raising such a
din. They wanted to torture me in that way, but I called on the name
of Jesus Christ and they could not do me any harm, *Deo gratias* . . .

[Perellós's account of the remainder of the journey through purgatory is
derived from Saltrey.]

[The Exit]

Then I went back weeping to the gate and they[55] came with me. I

53 Brother Francis del Pueh or Frayre Franses del Pueg (Des Puig) was a Franciscan from the
convent in Gerona. He was closely connected to Perellós; in a letter to Perellós dated 6 January
1382, King John I asked for some books and added: '. . . and send Frare Francesc dez Puig to us . .
.' (Riquer, *Història,* ii, 323).

54 Na Aldolsa de Quaralt or Na Aldonça de Quaralt was a niece of Perellós. Two of his sisters
married members of the Quaralt family, lords of Santa Coloma.

55 i.e. two archbishops who guided Perellós in the terrestrial paradise but who now direct him,
against his will, back to purgatory.

left against my will and the gate was very soon closed behind me. I returned the way I had come till I got to the hall where the devils who had come to meet me fled before me as if they were very frightened. And the torments did me no harm. I came to the hall through which I had first passed and the twelve men whom I met on my way [to the purgatory] came to meet me. They greatly praised God who had sustained me with such strong and holy courage. [To this place] came my companion whom I had not seen since he came into the pit with me and he was very seriously hurt by the evils he had experienced. By God's grace, I helped him to leave that hall. Then the twelve monks said to me: 'You are absolved from all the sins you have ever committed up to now. But you must return by the dawn of day to the earth, for if the prior and those who are waiting for you at the gate were not to find you, they would fear that you had perished and would never return and they would go away again'. Then they gave both me and my companion their blessing and we hurried to get out as soon as we could. We got to the end of the pit and could go no further. Then my companion and I became very frightened and alarmed, thinking that we were shut in. We sat down and devoutly beseeched God, who had already delivered us from so many dangers, to get us out and to save us from this danger also, so that we might not perish. And while we were sitting there we fell asleep from exhaustion due to the weariness and hardship we had undergone, as one can well imagine. We were thus sleeping fitfully till we heard a thunderclap — but not as great as the one we heard before, when we first came in — which woke myself and my companion up in great fear. We found ourselves at the gate by which we had entered the first pit. And while we were wondering where those who had conducted us to the Purgatory might be — for they were to come from the monastery to fetch us — we found them at the gate as soon as we reached it. When they saw us coming, we were received with great joy and we were immediately brought to the church where we said our prayers as God had instructed us. And the canons came with us.

[The return journey]

We set off from there, going back the way we had come and we got to King O'Neill's [land]. We were very well received, with great joy and delight, and I spent the feast of Christmas with him. He held a great court in their fashion which to us seems very strange for someone of his status. Nevertheless, there was a great number of people with him. Leaving him, we reached the land which the English have in the island of Ireland. We spent New Year's Day with the countess of March in one of her castles. We were very honourably received and she gave us gifts. And, in general, everyone, wherever we went, received us with great honour. It seemed they all held our journey in great esteem, as we had been delivered from such great peril, and they would very willingly have given me anything I wanted. I was asked a great deal of questions, especially within the island [of Ireland], but not afterwards. The earl of March had gone to England. Leaving there, we arrived in Dublin where I set out by sea to cross over to England. And [in] that city [Dublin] I was notably received by the gentlemen and the citizens and especially by the monks. After that, I crossed the sea and arrived in Wales at a harbour called Holyhead. Setting out from there I reached England a few days later and I met the king in a town called Liquefiel,[56] where there is a large and very beautiful abbey of black monks, where the king was staying most of the time. The queen was there and I was notably received. I left that place and a few days later I had traversed the island of England, passing by London, and I reached the port of Dover where we saw the head of Gawain,[57] for he died there, and we saw the *cota mantalea*,[58] for that is how the one who always wore it was called. When we had seen those things, [preserved] in the castle because [of their merit in terms] of chivalry, I set off by sea and crossed over to Calais. From there I made my way, travelling for a few days through Picardy, to the court of the king of France in Paris, where I was well received because I was his servant and chamberlain and had [also] been that of his father — [the king] who brought me up. I stayed there for four months, by order of the pope, and I went with him to the jousting which was held [in honour of] the emperor of Germany,[59] who was then king of Bohemia. The king of Navarre[60] was also there and

56 This is taken by Riquer and others to be the city of Lichfield. Wylie, however, considers it to be the Abbey at Lilleshall in Shropshire.

57 Sir Gawain, a knight of the Round Table, is said to have died at Dover. His preserved head was a famous Arthurian relic.

58 The reference is to the Arthurian legend of Brewnor le Noyre, nicknamed 'La Cote Male Tayle' or 'The Evyll-Shapyn Cote'. See Sir Thomas Malory *Works,* edited by Eugene Vinaver (second edition, Oxford, 1971), p. 282.

59 Wenzel or Wenceslas, emperor of Germany.

60 Charles III ('le noble'), king of Navarre.

several dukes and lords. When the king returned to Paris, I left and went back to Avignon, where the pope received me notably.

Let us now beseech our Lord Jesus Christ, who holds everything in His power, that by His holy grace He may allow us to live in this world in such a way that we can purge our sins on earth, so that at the end and at the moment of our death and decease, we may avoid the pains and torments which you have heard described and may go to that peace which never fails. Amen. May all those who read this book pray to God for me.

Mossen Raymond, viscount of Perellós and Roda.
Lord of the Barony of Céret. *Requiescat in passe* [sic].

DOROTHY M. CARPENTER

VI. Two Hungarian Pilgrims

The historical context

Among the medieval pilgrimages to St Patrick's Purgatory those of the Hungarian noblemen, George Grissaphan and Laurence of Pászthó, in 1353 and 1411 respectively, are of outstanding historical interest in that their context and circumstantial detail is in each case exceptionally well established. The relation of George's visions is in the principal manuscript tradition accompanied by six testimonial letters whose specific content puts their own authenticity above dispute: (1) a letter of Archbishop Richard FitzRalph of Armagh, dated 'at our manor above written' [sc. of Dromiskin, co. Louth] on a Wednesday, most likely 19 February 1354 but possibly a week or even two weeks earlier, and directed 'to George of Hungary' — the archbishop in his letters, by contrast with the prior of Lough Derg, the bishop of Clogher and the prior of Kilmainham in theirs, does not use George's surname, neither does he here address him as being noble — 'inhabitant of the realm of Apulia, pilgrim of God and of St Patrick'. The letter states that on the preceding Monday, at Vespers, FitzRalph had received from the archdeacon of Armagh a letter to the effect that George could not await the archbishop's arrival beyond Tuesday; that the archbishop had accordingly set off in the middle of the night, had come to Dundalk and was now at Dromiskin after a harder day's journey than he had passed for a long time. George is implored, 'that we may not be deprived of the fruits of the revelation made to you and may in spiritual matters contract no contumacy', to come to Dromiskin or elsewhere at his choice to converse with the archbishop over those things for which it is said he has divine mandate to do so. If he needs horses the archbishop will send them on request.[1] (2) A letter patent of the archbishop testifying that George, a young man of almost[2] twenty-four years and of noble Hungarian parentage, as certified by letters of certain Knights Hospitallers, had come to him seeking a conduct to the Purgatory of St Patrick, 'our patron', 'which place is situated in the diocese of Clogher among a wild people'.[3] He had

[1] *Visiones Georgii Visiones Quas in Purgatorio Sancti Patricii Vidit Georgius Miles de Ungaria A. D. MCCCLIII*, ed. L. L. Hammerich (Det Kgl. Danske Videnskabernes Selskab. Historisk-filologiske Meddelelser. xviii, 2. Copenhagen, 1930), pp. 78-80.

[2] *quasi, ibid.*, p. 80.

[3] *qui locus in diocesi Clochorensi inter homines minus domitos situatur, ibid.*

obtained letters of conduct and the archbishop had learned on the testimony of the bishop of Clogher and the prior and convent of Lough Derg that he had entered the Purgatory and completed the pilgrimage. George is referred to moreover as having taken an oath to this effect, apparently before the archbishop, a point which is repeated in the next document discussed below. The letter is dated at Dromiskin, on 22 February 1354 — or rather 1353, the new year being reckoned as commencing on 25 March, an aspect which the archbishop rather self-consciously explained as being 'according to the computation of our church of Ireland', though in fact as he well knew it was widespread practice in contemporary Europe including, not least, at the papal curia. Since he used the same phrase in dating the letter to his nephew it would seem less a concession to George's exotic background than intended to put the chronology beyond doubt. (3) A letter of the same date from the archbishop to his nephew and namesake, rector of the church of Trim and canon of Emly. This set out the broad details contained in the letter patent, to which was added the information that George's father was a resident of Naples, though of Hungarian origin, and that George was accompanied on his pilgrimage by one servant. The interview with George envisaged in item (1) above had taken place since the archbishop told his nephew that 'what he said to us concerning our own person you can perhaps, when he comes to you, hear freely or prudently elicit from him',[4] a remark which seems to suggest something of the reticence which the compiler of the narrative of George's visions attributes to him on several points. This personal communication is presented as following from George's experiences in the Purgatory, 'where as he alleges, he saw, on the revelation of an angel, many marvels concerning the living and the dead, concerning those saved and those lost'.[5] A certain measure of critical reserve is explicit in the archbishop's report as it was implicit in his testimonial letter, which had confined itself to the witnessed facts: George, as he has 'most strictly sworn' and 'as the prior and canons regular who have custody of the place testify to the same by their letter patent', entered the Purgatory, stayed there the customary time and 'as he alleges' had the revelations. As will be noted from the next item, the prior of Lough Derg had been less cautious. Finally and without further explanation, though the fact might in the abstract be thought to occasion some surprise, the

[4] *ibid.*, p. 82.
[5] *ibid.*

episode is being treated as of interest to the papal curia. FitzRalph tells his nephew, apparently resident at Avignon in this period,[6] that he may show the present letter, 'as being testimonial' in the matter, to 'your lords, the cardinals'. (4) A letter patent, presumably that referred to in FitzRalph's letter to his nephew, of Prior Paul and the convent 'of the isle of the Purgatory of St Patrick, in the diocese of Clogher', dated 'in the monastery *(cenobio)* of the Purgatory of St Patrick, our patron, in the ends or final parts of the world, on the morrow of St Nicholas [sc. 7 December], AD 1353.'[7] The letter certifies that 'George — son of the lord Grissaphan, a knight of Hungary — bearer of the present, has laudably made the pilgrimage of the said Purgatory in accordance with the ordinance and rule of our monastery *(cenobii nostri)*, in which Purgatory indeed he suffered diverse torments and after the said torments St Michael the Archangel appeared to him and remained with him for one natural day and finally conducted *(perduxit)* the said George in his human body to paradise. Wherefore we strongly beseech you, with what prayers we can, that out of regard for piety and by the intervention of our prayers, you act beneficently towards the said George and his servant, for such time as he shall spend with you, and firmly believe him in what he shall have said to you about the miracles of our isle, because we are fully satisfied concerning the confession and conscience of the said pilgrim *(quoniam nobis ad plenum constat de confessione et consciencia dicti peregrini)*, and having heard his confession we absolved him by authority of St Patrick and of the order and thus we permitted him, being absolved, to go and to enter the pit or the stairway into the pit and very deep *(intrare puteum seu scalam putealem et profundam valde)*, by which one descends to the Purgatory of St Patrick, and so we remit him to you as being he who truly saw the said Purgatory and numerous wonders.'[8] (5) A letter patent of Nicholas [MacCathasaigh], bishop of Clogher, 'by the ends of the world'. It seems to have been influenced by the phraseology of the prior and convent's letter but is notably more laconic: George — son of the lord Grissaphan, knight of Hungary — has laudably made the pilgrimage and the bishop asks, in the same terms as the prior, that he be given credence 'concerning his pilgrimage and concerning the other diverse

---

[6] Cf. K. Walsh, *A Fourteenth-Century Scholar and Primate: Richard FitzRalph in Oxford, Avignon and Armagh* (Oxford, 1981), p. 317.

[7] *Visiones Georgii*, p. 84.

[8] *ibid.*

torments of the said Purgatory'; there is no mention of miracles nor of angelic visitation. The date of the letter, 'on the morrow of the Nativity of Our Lord, 1353', suggests that George had spent the Christmas feast with the bishop — the account of his pilgrimage stresses how graciously he had been received by him when he arrived seeking authorisation to enter the Purgatory in the first place[9] — and may now have been about to set off again. (6) A letter patent of John de Frowick, prior of the Hospital of St John of Jerusalem at Kilmainham, outside of Dublin. The import of this too is limited. George — son of the lord Grissaphan, knight of Hungary — 'has been in our parts of Ireland out of devotion for the pilgrimage of the Purgatory of St Patrick; he has laudably completed the said pilgrimage, as also the bishop of Clogher and the prior and convent of the isle of the Purgatory . . . have by their letters . . . fully and clearly manifested to us, asserting, as we too write, that this is truly the case.' The prior then requests 'that you wholly believe and will believe, as we are piously bound to believe, the said George concerning his pilgrimage and the diverse other torments of the said Purgatory'.[10] The letter is dated 'in our manor of Kylmainam, on the Wednesday next after the feast of the conversion of St Paul the Apostle', that is, on 29 January 1354. If one assumes that the bishop's letter was indeed issued on George's departure, there is a gap of just less than five weeks in the itinerary. The most likely construction is that George set out on foot, on 26 December, to seek Archbishop FitzRalph — for what purpose will be discussed later — that either he failed to find him or failed to secure an interview with him[11] and that he then, or eventually, had recourse to the Knights Hospitallers in Dublin to whom he may have had some form of introduction.[12] FitzRalph's letter of 22 February (item 2 above) cites 'letters of certain knights of the hospital of St John of Jerusalem' as his source of information about George's parentage. 'Certain knights' seems odd as a reference to the prior of Kilmainham's testimonial (the letter to FitzRalph junior says 'the Knights Hospitallers' or possibly 'Knights Hospitallers',

[9] ibid., pp. 92-3.

[10] ibid., p. 86.

[11] It has been suggested, partly on the basis of his letter of (?)19 February 1354 (above item 1), with its reference to a day's journey harder than what the archbishop had experienced for some time, and partly on the fact that the archbishop's sermon diary lacks any sermons between 1352 and the spring of 1354, that FitzRalph was ill at this time. See Walsh, A Fourteenth-Century Scholar, pp. 234, 314.

[12] as also suggested ibid., p. 313.

per literas militum hospitaliorum) and this in any case gave neither more information nor more authentic information as to George's pedigree than had been supplied by the prior of Lough Derg and the bishop, though it is conceivable that as a reference on nobility it may have weighed more heavily with FitzRalph. It is possible that George had arrived in Ireland furnished with credences from some continental house of the great international military order[13] though in that case one might have expected the prior of Kilmainham to take the same account of them as the archbishop.

The second pilgrim of this chapter, Laurence Rathold of Pászthó, is known independently to history as an emissary of Emperor Sigismund in Venice in 1413.[14] His visit to Archbishop Nicholas Fleming is recorded in the Armagh registers.[15] For the rest, we rely on the account of his experiences (the *Memoriale*) compiled by James Yonge, 'imperial notary, the least of the citizens and scribes of the city of Dublin',[16] who wrote, as he claims, on the basis of lengthy conversations with him, but the circumstantial particulars which Yonge furnishes fit well with the two major pieces of external evidence already cited. Yonge's account includes a copy of a letter of Archbishop Fleming (dated at his manor of Dromiskin on 27 December 1411) testifying to Laurence's pilgrimage and containing an exemplification of the testimonial issued in Laurence's favour by Matthew, prior of Lough Derg (dated on Saints' Island, 12 November 1411).[17] Yonge also rehearses the text of Sigismund's letter of safe conduct, dated 10 January 1408, introducing Laurence as his chief steward,[18] 'a scion of the senior barons of our kingdoms, nurtured and known in our royal palace from his childhood and one found faithful and constant in numberless affairs, happy and

---

[13] Cf. *ibid.*

[14] S. Ljubic, in *Monumenta spectantia historiam Slavorum meridionalium,* xii (Zagreb, 1882), 72-76; cited in Delehaye, 'Le pèlerinage', 41.

[15] H. J. Lawlor, 'A calendar of the register of Archbishop Fleming', *Proceedings of the Royal Irish Academy,* xxx, sect. C, no. 5 (1912-3), [94-190], 122, 144.

[16] Delehaye, 'Le pèlerinage', 58. James Yonge is known independently of his account of Laurence's pilgrimage; see *The Whole Works of Sir James Ware,* ed. Harris, ii (Dublin, 1746), part 2, 88. J. L. Robinson, 'On the ancient deeds of the parish of St John, Dublin, preserved in the library of Trinity College, Dublin', *Proceedings of the Royal Irish Academy,* xxxiii, sect. C, no. 7 (1916-7), [175-224], 192 (no. 68), 194 (nos. 86, 88). There is an indication that Yonge may not have completed the surviving version of his account until after the death of Archbishop Nicholas Fleming (who died *post* 22 June 1416), since he refers to him as 'the then primate' *(tunc primatem).* See Delehaye, 'Le pèlerinage', 45, lines 14-15. However it is hazardous to assert this on the basis of a single manuscript.

[17] *ibid.,* 57-8.

[18] *magister dapiferorum, ibid.,* 46.

unhappy,'[19] now setting out on pilgrimage to the shrine of St James in Compostella and to the Purgatory of St Patrick in Ireland. There is no indication of any motive beyond pure devotion or perhaps the spirit of adventure — the letter also states that Laurence 'led by the fineness of his mind, intends to traverse the various climates of the world in the exercise and increase of feats of knighthood'[20] — and Laurence's pilgrimage is elsewhere attributed to the desire to resolve problems of faith.[21] However, the fact that Laurence's visit to Venice in 1413 for discussions with the Signoria was conducted under cloak of a religious expedition raises the question whether his Irish trip may have had any diplomatic aspect. On the whole it seems improbable. The great Bollandist, Hippolyte Delehaye, to whom we owe the edition of the account of Laurence's pilgrimage to Lough Derg, commented on the concealed nature of his mission to Venice and on the likelihood that in other cases the pilgrimages of great lords served to cover business which they wished to be kept secret, but thought it unlikely that this applied in the present instance.[22] By 1411, Sigismund was dealing with the English king over the prospect of an end to the Great Schism of the west (1378-1417) through a general council,[23] and if Laurence were in touch with these developments it is not impossible that advantage might have been taken of his contact with a remote archbishop to sound opinion. But the crucial alignments in these matters were settled at governmental level; any diplomatic element would at most have been peripheral even by the date of Laurence's arrival in Ireland and in view of the significant changes in the interval could not have been part of a project determined by 1408. The religious disguise of his mission to Venice may itself have been prompted by his reputation as a pilgrim.

Such are the particular historical details. A brief notice of the wider background will serve as a final preliminary to considering the accounts of the two pilgrimages and indeed is required in George's case. The Hungary of which the pilgrims were natives although, like Ireland, on the margin of western christendom, was politically and dynastically closely connected with it. Charles Robert of Naples (of the French house of Anjou) had in 1307-10 succeeded in establishing his claim to the Hungarian throne against the rival

[19] *ibid.*

[20] *ibid.*

[21] See below, p. 167.

[22] Delehaye, 'Le pèlerinage', 41.

[23] Cf. E. F. Jacob, *The Fifteenth Century 1399-1485,* (corrected reprint Oxford, 1969), p. 161.

interests of Wenceslas of Bohemia and Otto of Bavaria. By skilful political manoeuvring and military campaigning he broke the power of the Hungarian nobility and established a measure of centralised royal authority which the country had lacked for at least forty years. This policy was ably maintained by his son, Louis I, 'the Great' (1342-82). The latter's success in ruling Hungary stood however in contrast to his efforts, in the period 1347-52, to wrest the kingdom of Naples from Queen Joanna (1343-82). Her claim, derived from her grandfather, to the throne of Naples was the object of contention by two rival branches of the Angevin house, one locally based and represented by the dukes of Durazzo and the other represented, after the murder of her husband, Louis' brother, Andrew of Hungary, by Louis himself. Having at first made considerable progress in his invasion of southern Italy, Louis quickly alienated the nobility and Joanna managed to reestablish herself precariously. It was in the course of this war that George Grissaphan committed the excesses which moved him to make his pilgrimage.

Laurence of Pászthó's lord, Sigismund, king of Hungary (1387) and Holy Roman Emperor (1411-37), was the son of Charles IV of the house of Luxembourg, king of Bohemia (1346-78) and Holy Roman Emperor. After the death of his elder brother, Wenceslas, in 1419, Sigismund was to press his claim to the throne of Bohemia against a nation which rejected him as the perceived betrayer of their condemned religious leader John Hus, burned as a heretic at the Council of Constance in 1415. Only after seventeen years of war and on the final dissolution of Hussite unity was he allowed, in 1436, to take possession of his Bohemian kingdom. His claim to the throne of Hungary derived from his betrothal and subsequent marriage to the elder daughter of Louis the Great, who died without male issue in 1382. Here he had to face the opposition of the Angevin claimant, Charles of Durazzo, king of Naples, and not until after Charles' murder did Sigismund succeed in establishing himself on the Hungarian throne in 1387. It is by reference to his accession in this year that the letter of conduct issued for Laurence of Pászthó is dated: 1408, 'in the twentieth year of our reigning' *(regnorum autem nostrorum anno vicesimo)*.

George's Pilgrimage — the Character of the Account

The presentation of the text of the testimonial letters concerning

George's pilgrimage was intended to lend authority to the narrative that followed. So much is clear even from their ordering. The three from Archbishop FitzRalph, although chronologically the latest of the batch, are given pride of place; aside from his ecclesiastical preeminence he was a well-known figure at the papal curia at Avignon both as a litigant and more recently as a critic of the mendicant friars, a preoccupation for which he was soon to be notorious through most of Europe; he was moreover a preacher of note and had an academic reputation already firmly established as a master of theology and former chancellor of Oxford university.[24] George could not but benefit from the association. The other letters, of the prior of Lough Derg, of the bishop of Clogher and of the prior of the Hospitallers, are presented in simple chronological or logical order.

In addition to confirming the basic historicity of the pilgrimage, the letters provide a rudimentary control over the elaborated account of it. The account itself has been demonstrated on internal evidence to be the work of a Provencal speaking Augustinian friar, who was evidently writing in the area of Avignon.[25] The suggestion that he may have been engaged for the compilation by Richard

[24] His fame as a theologian of first rank was owed to two treatises — the *Summa de Quaestionibus Armenorum,* an argued statement of western catholic doctrine designed to promote union with the eastern rite, and the *De Pauperie Salvatoris,* a theoretical analysis of the foundation of dominion or right to property. However, although the first of these works had been completed (as probably, indeed, had most of the second) and had been presented to Pope Clement VI, FitzRalph's reputation would not yet have been widely established on the basis of it. Since in the course of the *Summa* FitzRalph had had to defend Purgatory against Greek denial of the doctrine, he was an entirely appropriate patron of someone with alleged experience of that state. George would not have been aware of this point though it is not impossible that the compiler of his account may have been. But there was ample motive otherwise for highlighting the archbishop's connection with the episode.

[25] The pioneering work in this regard was done by Voigt, *Beiträge zur Geschichte der Visionenliteratur,* whose conclusions were accepted by the editor of the text, *Visiones Georgii,* and *idem,* 'Eine Pilgerfahrt des XIV Jahrhunderts nach dem Fegfeuer des h. Patrizius', *Zeitschrift für Deutsche Philologie,* liii (1928), [25-40], 27, 37, 39. It would seem that some further inquiry was made into George's pedigree at the papal curia either by the author or, as is more likely, by his principal. The author is at pains to describe George as 'son of the noble and puissant man, the lord Grissaphan of Hungary, knight, as has been most clearly proved in the Roman curia by very many knights and squires and also religious men [sc., probably, regular clerics] of the Hungarian nation, who allege that the said George is a true noble and of great nobility, that is to say, the son of the right noble man, the lord Grissaphan, the latter being not only a knight but also a great and noble baron'. *Visiones Georgii,* 86-87. Since of the several letter writers only the archbishop shows enough concern with the point to alert us to the source of his knowledge of George's background, it is reasonable to think of him as having been the instigator of a further inquiry. This would agree well with the suggestion that his nephew was active in the compilation of the account (see the following note).

FitzRalph junior[26] is entirely plausible in view of the latter's residence at the papal court during the period and his uncle's letter introducing George to him. The account claims, with verisimilitude, that it is based on conversations with George. Nothing conflicts with the claim and that the author had had some contact, at least indirectly, with him is clearly presupposed by his being in possession of the texts of the testimonials. The latter too, especially that of the prior of Lough Derg, the letter from FitzRalph to George inviting him to an interview and the letter from FitzRalph to his nephew, show that certain salient features of the elaborated version were present from the immediate aftermath of the pilgrimage. According to the prior, George had suffered various torments, had had a vision of St Michael and had been led by him to paradise; the archbishop knew of the angel, though strangely he does not refer to him by name, and is the first to mention revelations; these revelations included something pertaining to the archbishop, a fact which had been signified to him by the time he wrote the first letter. For the rest one depends on the literary version. This is a lengthy document, of some 30,000 words. After a brief introduction and an outline of the circumstances of George's pilgrimage — prefaced by the testimonial letters — it distinguishes twenty-six visions experienced by George in the Purgatory, followed by details of four supplications made by him to the angel and six commissions received by him. It concludes with George's exit from the Purgatory.

L. L. Hammerich, discussing the genesis of the surviving record of the pilgrimage, differentiated the motives of the compiler of the account from those in Ireland who had a propagandist interest in exploiting George's story, to which they may also be thought to have contributed.[27] Hammerich was certainly right in diagnosing that the compiler had no concern for promoting the Purgatory. It is less easy, though, to agree with the remainder of his judgement:

[26] See Walsh, *A Fourteenth-Century Scholar*, p. 317. The fact that the author of the account deliberately links the Purgatory to the see of Armagh, describing it *(Visiones Georgii*, pp. 76-7) as 'the Purgatory of the most blessed Patrick, bishop and confessor, formerly archbishop of Armagh, primate of Ireland', may be thought to offer some confirmation of the hypothesis. Walsh, *op. cit.*, p. 318, adverts to the propagandist advantage to the archbishop of the promotion of the cult.

[27] Hammerich, 'Eine Pilgerfahrt', 37. Hammerich noted in particular the guarded and deferential tone of the angel's communication for FitzRalph as suggesting composition by a cleric of the archbishop's jurisdiction. The circumspection might of course be explained if FitzRalph junior was indeed the patron of the compilation.

that his purpose included the edification and entertainment of layfolk. Not only is the language of the account against this — it is written in Latin — but the theological and philosophical overlay which the author imposes on the narrative of George's visions is of a thoroughly serious, clerical, character. The work was translated into the vernacular, and in German and even in Czech enjoyed an important second level of circulation in central Europe, but it does not seem that the compiler had this type of readership mainly in view. The possibility does occur to him that layfolk might have access to the account but it is rather a consideration which necessitates the precaution of countering the demons' propaganda than a prospect to be cultivated in its own right.[28] There was indeed much in George's story to appeal to the lay imagination as the demand for translations and the subsequent expansion of the pilgrimage show. However, the initial success, to which the visions as they have been transmitted owed their formulation, lay in the story's appeal for the academically trained clerical imagination.[29] Unless this point is given due weight a large part of the significance of the episode is missed. The compiler gives his own startling verdict on the importance of George's experiences in the preface to his account: 'God and Our Lord Jesus Christ formerly showing the way of salvation multifariously and in many manners by his evangelists, apostles, disciples, doctors and preachers, preaching the word of God, has most recently in our own days, namely in the year of Our Lord 1353, deigned to speak to us of the same way of salvation, by which it is possible to arrive immediately at contrition and penance and consequently at the grace of God and glory, through a certain man beloved of him and his dear son by adoption, called George of Hungary . . .'[30] The later middle ages were peculiarly open to the idea of private revelation, a fact which is readily demonstrated by examples as diverse as the burgeoning literature of mysticism and the initial impact of Joan of Arc. Not that a measure of critical reserve was lacking, but reserve was tempered by an apprehension of the risk as expressed by the archbishop himself, that in spiritual

[28] See *Visiones Georgii*, p. 129, and below, p. 137.

[29] It is quite clear from the philosophical content of the account that the anonymous Augustinian compiler had been academically trained, and the archbishop, while a great deal more circumspect than the prior of Lough Derg in his endorsement of George's claims, had treated them with a high seriousness.

[30] *ibid.*, pp. 75-6.

matters one might contract contumacy.[31] This cultural trait, rendering credible what might otherwise be dismissed as fantastic, at once explains the reception accorded to the visionary and in no small part constitutes the importance of the visionary genre to wider history.

George's Pilgrimage

The occasion of George's pilgrimage was the war in southern Italy. In precisely what phase, is not clear; the author in narrating the Italian context describes him as 'a young and robust man of twenty-four years or less' but since the archbishop's letters refer to him as 'almost twenty-four' at the time of the pilgrimage, age gives only a general guidance. According to the account, George had been constituted by King Louis as a captain in Apulia over a large number of cities and fortresses, in particular over the city of Trani, described as 'situated on the coast near the cities of Bari and Barletta', and over the fortress of Canosa di Puglia. In the office committed to him he was 'exceedingly strict' and in his harrying of those opposed to his cause he 'perpetrated both personally and through his accomplices innumerable evils and wrongs, namely numerous depredations and the slaying of at least 350 persons, killed unjustly and against conscience.'[32] Then one night, lying awake in his bed, 'seeing all his sins and those of his accomplices to be horrible and truly abominable in the sight of God and man',[33] he was struck by remorse and the fear of God and damnation, so that he promised wholly to abstain from deeds of arms. Next morning, unknown to his friends and kinsfolk, he set off at once with one servant but without horse or beast for the Roman curia,[34] in order to seek absolution. The penance which was assigned to him there in accordance with the standard practice did not however seem to him sufficient or in proportion to the magnitude of his crimes and as a supplement he decided to make his way to the great Spanish pilgrim

[31] The problem of new revelation was examined with characteristic incisiveness by Jean Gerson, in his treatise *De Distinctione Verarum Revelationum a Falsis,* written early in 1402: Jean Gerson, *Oeuvres Complètes,* ed. P. Glorieux, iii, *L'Oeuvre Magistrale* (Paris, Tournai, Rome, New York, 1962), 36-56.

[32] *ed. cit.,* p. 88. In the Preface to the account, *ibid.,* p. 76, the number of homicides is given as two hundred and fifty. The lower number may reflect those for which George felt particularly responsible but it may equally be an insignificant variant.

[33] *ibid.*

[34] The papacy was during this period resident at Avignon in the south of France. George would probably have travelled by sea from southern Italy.

centre of Santiago in Compostela and to remain there leading a life of penance and austerity 'until, feeling the effect of divine mercy, he should experience in his mind that his truly unspeakable sins had been remitted him'.[35] The account emphasises the hardship of this journey, completed on foot, to Compostela for one who had always been used to travelling on the best horses. Having arrived and made his reverence at the shrine, George enquired of the clergy of the church of St James whether there was somewhere in the locality secluded and fit for his purpose. They directed him to a district at two days journey off, apparently bearing the name 'St William', near the church of Santa Maria Finistierra, situated among very high mountains and not much visited. George betook himself to the spot, still accompanied by his servant, and remained there for five months on a strict regime of bread and water until word went round of this devout man leading the eremitical life so that people began to flock to him. At this point, he determined on a visit to the 'place of St Patrick in the ends of the earth, namely in Ireland, which is the last province of the world in the western part', having already heard many marvels and devout reports of the Purgatory. So, again on foot and with great hardship, 'traversing the whole of Gascony, Navarre and the whole realm of France and all of England', he came finally to the church of St Patrick with its convent of regular canons, leading a most devout life, presided over by their prior, Paul, a centenarian almost, with a reputation for sanctity.[36]

Whatever the source of George's knowledge of the Purgatory, it cannot have been precisely detailed because he now discovered a difficulty for which the 'History of Knight Owein' could in part have prepared him. The monk of Saltrey's treatise advises that in accordance with custom established by St Patrick no one enters the Purgatory without obtaining permission of the local bishop.[37] In fact, the prior and canons specified two licences, of which the first-mentioned is that of the archbishop of Armagh and the second that of the bishop of Clogher, the diocesan. George accordingly withdrew for a journey lasting about eight days and came first to the archbishop, from whom he sought 'most devoutly and with a flood of tears' — there may have been some initial resistance — licence to enter the Purgatory and mandate by his authentic letters to the

---

[35] *Visiones Georgii,* p. 89.
[36] *ibid.,* p. 91.
[37] See Picard and Pontfarcy, *Saint Patrick's Purgatory,* p. 49. Cf. above, p. 9.

bishop of Clogher and the prior and canons that they permit him to do so. Having obtained from the archbishop licence, letter (or letters) and, interestingly, a safe conduct, George presented himself to the bishop, by whom he was very graciously received — there seems to be a hint of contrast here — and from whom he obtained mandatory letters to the prior and canons to give him admittance. Full of joy, he then returned to the Purgatory where his letters were inspected and accorded due reverence.

The account next describes the ritual of admission. The applicant must first confess to and be absolved by the penitentiary appointed for the purpose in the church of St Patrick 'and having faculty and power from the lord pope to absolve such cases'. Secondly, when he has performed the ensuing penance, he must fast for fifteen days on limited quantities of bread of some sort and water. At the end of the fast, the office of the dead is said for him night and morning, 'as though he were dead', after five days, in this fashion: a bier is set up in the middle of the choir of the church, covered with black cloth and the pilgrim is placed on it as though dead, with priest, deacon, subdeacon and acolytes in funeral vestments and carrying cross, thurible and holy water. In the mornings, the office for the dead is followed by requiem mass, after which the pilgrim is absolved as though before burial and bells are rung as for the dead.[39]

All this was done for George, who was then conducted 'to a very small island quite close to their monastery, on which island there is a very small chapel and in the chapel an entrance like the gate of a pit or cellar, as one finds in France, the length of the door of which is four palms and the breadth three palms'. Upon the door were three great stones, 'of which the weight in each case was seven or eight quintals'. These had not been moved for thirty whole years, as the prior affirmed. While the company was pondering the problem of moving the stones, George, having made the sign of the cross, moved them as though they were only the weight of a feather. The prior, who alone keeps the key to the door, then opened it at George's request, in the sight of all. Party to these proceedings were

[38] This seems to imply that the penitentiary is being credited with power to absolve in papally reserved cases. As the convent was one of Augustinian canons, it should not refer to a licence under *Super cathedram/Dudum (Extravag. Commun.* 3.6.2; *Clementin.* 3.7.2). However, it is noteworthy that the prior of Lough Derg in his testimonial says that he absolved George 'by authority of St Patrick and of the order' and makes no reference to papal privilege in the matter.

[39] *Visiones Georgii,* pp. 94-5.

not only the convent but the king of that country — probably MacGrath[40] — who from devotion wished to be there for the occasion, with many other noblemen.

When the door had been opened, the prior, solemnly vested, with his servants, 'as is the customary practice', blessed George. Dressed 'in the prescribed manner' in three white tunics, without belt or hood, barefoot, bareheaded and ungirt, having made the sign of the cross and saying 'Jesus Christ, son of the living God, have mercy on me a sinner', George entered the door of the Purgatory, 'which entrance is a pit, exceedingly deep, of depth two miles and more, with turning, twisting steps in the manner of a (?) spiral staircase, which one finds in bell-towers and in the ascent and descent thereof'.[41] When he had descended almost to his waist, the prior — at the request of the king mentioned above and other bystanders — bound in George's left hand 'the cross of St Patrick, of great nobility and of great price'.[42] Full of confidence, George descended. The prior shut the door firmly, with key and stones, and went off, with the others, to return next day, precisely twenty-four hours afterwards.

George's Reception in the Purgatory

George descended by the steps 'for the space or length of a mile and a half' in total darkness, seeing nothing and feeling nothing but the solid steps beneath his feet. Then, turning in prayer to Our Lord

[40] *ibid.*, p. 95 (and again at pp. 315, 319) supplies the name 'Magrath' on the basis that this was the coarb. Walsh, *A Fourteenth-Century Scholar*, p. 311, rightly noting that the readings of the manuscripts from which Hammerich edits favour Macmahon, takes this to be the personage in question. However, although the king's presence is attributed to his 'devotion', there is a hint that he had a ritual function in the committal of the cross to George and this suggests MacGrath. It does seem that the compiler of the account meant to record the name as Macmahon but it may be doubted whether George could have been certain in his information on the point. On the hypothesis that Richard FitzRalph, junior, organised the compilation, he would be the obvious authority to interpret George's references to the king and supply what would seem an appropriate name. While Hammerich, 'Eine Pilgerfahrt', 37, remarks on the distortion of names arising from the cosmopolitan provenance of the account and the manuscript transmission, in fact the spellings in this case, 'Mathamathan' 'Machamatary', 'Machani', 'Machamatam', 'Machamatan', witness surprisingly well to the name Macmahon by comparison for instance with spellings of Irish names in the papal registers; too well perhaps for the archetypal spelling to have been a rendering of George's recollection and pronunciation.

[41] *qui quidem introitus est puteus profundissimus profunditatis duorum miliarium et ultra, habens gradus vertiles et volutuosos ad modum vitis gradualis, qui in campanilibus et ipsorum ascensu et descensu fieri consuevit'*, *Visiones Georgii*, p. 97. For discussion, see P. Dinzelbacher, *Die Jenseitsbrücke im Mittelalter* (Vienna, 1973), pp. 156-7.

[42] *ibid.*, p. 98.

Jesus Christ, he supplicated for a light by which to discern the limit of his descent. Immediately, he saw a light — akin to the light of the setting sun in this world[43] — which seemed to derive from above, from a little aperture the size of an ox's eye. Thus comforted, he continued his descent till at the last step he found a small door through which he left behind the staircase. He now crossed a plain, devoid of vegetation or stones, containing nothing but earth and a solitary path. This led him to a chapel of singular whiteness, through the centre of which he must pass, entering by one door and exiting by another. Disappointed in his hope of finding a hermit and seeing no one there, he prayed on bended knees before the entrance for guidance in the predicament. Immediately there appeared, entering from the other door, three men of great age and whiteness, bearded to the waist, as like to one another as bee to bee, so that it seemed to George that although he was seeing three he was only seeing one.

> One of these stepped forth and approached him saying, 'George, what do you seek?', to which he replied: 'Most devoutly and with the whole intent of my mind I seek the grace of Our Lord Jesus Christ and of the whole most holy Trinity and also the grace of the most holy Virgin Mary and of all the saints, if I will be able to win and have it by the help of his mother.' But he, somewhat indignantly, as to his manner of speaking, replied, saying: 'You will not be able to have it.' And when George had said to him, 'And why will I not be able to have it, if not in consideration of my own merits, yet in consideration of his infinite mercy?', he replied saying, 'Because just as you cannot support even the least torment of purgatory, so you cannot in any way behold its pains.' To whom George, very humbly and devoutly replied, saying, 'All things will be easy for me, so I trust, by the power of the Holy Spirit and Our Lord Jesus Christ, father of mercies and God of all consolation, who consoles us in all our tribulation.' So, seeing and hearing George's devotion and most devout will that most ancient and right venerable brother took him by the hand and led him into the said chapel and signing him with the sign of the most holy cross blessed him and speaking to him most secretly related to him in his right ear what things were in store for him on his pilgrimage, whether good or evil, namely, visions and illusions in great number of demons and at length the vision of purgatory, of hell and of paradise, teaching him in what manner he should bear himself in the visions of

---

[43] There seems to be a reminiscence here of H. of Saltrey (see Picard and Pontfarcy, *St Patrick's Purgatory*, p. 53) but the correspondence is inexact.

the demons, saying, 'When the demons shall have appeared to you in this form or that, you shall, after having made the sign of the cross, say these words, "Lord Jesus Christ, son of the living God, have mercy on me a sinner", and immediately the demons, fleeing with a most mighty clamour, will be unable to harm you and will in no way be able to overcome you in their various temptations and especially concerning the catholic faith.' The same religious man continued, saying, 'But when you shall have come to the pit or iron bridge of hell, if anyone appears to you, adjure him, saying, "I adjure you by the living God, true and holy, and by the merit of the passion of Our Lord Jesus Christ, that you tell me, whether you are of the part of paradise or of hell." Thus adjured, he will not be able to lie to you but will in answer tell most certain truth. And there by the said pit of hell you shall persist in prayer until the angel of God shall appear to you, who will truly show you the pains of hell and purgatory and also the glory of paradise.'[44]

While he was receiving this counsel, it seemed to George that he was being fed to satiety with a divine food which percolated through all his limbs. The other two ancients meantime sang the passion of Christ with ineffable sweetness and skill. When counsel and singing were complete the ancients disappeared, leaving George in the chapel alone.

George's Visions

The ancient's counsel provides a broad schema of George's subsequent experiences, of which only an outline can be given here.

First Vision: Demons in the shape of various terrible beasts

Having left the chapel, George entered another plain in which he found more than three thousand demons in the guise of various terrifying animals — lions, bears and so on — breathing fire, terrible and fetid, through which, as they faced the path, he was obliged to pass. The largest and most terrible of these demons demanded of him what he sought, and on being told 'The grace of Our Lord Jesus Christ', replied that Jesus Christ was a most wicked sinner, justly crucified, who was dead and had not risen but was now in hell. The Christian faith was perfidy and insanity. In return for the promise of perpetual obedience and George's soul and body,

[44] *Visiones Georgii*, pp. 102-4.

the demons would return him to his homeland or elsewhere, with as much treasure as he wished, and after death he would have a high place in their kingdom. George countered by a spirited defence of Christian teaching (though with rather more Scriptural references and exegetical nicety than might be expected of him). When this provoked the demons to seize him and plunge him in the fire he retained just enough recollection to use the formula which had been recommended to him. Immediately, he found himself unscathed and the demons departed with earth-shaking clamour.

Second Vision: Demons in the guise of horsemen and horses

A little further along, George encountered two thousand horsemen, armed men, knights and barons, whom he had known in this life. These in friendly and gracious tones repeated the attack on Christ and Christian faith and boasted the advantages of the world to which they had come, where they eternally and without injury practised noble and warlike feats in tournaments and jousting. If George joined them they would make him king and captain. On his using the formula, they fled at once, amidst a great storm of winds, blizzards, stones and thunderbolts.

Third Vision: Devil in the guise of a beautiful woman

Proceeding further, George saw from afar a very great and powerful city from whose gate issued to meet him a lady, wonderfully lovable and exceedingly beautiful, clothed in scarlet and wearing a most beautiful crown, accompanied by two hundred or more damsels of similar beauty. As she came closer to him, however, he noticed the lady's feet, of which one was the foot of a cow and the other of a horse. These she attempted to cover but without success as they were clearly visible a third way up her shin. After repeating the attack on Christ and faith, the lady offered her hand in marriage and her kingdom, explaining that she was an orphan and that when she had heard of George's prowess she had decided on him as her defender. He however kept an eye on her feet and resisted the advance, proclaiming his faith and concluding with the formula as before, at which the devil who had thus appeared to him vanished with his accomplices, leaving behind a smoke fetid beyond all the corruptions of the world.

Fourth Vision: Demons in the form of merchants, male and female

George entered the great city, where he found a market in course with all imaginable merchandise. As he passed by, the tradespeople called on him by name, commenting on the poverty of his attire, and offering him (most insidious temptation) goods on credit, or even free, and refreshment while clothes were made for him. He however deviated neither to right nor left, giving them no reply but his formula. When he had passed through the city it was swallowed up in hell.

Fifth Vision: Demons in the form of terrible serpents

George now saw on either side of his path demons tormenting innumerable souls, chained in the midst of a great fire. Blocking his way was an infinite multitude of demons in the form of most horrible serpents, capable of eating an ox or two or three men, and breathing fire. In fear for body and soul he repeated his formula and made the sign of the cross, following which the serpents were totally vanquished and as if dead.

Sixth Vision: Demons in the form of Dominican and Franciscan friars

Crossing a plain, George encountered a double procession of more than five hundred friars, Preachers and Minors, who greeted him joyfully and, as being themselves formerly great religious, lectors, bachelors, masters and clerics of high status, urged on him the necessity of changing his faith. They pursued their point with close theological argument on the impossibility of the doctrine of the incarnation, pressing him as unlettered *(laicus)* and ignorant to defer to their knowledge. George, though firm in faith, was perplexed by the contrast between their outward appearance and devotion and their doctrine. The compiler intervenes to explain that the devil takes on various shapes, even that of Christ or the Blessed Virgin and those of the saints: of Christ, as recounted in Sulpicius Severus' life of St Martin; of the Blessed Virgin, as in a case in Tours during the compiler's own lifetime; of the saints, as witnessed in the *Golden Legend* and the Lives of the Fathers. George, in any case, admonished them sternly and banished them as usual. The compiler intervenes again to reply to the 'diabolical and sophistical reasons, in which also the perfidy of the Jews is founded'[45] advanced against the incarnation, lest they deceive the souls of simple laymen perhaps reading the book.

[45] *ibid.*, p. 129.

Seventh Vision: Demons in the form of clerics and canons

Another procession appeared, this time of regular canons, priests and other clerics, in surplices, who seemed to be singing devoutly in praise of God and chanting. At the end, was a venerable and devout man, as it seemed, dressed in pontificals as a bishop, holding in his hand a tiny wooden cross, the size of a finger. He saluted George graciously and welcomed him to his episcopate, explaining that he had heard 'by a revelation of the Holy Spirit and the grace of Jesus Christ' that he was a man 'very devout and with that prudent and right noble, although lay and without knowledge of letters, and yet deficient in rectitude of faith'.[46] This defect the demon bishop now tackled, urging that 'although Jesus Christ was a good man and a great prophet, yet it is not possible that he was God, because from so vile a creature and fetid as is woman, God, who by nature is most clean, cannot be born, nor be polluted and made unclean by her.'[47] This fatuity of Christians, heretically contriving Christ to be God, was displeasing both to God and Christ. If George gave heed to the bishop's counsel, he would be a great lord, governing the bishop's whole diocese, his treasurer and principal counsellor. George replied with a statement of faith including an affirmation of the resurrection. At this, the bishop, gnashing his teeth, with his hand struck the wooden cross (though apparently more for emphasis than insult), launched into a denial of the resurrection, repeated the impossibility of the incarnation — this time appealing to the episcopal dignity of which he was the unworthy executive — and returned to a denial of the resurrection, taxing George with being 'only a layman and a youth who have never learned the truth of the scriptures and the secret of the sciences'.[48] George however remained constant in his previous affirmation. The bishop, now quite abandoned, threw down the cross and tramped it into pieces. George recognised with what he was dealing and had recourse to his formula, whereupon the bishop and his associates vanished with the usual stench.

Here too the compiler intervenes to defend the incarnation against the above attack. The most interesting aspect of the defence is the hint which it contains of the doctrine of the Immaculate Conception — not however explicitly formulated here, though

---

[46] *ibid.*, p. 131.
[47] *ibid.*
[48] *ibid.*, p. 133.

Mary is described as having been 'sanctified and filled with grace in her mother's womb'.[49] The doctrine was a topic of contemporary theological controversy, especially between the Franciscans, who for the most part championed it, and the Dominicans, who were for the most part opposed.[50]

Eighth Vision: Demons in the form of the Lord Grissaphan and George's brothers

Next on his way George met a devil in the form of his father accompanied by three others in the form of his own brothers, including George's youngest brother, Stephen, of whom he was especially fond. His father saluted him joyfully and embraced him, reminding him what a long time it was since they had seen him. He told him that he and George's brothers were dead and that their souls in this life of the other world were placed in the highest state and in honour beyond their state in their other life; the reason for this was that having been certified by the Holy Spirit of the falsity of the Christian faith and of Christ's claim to be God, he denied him and his faith and was thus made acceptable to God. He counselled George and ordered him as a father to do likewise, under penalty of his curse, adding as a further consideration that if he did not do so at once he would then and there cut the head off Stephen. Although George did not defect, he was frightened by these threats and was more tempted than in all the previous temptations. In trembling he made his affirmation of faith, whereupon Grissaphan *père*, in a fit of temper, seized Stephen by the hair of the head and decapitated him. George, seeing by divine inspiration that all this was devilish and evil, most devoutly repeated his formula, at which the devil with his accomplices vanished in anger and stench, leaving him comforted, firmly rooted in faith and giving thanks.

Ninth Vision: Demon in form of George's damsel

On his departure from Apulia George had entrusted his jewels, including three belts embellished with silver, to a most noble,

[49] *ibid.,* p. 135.

[50] For general treatments of the matter, see F. da Leire Guimaraens, 'La doctrine des théologiens sur l'Immaculée Conception de 1250 à 1350', *Etudes Franciscaines,* new series iii (1952), 181-203, iv (1953), 23-51, 167-87; I. Brady, 'The development of the doctrine of the Immaculate Conception in the fourteenth century after Aureoli', *Franciscan Studies,* xv (1955), 175-202. On the Augustinians, A. Zumkeller, 'Die Augustinerschule des Mittelalters: Vertreter und philosophisch-theologische Lehre', *Analecta Augustiniana,* xxvii (1964), [167-262], 191-2.

trustworthy and devout damsel in whom he much confided. A demon now appeared to him in her form and dress and carrying the casket with his jewels. She was overjoyed to see him after so long and in that she perceived how he had been tormented by demons. The angel of God had wished her to participate in George's pilgrimage and had directed her to bring the casket as consolation to him after his trials. She urged him now to put on one of his belts and his precious headpiece *(caputium),* so that he would be fitter, in accordance with his nobility, to appear in paradise, where ornament was worn. Despite the eloquence and devotion of the damsel, and the other convincing appearances, George realised that this was a deception aimed at causing him to commit the sin of vainglory, foulness and luxury. Accordingly he replied that it was unbecoming for a pilgrim to use ornament but that he must follow the ordinance of St Patrick, in whose footsteps he trod, as taught him by Prior Paul, that he wear nothing but the three tunics. Let her therefore keep her belts etc., for which he cared nothing. The damsel however persisted. The holiness of Prior Paul, though admitted, was less than that of an angel, and although St Patrick had ordained that clothing, the ordinance did not apply to the whole pilgrimage but only for the time that the vision of demons lasted, which by the grace of God he had now passed and conquered. It was time to accept the ornaments, in accordance with the angel's direction and the commandment of God. As the devout in the other world dressed specially for feastdays, so must he for paradise. If not, he would be ejected as was, in the parable, the guest without the wedding garment. George, finding his resources insufficient in the face of these and similar promptings, resorted to his formula, with the usual happy result.

Tenth Vision: Of the lake of fire

Proceeding on his way, George saw a great lake of fire, full of boiling lead, pitch and sulphur, and most fetid, in which innumerable souls were being tortured. In the middle of the lake was an iron wheel, all ablaze, equipped with iron teeth, and rotated like a mill-wheel by three thousand demons. In each revolution the wheel seemed to tear innumerable souls in their various limbs — head, kneck, face, breast, belly, shanks, shins and so on. In each revolution and elevation it spued out and cast forth more than fifty souls pinned on its iron teeth, of whom some fell into the boiling pitch, some into the liquefied copper, some into the liquefied lead.

They meanwhile lamented most horribly not only from the pain of the fire and the wheel but from the horrible prospect and the derision of the demons who turned it. George was greatly frightened but much comforted in the Lord.

The episode is reminiscent of the sixth and seventh torments of Knight Owein.[51]

Eleventh Vision: Of the house of great length and breadth

Next, George saw a house which at first glance seemed a mile long and a mile broad.[52] It seemed to be covered with iron or copper, all aglow, and inside was filled with fire. The house was open on every side so that there was a clear view of the interior. It was completely occupied by brazen pots and cauldrons, full of liquefied lead, copper, sulphur, pitch and resin. The cauldrons were huge and 'on a common estimation' each held two or three hundred souls, much afflicted, who cried to Christ and the saints at the top of their voices, applying to the various saints in accordance with their devotion in this world. The compiler takes note that the souls, having first invoked Christ, then invoked Mary and then the various saints of their devotion. Beside the house was a river of water as cold as the fire of hell and purgatory is hot, that is in accordance with the measure of the strength of mortal sin, which is of infinite intensity. Innumerable demons stood eager to catch souls from the cauldrons with forks and hooks of iron, very sharp and fiery, and plunge them into the icy river, transferring them again after a time. George's way lay through the middle of the house, so he prayed to the Blessed Virgin, 'mother of my lord Jesus Christ, lady of pirgatory and of hell, paradise and the whole world, in whose power and piety next after your son Our Lord Jesus Christ all things consist, by whose humility [in response to the angelic salutation] the world was radically saved',[53] for another way or to be preserved if he must enter the house. No sooner had he finished his prayer than he saw his way made broad on the other side of the house.

Twelfth Vision: Of the pit of great depth

Having left behind the house, George found a pit of such depth that its bottom could not be seen, in which was a multitude of souls,

---

[51] Picard and Pontfarcy, *St Patrick's Purgatory*, pp. 60-2.

[52] Cf. the building of Knight Owein's seventh torment, *ibid.*, p. 61. For the icy river, cf. Knight Owein's eighth torment, *ibid.*, 62-3.

[53] *Visiones Georgii*, p. 153.

crying miserably. From it issued smoke most dark and fetid. When he reached the pit, past which he must go, he fell in, as would a very round ball or apple, without knowing by whom or how he had been pushed. Near the bottom of the pit he had recourse to his formula and was raised as suddenly as he had been precipitated.

Thirteenth Vision: Of the mountain, great and high

George came to a place near which, about a mile off, he saw a mountain, great and high, covered in cloud. On it was a very great number of souls, crying miserably and calling on Christ and the Blessed Virgin. Such was the covering of dark cloud and smoke that the souls could not be seen though they could be clearly heard. A most icy wind blew from the mountain, such that it could topple all the buildings of the world even if they were converted into one tower of immense strength and cause them to fly as though a feather or straw. Filled with compassion, George prayed for them, internally and without sound of voice, at the end of which most secret prayer the souls replied 'Amen' and made their own prayer on George's behalf. At this he greatly wondered.

The vision recalls the eighth torment of Knight Owein.[54] However, the compiler's principal interest is in the moral: that the souls in purgatory are conscious of their benefactors.

Fourteenth Vision: Of the pit of hell

As he walked on, George next came to a pit of great depth, which is the pit of hell, through the middle of which is an iron bridge like a sword of extreme sharpness and cutting edge, twisting and turning continually and with speed, like the leaves of a poplar in wind, so that there is no bird or creature, however light or agile, which could cross it of its own strength. The pit boils all the species of metals so that they resemble one liquid and gives off such smoke and stench that there is no one who dare look in but that he would at once die, even if he possessed the lives not only of all men living, but of all past, present and future, and even of the whole human race, which in its *esse possibile* includes infinite men: unless, that is, he were conserved by a miracle. And although hell is constituted within the elemental earth, in accordance with Psalm 62, 10, yet it has by divine power, for the exercise of divine judgment on the damned, such capacity as is that between heaven and earth, so that to a man

---

[54] Picard and Pontfarcy, *St Patrick's Purgatory*, pp. 62-3.

on the bridge of hell it seems to have depth and breadth as though he were in heaven looking at the depth and breadth of the whole world. Stupefied at this, George fell on his knees and prayed to Christ.

Fifteenth Vision: Of the apparition of the Archangel Michael

When George had finished his prayer, behold a young man, about the age of Christ, that is about thirty-four years or less, of great beauty, clothed in green garments, barefoot, having on his head a golden crown most richly ornate with precious stones (jacinths and all other kinds) and in his left hand, honourably borne, a most beautiful golden cross, similarly ornate, from which crown and cross gleamed a light most splendid, that seemed to surpass the light of the sun. He wore a cloak of green colour in the manner of the Spaniards or the brothers of St John and in the manner in which the cloaks of the apostles or angels are wont to be painted. His face was especially beautiful and joyful, such that no artist could depict it. He greeted George and asked him what he sought; to George's reply that he sought the grace of Our Lord Jesus Christ, he answered that he should find and have it. George, however, remembered the counsel which he had been given and conjured the young man thrice, receiving each time further reassurance and on the third time his name. On bended knees he kissed the feet of the angel, who as the ambassador of God permitted himself to be kissed, although in the Apocalypse the opposite is found of the angel who appeared to St John but forbade him to reverence him (Rev. 19, 10. 22, 9). It is evident that like the visitation itself, referred to already in the prior of Lough Derg's letter, George's obeisance to the archangel is part of the original story, since the compiler is much exercised by the disparity in angelic behaviour and seeks to account for it. The reason is twofold. First, George was simply a man *(homo precise)* — and it is the case that not only does man do reverence but the whole church militant does so on the feast of St Michael; the angel did not permit reverence in the case of St John because he knew that he was most holy, an apostle and evangelist, and the most blessed apostles and evangelists are of greater degree than all the angels; this however was not the case with George, 'as manifestly appears'.[55] (The compiler appears to have forgotten the extravagant implications of his preface.) Secondly, St John perhaps, suddenly seeing the angel, wished to

[55] *Visiones Georgii,* p. 165.

show reverence to him as an angel and the latter, being of lower status, would not receive this for the reason stated. In this case, the archangel Michael accepted the reverence from George, a simple man, not precisely as archangel but as the ambassador and vicegerent of God.

Sixteenth Vision: Of the diverse pains of purgatory

George was now associated with the archangel as pupil with master. The archangel invited him to see the pains of purgatory, telling him that in comparison with what he would show him, what he had seen so far was as nothing. He led him from the side of the pit of hell to a place of great size, full like a great lake or sea with fire, the heat of which, although temporal, was equal to that of hell-fire. In the fiery lake George saw three hundred principal manners of punishment, so horrible that if all heaven were a parchment and all the stars and all the leaves of trees and grasses were scribes and the whole sea-shore were an ink-pot and all the angels were associated with the stars and leaves as scribes, the whole would be insufficient to write and notify to men the pains of purgatory, their manner and the infinite horror of the tribulations. George saw innumerable souls of men and women, in human form, and in the state which they had held in this life, the soul of king as king, of queen as queen, of pope as pope, of cardinal as cardinal, and so on, religious (that is regular clergy) being in the appropriate habit. The three hundred principal pains referred to are in addition to the common and principal pains of fire and freezing water, and are special pains suffered by some souls as appropriate to special sins. He saw souls hung by fiery ropes or serpentine cords, like living serpents, which were demons in the form of serpents. Those thus hung up and bound were fiercely and horribly bitten in all parts of the body. Also, some were hung up by their hair, some by their eyes, some by their nose, some by their tongue, some by their lips, some by their neck and so on, according as they had sinned. He also saw things described in the book of Lazarus, on the pains of purgatory, as read publicly and commonly in the churches of Marseilles.[56] Details follow of the punishments of the proud, the avaricious, the lecherous, the wrathful, the gluttonous, the envious and the slothful (among the last are given special mention religious and clerics who

---

[56] On the *Visio Lazari*, see Voigt, *Visionenliteratur*, i. Cf. Hammerich, 'Eine Pilgerfahrt', 25-6.

do not rise in the morning for divine office and the canonical hours or who have omitted the latter through idleness).

The compiler now explains a number of details.[57] The clothes and ornaments referred to, as reflecting the former state of the souls, are not real but rather demons which scorch those whom they thus decorate. Neither are the bodies real bodies, because separated souls do not assume their bodies before the general resurrection nor can they do so of themselves; they only assume the figures of their bodies, in which they appear as living men, and otherwise they could not be observed by corporal eyes. They do this by divine permission. It is also to be understood that the pain of purgatory differs from that of hell only in duration. Then, in that it is said that the souls are punished by corporeal fire, as though they had bodies, unbelievers, denying purgatory and hell, object that the soul as an indivisible spirit cannot suffer from a divisible body [sc. corporeal fire] because the latter lacks the force, *acumen indivisibile,* with which to make contact with a spirit.[58] Moreover, the truth of natural philosophy [sc. Aristotelian science] teaches that every agent, considered as an agent and in respect of its activity, is more outstanding and noble than the patient, in that it is more noble to be active than to be passive. But the fire of hell or purgatory is not more noble than a spirit. Therefore the soul cannot suffer from a body, nor in consequence from infernal or purgatorial fire. One must say, however, according to the truth of catholic faith, that although infernal and purgatorial fire, which is not naturally joined to the soul and to demons, cannot naturally join its activity to them or naturally act upon them, it can act in so far as it is the instrument of divine justice. And when it is said that a body does not and cannot have the force, *acumen indivisibile,* to make contact with souls and indivisible spirits, although it does not have this naturally, it does have it supernaturally communicated to it by divine power.[59] This point is elaborated. The argument is also pursued from a consideration of the soul. The rational soul naturally conjoined to

---

[57] *Visiones Georgii*, pp. 177-185.

[58] That the separated soul did not suffer from corporeal fire was one of the errors of the arts faculty of Paris university condemned by Bishop Tempier in 1270. Cf. M. Haren, *Medieval Thought The Western Intellectual Tradition from Antiquity to the Thirteenth Century* (London, 1985), pp. 199-200. In what follows concerning the two truths, there may be an echo of the 1277 controversy at Paris. Cf. *ibid.*, pp. 194-5.

[59] The argument, which has its foundation in Aristotelian and fourteenth century physics, appears also to be influenced by the contemporary theological distinction between the *potentia ordinata* and the *potentia absoluta* of God, though this distinction is not explicitly drawn.

the human body and constituting an essential unity with it, that is the essence 'humanity', a combination from two partial substances, soul and body, suffers naturally all the corporal passions. Indeed it does so principally, for the sensitive potencies are potencies of the soul, not of the body, which on the separation of the soul retains no potency of it. Accordingly, the soul separated from the body can suffer corporal pain for it retains its natural capacity in this regard. Though the authority quoted for this analysis is Book 2 of Aristotle's *De Anima,* the psychological theory by which it is chiefly influenced is that of St Augustine. In an extension of the argument, the compiler advances the view that corporeity can be called the first degree of form, citing in support the Augustinian theologian John de Lana (d. 1350), whom he refers to as 'one of ours'.[60] The whole passage, while technical, is of considerable interest as reflecting the compiler's anxiety and determination to accommodate the experiences credited to George within a contemporary philosophical and scientific understanding.

Seventeenth Vision: Of the torment of the souls in purgatory

George not only saw souls in mass; he saw individuals too. He recognised his mother and others, including friends (unnamed) whom he had known in this world, standing within the fire. His mother was too far off for him to talk to her but they regarded one another tenderly as befitted those linked not only by natural love but also by love in the Lord. For the mother rejoiced at such grace conferred on her son and most avidly hoped for greater merit for him, being as it were certified concerning the same, while the son at once grieved and rejoiced, rejoicing in the certainty of his mother's salvation and grieving at her present condition. George was also notified by the archangel, in a brief hour, of more than two thousand persons in purgatory, of various degrees, whose names are not given except for three: Robert, late king of Jerusalem and Sicily [sc. Robert of Anjou, who died in 1343 and from whom the contested claims to the southern Italian kingdom derived]; Philip, king of France, 'recently deceased' [sc. Philip VI, who died in 1350]; and Alfonso, king of Castile [who also died in 1350]. He saw too a cauldron of a huge size exceeding all others in purgatory, in which no one was nor shall be, as the archangel said, in which St Patrick had sustained his penance for seven whole years. While they both

60 *Visiones Georgii,* p. 182.

stood there, another angel descended from heaven to comfort the souls by reminding them of the eternal rest shortly awaiting.[61] Michael told George that this took place every week, from which the souls derived great consolation.

Eighteenth Vision: Of hell and the damned

St Michael brought George by the hand back to the pit of hell. This was full to the brim with lead and all metals, as with sulphur, pitch and resin, liquefied and burning. The stench was such that no one, however many lives he possessed, could sustain it without instant death, unless he were conserved by special grace, as was the case with St Patrick, George and 'many other devout and penitent', who by divine will and help have devoutly visited purgatory and hell in this life. In the middle of the pit was the bridge previously mentioned, a mile long and a finger's breadth. After receiving from him a declaration of faith and having blessed him in the name of the Trinity and of the Blessed Virgin, St Michael led him by the hand across. Under their feet the bridge became stable and widened as they progressed, until by the middle it was one and a half yards *(unius canne cum dimidio),* that is twelve palms, across. Though the detail varies, the bridge resembles that of Knight Owein's tenth torment.[62]

In the middle of the bridge they stopped and hell opened at the archangel's command. Here were many more demons than in purgatory, for so full is hell of demons that they seem like flies on a corpse, congregated to feast. They saw innumerable souls of Jews, Saracens, pagans, heretics and evil Christians. There are incomparably more souls in hell than in purgatory. Thus, if one divides the world into four parts, in that catholic Christians occupy a fourth part, which is called Europe, three parts are certainly damned, namely Africa and 'greater India', which contains half the world, since it is certain that these are inhabited by infidels. Indeed, the division is a fivefold one if Europe is treated as being two parts, allowing for the Jews, Saracens and evil Christians which it contains, so that by this calculation four parts of the human race is damned and only one-fifth saved. George saw persons of all classes, lay and clerical, including 'pontiffs' and prelates of every state and members of all religious orders (including the Templars). Among

[61] *ibid.,* p. 188.
[62] Picard and Pontfarcy, *Purgatory,* pp. 64-5. Cf. Dinzelbacher, *Die Jenseitsbrücke,* pp. 64-6.

the sins for which the damned suffer are specified envy, sloth in respect of the canonical hours and 'another sin not to be mentioned here'. Although George saw many persons whom he had known in this life and although St Michael is said to have named to him a great multitude, 'whom George had not personally seen in this world', there are no identifications in the account.

Nineteenth Vision: Of the meadow of great beauty

When they descended from the bridge it again narrowed and became unstable. George asked the archangel whether the souls in hell will ever possess eternal life and he replied that Christ, 'who is the most powerful king of the universe', could by his mere will and command annihilate hell or even, while leaving hell as it is, snatch souls from it and glorify them. However, he does not and will not care to do so as they are condemned most justly.

After this, they passed through a meadow of great beauty and delight whose limit could not be seen.

Twentieth Vision: Of the wood

After the meadow, George saw a wood, filled with flowering trees, in which birds sang with surpassing sweetness. It seemed to George that this was paradise and it was not imagined that there was another paradise.

Twenty-first Vision: Of the golden wall and the gate of paradise

St Michael explained that although the birds in the wood were angels in that form, constituted amid the flowers of natural and supernatural virginity, the wood was not paradise but a foretaste of it, which God wished to show him so that he would perceive paradise by degrees.

Proceeding further, George saw a circular wall as of a great city, golden and gleaming. In the middle was a great gate, closed and as it seemed on fire. The fire was not true fire but light which occasioned ineffable delight and joy to such as saw and felt it. St Michael explained that the wall and gate were of paradise, not the heavenly paradise but an image of it, for the angels and souls of the saints, being indivisible spirits, could not be seen by the corporal eye 'in their proper substance and nature', like God, 'of whom they are the natural image'. It had been granted them on George's account to assume the figures of bodies. Since no one living could see God (for which is cited, slightly modified, Exodus 33, 20) either with the corporal eye or the eye of the intellect, because that is the beatific vision, which excludes all mortality, George might not ascend to the empyreal heaven nor see the proper glory of the saints, even with the mental eye, but he would see the paradise which is the image of the true, heavenly paradise. Accordingly, he took George by the hand and holding up the cross ordered the gate to open.

Twenty-second Vision: Of the entrance and view of paradise

Inside, George saw a great plain, whose limit could not be seen. It was even in all its parts except in the middle where it rose to form an altar. There was to be seen no stone, grass, plant or tree nor gold or silver nor any body, great or small, except for precious stones. The sight absorbed hunger, thirst and all misery and all memory of this world. By comparison with it the world is most vile, most especially on account of sin, whose foulness is such that were it not for the prayer of the Blessed Virgin Mary to her son, Jesus Christ, the world would be cast down into hell. This foulness offends the will of God more than that of hell, because hell is incorrigible while the world is corrigible.

Twenty-third Vision: Of the procession of the holy angels

George saw a multitude of angels in the form of young men, who chanted the 'Sanctus', which is the common canticle of the angels, though every order has too its own chants and hymns as do the saints. Afterwards they formed a procession, those of lower dignity preceding, as in the church militant. The angels are crowned with crowns of gold interworked with precious stones.

Twenty-fourth Vision: Of the procession of human kind

He saw too the innumerable multitude of saints, distinguished in nine societies: patriarchs, prophets, doctors of Old and New testaments, the apostles, the evangelists, the seventy-two disciples, and the orders of martyrs, of confessors and of virgins. Their order of processing is recounted. All have a crown of gold; some have in addition a small crown placed over, called an aureole, a circle of gold ornate with precious stones, 'like the circle which is placed over the crown imperial'.[63] The colour of the clothing of the various degrees is described.

---

[63] *Visiones Georgii*, p. 224. Cf. *ibid.*, p. 228.

The compiler repeats that the principal glory of the saints cannot be seen by the corporal eye. The reason for this is that incorporeal things are indivisible and the indivisible cannot make a corporal angle, whereas all that is seen sensibly is seen in respect of an angle *(sub angulo)*, 'as the truth of the science of perspective teaches'.[64]

Twenty-fifth Vision: Of the elevation of George

The archangel suddenly lifted George and placed him on the height, like an altar, in the middle of paradise. From here he viewed. There is an account again of the processing, which resembles that at a papal coronation.[65] The differing rewards of the saints are discussed with theological precision. Merit is the measure of reward, but the measure is in accordance with geometrical proportion not with arithmetical equality. However although in the kingdom of heaven there is difference within the same beatitude, 'George says'[66] that the glory seems such in the praises and musical instruments of the saints 'that there seems almost no or little difference in them'. (There is a pleasing suggestion of tension here between theory and 'fact'. It appears as though George may have been quizzed on the point.) 'He also says' that such suavity of odour emanates from paradise and the saints there that if the least part of it were felt in this world the whole world would be so sated that hunger and thirst would be removed.

Twenty-sixth Vision: On the opening of heaven

At the archangel's bidding George looked heavenward and saw heaven opened, with issue of as it were infinite light like that of a great fire, though the fire was not true fire but most resplendent light. Within the fire he saw a palace of immense size and ineffable beauty. In the middle of the palace were two thrones, most high. On one, a little the higher *(aliquantulum altiori),* sat a most beautiful king, and on the other, slightly the lower, sat a most beautiful queen. The significance of this was explained by St Michael and also the reason why heaven was thus opened: it was a special grace to George so that he might see heaven, as had Stephen the protomartyr, in so far as was possible for the corporal eye. The latter point is again explained with a further disquisition on

---

[64] *ibid.*, p. 230.
[65] *prout fit in coronacione pape, ibid.*, p. 232.
[66] *tamen dicit idem Georgius, ibid.*, p. 241. *dicit etiam, ibid.*, p. 242.

perspective. George asked to be transported to heaven but was told to content himself with the graces received. These included having been taught by God himself, as the archangel explained, in the persons of the three ancients in the white chapel, who were three angels representing *(figurantes)* the Trinity. The doctrine of the Trinity is set out.

Twenty-seventh Vision: Of George's four supplications

Such was George's rapture that the angel had to shake him in friendly fashion, smilingly asking him whether he wished to remain or return to the misery of the world. George replied that he preferred to stay here in the company of the saints. Michael, addressing him as 'my most dear brother', gave two reasons why this was impossible: because the inferior paradise which he saw was ephemeral and of a day's duration only, and would be annihilated after George's departure; and because George was mortal. He invited him however to make other, reasonable and possible supplications. George, on bended knees and still on the altar, then made four supplications: 1) that he might escape the pains of hell; 2) that the angel would reveal to him the length of his life; 3) that he would let him know what he must do to secure the early release of his mother's soul from purgatory; 4) and that he would assist him before God in the latter enterprise. Michael replied that the first had been granted by God (with a double *Fiat* and signature, in the manner of granting of supplications in the papal court). The second was 'truly unaccustomed' and had never been granted to anyone else. However, since God with all the saints now singularly loved George, his supplication was heard; he would live a little while after completing his embassies and after his death would come to heaven. The compiler adds that 'although the angel precisely expressed that time, clearly, and its precise duration, George would not express it to me nor to anyone else, to my knowledge, and therefore I have not written down here the certainty of that time'.[67]

To the third supplication, the archangel replied by setting out the means by which the souls in purgatory are aided: masses (the mass includes the whole efficacy of the passion of Christ); prayers (which singularly pertain to the contemplative life. Such are the Lord's Prayer, the Ave Maria, the Creed and the prayer 'Quicumque vult salvus esse'.); and the works of the active life, including almsgiving,

[67] *ibid.*, pp. 260-1.

which is both corporal and spiritual (both of which parts are
subdivided into seven). This whole section is used by the compiler
as a vehicle of doctrine and as an occasion to make particular points,
such as that although the mass is of infinite value no one knows
except by special revelation how far God applies it in liberating a
soul from purgatory,[68] and to discuss more general topics, such as
the superiority of the contemplative over the active life,[69] a
traditional argument but one with peculiar currency in the
fourteenth century. The seventh division of spiritual almsgiving is to
teach the untaught and to direct the wayward. Among the latter are
women, especially widows, on whose incapacity the author
digresses at some length,[70] citing Aristotle in support of his
assertion that women are deficient in constancy and prudence.[71] A
discussion of fasting[72] as a means of resolving the tension between
body and soul introduces an analysis of the intellective soul.

In response to the fourth supplication, St Michael promised not
only his own support but that of his fellow angels and of the Mother
of God, being certain of success.

Twenty-eighth Vision: Of George's embassies

The compiler now introduces 'the multiple embassies to diverse
persons prescribed to and enjoined on George by Michael the
archangel on the part of Our Lord Jesus Christ.'[73] Of these, the first
was to Richard, archbishop of Armagh, primate of Ireland; the
second was to King Edward [III] of England and his mother [Queen
Isabella]; the third was to King John [II] of France; the fourth was to
Pope Innocent [VI]; the fifth was to 'the Sultan of Babylon now
living and reigning over the kingdom of Babylon and Egypt'. The
compiler does not know the details of the embassies as George has
not given them 'singly or as a whole, anywhere or to anyone, except
those to whom he was sent and where he was sent'.[74] This need not
perhaps be read as a claim that more than one of the commissions
has been fulfilled. Later, at the end of this chapter, the compiler
says that after his exit George 'faithfully tried to fulfill the said

[68] *ibid.*, p. 287.
[69] *ibid.*, p. 290.
[70] *ibid.*, pp. 291-3.
[71] *ibid.*, p. 292. His use of Aristotle on the point is imprecise.
[72] *ibid.*, pp. 295-6.
[73] *ibid.*, p. 310.
[74] *ibid.*, p. 311.

embassies, giving the wonderful and most secret signs [sc. signs which would be recognised only by the recipients as evidence of George's authenticity] . . . revealed to him by the angel'.[75] He cites in confirmation of the truth of this 'the patent and evident letters of the Lord Armagh and of many others posited and described above in the beginning of this treatise',[76] but that collection of course confirms only one embassy. Perhaps 'tried to' *(conatus est)* indicates that he failed in some of the other approaches but no information is given. A later statement, in the context of the angel's final instructions, that George had put the divine will into effect as regards his embassies must be read with this weaker version.

Despite George's reticence as to the content of the embassies, titbits were dispensed. 'He expressed in general terms the embassy to the primate of Ireland and said that among other matters that embassy had to do with *(fundabatur super)* the absolution of a certain great city of his archiepiscopate, which the said primate unjustly interdicted and excommunicated and held subject to interdict and excommunication, although [sc. he did so] not from malice or injustice, in as much as seemed, but because it seemed to him that the city in certain points did not do its due, nor wished to do so.'[77] The embassies to the two kings 'contained many things but principally contained treating of peace and multiple admonition.'[78] The embassy to the pope contained also 'the treating of peace between the said kings' and in addition 'the absolution of a certain prince who died a long time ago and whom he [sc. George] did not care to name'.[79] George did not otherwise explain the embassy to the Sultan except that 'it contained the (or a) great and notable good of the whole of Christendom'.[80]

Twenty-ninth Vision: Of George's exit

Holding in his left hand the golden cross and taking George with

[75] *ibid.*, p. 313.

[76] *ibid.*, pp. 313-4.

[77] *ibid.*, p. 312.

[78] *ibid.* The 'treating of peace' here and in the following embassy refers to the war between England and France, now known as the Hundred Years War, which began in 1337. The Avignon popes were responsible for a number of initiatives to resolve the conflict, including an important conference in 1344. From the election of Innocent VI in late 1352 until 1355 new and vigorous papal diplomacy was in progress to achieve peace. See M. Mollat, 'Innocent VI et les tentatives de paix entre la France et l'Angleterre', *Revue d'Histoire Ecclésiastique,* x (1909), 729-43; E. Perroy, 'Quatre lettres du Cardinal Guy de Boulogne (1352-1354)', *Revue du Nord,* xxxvi (1954), 159-164.

[79] *Visiones Georgii, ioc. cit.*

[80] *ibid.*

his right hand, the archangel led him away 'to the chapel of St Patrick, where the door of the Purgatory is', and all that he had seen disappeared. At the end of the allotted twenty-four hours, the prior with his canons and the king with his nobles and a great multitude of other people saw George with another man, of age and appearance as described above. Of the two, they recognised George but did not know the other, though they thought in their heart that he was indeed an angel. In their sight, St Michael and George spoke together for a time, while St Michael cautioned him to keep the commandments and 'in the aforesaid embassies to keep the will of God and put it into effect, as also afterwards he did put it into effect'.[81] Then Michael, 'in the manner of a prelate', with his thumb made the sign of the cross on George's forehead, mouth and breast, saying 'Adiutorium nostrum in nomine domini [etc.]', 'Sit nomen domini benedictum [etc.]'. Having pronounced a general blessing (the text of which is given) over George and the crowd, he disappeared, though before doing so he confirmed George's fourth supplication by promising his intercession when he ascended to heaven. On the angel's departure, George 'wholly ascended the steps of the ladder of the Purgatory' to the joy of the prior and convent. The onlookers, who were singing in praise of God, 'affected by notable devotion not only on account of George's return but also of the vision of the angel and the wonderful and altogether ineffable odour which emanated from the place and from the clothing', tore strips off his clothing, 'as best they could, with knives or otherwise' and when they had thus left George naked, though with breeches,[82] they wanted to pull the hairs off his head and would have done so but for the intervention of the king already mentioned who most devoutly had George clothed in his own clothing.[83]

Retrospect on George's Pilgrimage

The account of George's pilgrimage raises a number of unresolved problems the answer to which must be speculative. On a

---

[81] *ibid.*, p. 317.

[82] *cum sic Georgium nudum, tamen in femoralibus, dimisissent, ibid.*, pp. 318-9.

[83] *qui ipsum Georgium vestimentis suis propriis devotissime indui fecit, ibid.*, p. 319. As George had donned special clothing for the Purgatory, this may mean either that his previous clothing was restored to him or that 'the king' provided him with a new outfit. In medieval Latin, 'suis' is consonant with either interpretation.

general level there is the question what language George used. This is not only a point of curiosity as to how he conducted his pilgrimage; it affects our interpretation of the genesis of the written account. The compiler gives no explicit guidance. However, George is taxed several times, by the demon friars and by the demon bishop, with being 'lay' and 'lay and illiterate',[84] and since this passes unchallenged it is implicit that he did not know Latin. If not from association with Angevin courtly circles, then from his residence in southern Italy and subsequent travels it may be assumed that he had a Romance language. Almost certainly he could speak French and interpretation from this into Latin is one possible medium of his communication with the prior and canons at Lough Derg. If the servant *(minister, famulus)* who is mentioned as accompanying him had been a clerk his role in the contacts would have been sufficiently prominent for one to expect his status to have been noted. With Archbishop FitzRalph George would no doubt have been able to communicate directly. His dealings with St Michael may be thought to pose less of a problem, except at one instance where the angel speaks aloud to bless the crowd — evidently in Latin since apart from the liturgical form he distinguishes carefully between male and female saints.[85] Unless George had brought with him a first draft of his visions from Lough Derg, by courtesy of the prior and canons — and the complete lack of evidence for this, both in the testimonial letters and in the final version, is enough to exclude it as more than a notional possibility — this sort of picturesque detail is wholly the product of the compiler's fluent pen and it is a useful measure of how much in the account, besides the overt intrusions and commentaries, we owe to him. It is worth restating here too that if George had nothing but his memory to rely on then he can hardly have been the authority for such a point as the spelling of the name of the king whom he had met at the Purgatory.

A second, crucial, problem is raised by the embassies. Prior Paul's testimonial witnesses to the presence of St Michael at an early stage in the narrative. Whether his appearance was dictated by George's preference or whether he was suggested to him as an appropriate guide by the prior and canons must be moot. His

---

[84] *tu autem es purus laicus, ibid.,* p. 125; *licet laicalem et sine noticia literarum, ibid.,* p. 131; *tu qui es purus laicus, ibid.,* p. 133.

[85] *Benediccio dei omnipotentis, patris* [etc.] *et omnium sanctorum et sanctarum descendat super vos et maneat semper. Amen.*

descent may be directly from the well disseminated *Visio Pauli* ('The Vision of Paul'), the early (perhaps third century) apocryphal description of St Paul's experiences of the otherworld, in which case a clerical prompt would be appropriate.[86] But George's recourse to this knightly champion against the powers of darkness, under whose banner the crusading Germans had campaigned against the Hungarians in the tenth century, may well have been spontaneous.[87] As regards the angelic messages themselves it is clear that one of them at least is of local inspiration. The late Professor Aubrey Gwynn over fifty years ago connected the embassy to FitzRalph — concerning the absolution of a 'certain great city of his archiepiscopate which had been censured for not doing its due' — with a sermon preserved in his sermon diary as preached by him to the merchant folk of Drogheda on the first Sunday of Advent, 2 December 1352, castigating the practice of setting losses against profits before tithing instead of paying immediately a profit arose.[88] Fr Gwynn felt that George's embassy might be taken 'as proof that the Archbishop followed up his sermon by the drastic step of imposing an interdict on the town and excommunicating those who failed to pay their tithes according to his requirement.' It might also he suggested 'be taken as good proof that the discontent had spread as far afield as the Augustinian monastery of Lough Derg: for it is impossible not to suspect that the canons of that monastery had some part in preparing the pilgrim for the reception of this particular message. He was with them for three weeks at least before his descent into the cave, in just the emotional condition that would make him most susceptible to such suggestions.'[89] Besides its inherent attractivenesss, this interpretation has the advantage of going some way towards explaining the apparent break in the archbishop's preaching activity in the period following.[90] The interpretation has however been criticised by Dr Walsh, justifiably I think, on the grounds that 'it is difficult to

---

[86] Hammerich, 'Eine Pilgerfahrt', 37. For the *Visio Pauli,* see Silverstein, *Visio Sancti Pauli,* and idem, 'The vision of St Paul: new links and patterns in the western tradition', *Archives d'Histoire Doctrinale et Littéraire du Moyen Age,* xxvi (1959), 199-248.

[87] On the cult of St Michael in this context, see M. Keen, *Chivalry* (New Haven and London, 1984), pp. 47, 53.

[88] I hope to deal elsewhere with the influences on FitzRalph's doctrine of tithing and restitution.

[89] A. Gwynn, 'Archbishop FitzRalph and George of Hungary', *Studies,* xxiv (1935), [558-572], 571.

[90] Cf. Walsh, *A Fourteenth-Century Scholar,* p. 315.

understand why a community of canons in a remote part of Gaelic
Ireland, in a part of the ecclesiastical province which was clearly
under the control of Gaelic clergy and Gaelic chieftains, and where
the canons by this late date must have been a largely, if not
exclusively Gaelic group, should have been so concerned'[91] as to
warrant their attempting to influence events in Drogheda. 'A more
probable object of their concern', she proposed, 'could have been
the primatial city of Armagh, which was never susceptible to
FitzRalph's jurisdiction and which he may well have had
opportunity to place under interdict. In such a case the phrase
"magne civitatis sui archiepiscopatus" would be inappropriate, but
the interest of the canons would be explained.'[92] In its own terms
this hypothesis is quite plausible and Armagh as the titular seat of
the archbishop might well qualify, especially at a remove, as 'a great
city'. However, we are not compelled to suppose that the
community at Lough Derg was the source of the mission to
FitzRalph. There is no evidence to that effect and — leaving aside
the strong reason for taking the city to have been Drogheda — some
little evidence, albeit an argument from silence, against. The
testimonial from Lough Derg asserts that George suffered
torments, had an apparition of the archangel Michael and was
conducted by him to paradise; it says nothing of revelations or
embassies and the omission is the more telling for what, by
comparison with the bishop of Clogher's letter, it does claim. Prior
Paul does not convey the impression of underplaying his hand and it
is reasonable to think that had he known of news for the great he
would have given some premonition of it. (That he should have
been silent as a cover for his inventiveness seems over-subtle). The
first indication that George has something to communicate to the
archbishop comes in the latter's invitation to him — the letter
probably written on 19 February, weeks after George may be
assumed to have left Clogher. Where he was between 26 December,
if he did leave the bishop on that day, and 29 January is a matter of
surmise but in the interval between his leaving Clogher and the date
of FitzRalph's writing to him he associated with people who would
have had greater interest in events at Drogheda than had the canons
of Lough Derg. Either the prior of Kilmainham, on behalf of more
general opinion within the Pale, or the (unnamed but presumably

[91] *ibid.*
[92] *ibid.*

Anglo-Irish) archdeacon of Armagh, on behalf of the immediate hinterland of Drogheda, is a more likely candidate to have briefed George on the point and to have tried to manipulate him. We do not know who else he may have talked to but of his two known contacts the evidence such as it is points rather more to the archdeacon: it was he after all who was instrumental in finally securing George an audience, though not necessarily at first application, on foot of a letter which, to judge by the sequel, must have contained the information that George had a message to deliver. No doubt George, on leaving the bishop, set out to find FitzRalph. He need not have had a message; his search for a further testimonial would have been sufficient motive and it is hardly to be thought that Prior Paul, having insisted on an archiepiscopal letter of authority in the first instance, would have failed to impress on his star pilgrim the desirability of obtaining the fullest possible confirmation. In any case and for whatever reason, George seems to have met some difficulty in his quest. The idea of a divine message may have been proposed to him as an *entrée* to the primatial ear and would thus happily have served a double purpose. Nor need one think George to have been merely cynical; it is just the kind of pious fraud for which medieval men of high principle seem to have had a peculiar weakness. The cause was just: he had completed his pilgrimage, with distinction, and for all he knew the 'great city' was being harshly treated. Many an abbot in defence of the privileges of his house ventured further into make-believe. It may be too that the nervous exhaustion which as Professor Gwynn hinted might have rendered George susceptible to influence at Lough Derg — and which may be thought also to be the best explanation of his visions — was not quite shaken off, or it might have been replaced or supplemented by a growing consciousness of his celebrity status.

What of the other missions? With one exception, they are too bland to require much comment. It is impossible to determine the identity or provenance of the dead prince whose absolution was to be sought from the pope. Professor Hammerich thought that he might be the excommunicate emperor Lewis of Bavaria (d. 1347).[93] Dr Walsh made the interesting suggestion of Edward Bruce as a more likely candidate, speculating that there may have been still some sympathy for him in Gaelic Ulster.[94] However, if the mission

[93] Hammerich, 'Eine Pilgerfahrt', 38.
[94] Walsh, *A Fourteenth-Century Scholar,* pp. 311-2.

to FitzRalph is judged rather to have emanated from the Pale, the identification with Bruce is improbable. The reference may well be continental, a piece (broadly speaking) with the other embassies. The prince may even have been Hungarian, a relic of Charles Robert's war against the magnates, in which he had enjoyed a measure of papal support. Whether the missions were conceived simultaneously is another difficult question. It would have been useful verisimilitude if FitzRalph should have been only one, the humblest, of a number of grandees to receive angelic direction and correction. The reference in his letter to his nephew to 'marvels concerning the living and the dead *(de vivis et mortuis)*'[95] suggests perhaps more than one message. On the other hand, George may have progressively warmed to his role. At all events, he had the good sense to remain mysterious and to keep his contemporaries as well as later historians guessing.

The Pilgrimage of Laurence of Pászthó

Yonge's account of Laurence's pilgrimage opens with a short, rhetorical[96] introduction on the origin of the Purgatory of St Patrick. It is one of the saintly places established by God as a testimony to truth and a remedy for ignorance, in this case the blindness of the Irish who were thereby given a salutary foretaste of the final judgment.[97] Those who do not believe the Gospels and the writings of dead saints may give heed to the enduring monuments of their works. In Ireland, the island from which St Patrick expelled noxious animals, they may see with their own eyes the evidence for belief and if they do not wish to or cannot tour the whole island, they may in proper fashion enter the Purgatory where they can have bodily experience of the evidence. Alternatively they may give credence to the reports of modern visitors, and especially of the subject of this treatise, the nobleman, Laurence, who has recently visited not only the Purgatory but most parts of the world. And whereas many in our time have visited the place few have from saintly motives actually entered it. Of these few, Laurence is one.[98]

Laurence arrived in Dublin in knightly attire, with herald and servants. In the cathedral of Holy Trinity, he venerated *(adoravit)*

[95] *Visiones Georgii*, p. 82.
[96] Yonge's Latin style is stilted and marked by a straining for effect.
[97] Delehaye, 'Le pèlerinage', 43.
[98] *ibid.*, 44.

the *bachall Íosa (baculus Ihesu)*, described as the staff with which St Patrick had, among other works, expelled the snakes.[99] Having exhibited there his letter of credence from King Sigismund stating the reason for his coming, he set out with his company to find the primate, Archbishop Nicholas Fleming. He was received honourably by the latter, again on display of his credence, and obtained from him the customary letter for his pilgrimage.[100] He then proceeded to Downpatrick[101] and remained there for some days in prayer and fasting for the safe completion of his journey. While lying in bed there one night,[102] the successful outcome of his pilgrimage was revealed to him by St Patrick, 'in whom he fixed the spiritual anchor of his proposal'.[103] Next morning, he started for 'the island called Saints' Island on the western shore of Ulster'.[104] When the prior saw the primate's letter he rejoiced but recalling the fate of very many who entered the place of the Purgatory and did not come back, he cautioned the knight: 'Brother and most dear friend, let your worship be aware of how many in my time have entered the place which you propose to have opened and suffered there an anguished death; of how others too have by the infestation of unclean spirits contracted permanent idiocy, and the remainder have vanished, body and soul. I counsel you therefore, brother in love, with devout prayer, in the name of divine pity, that unless you shall have fullest faith in Christ and shall have confessed and shall be contrite, you do not presume to enter the place of the Purgatory.'[105] To this the knight humbly made a declaration of faith in the Trinity, and the prior, rejoicing at the reply, informed him that in order to perform the pilgrimage he must first spend fifteen days on bread and water and in other works of piety, followed by confession, contrition and communion. The knight (a diplomat to his fingertips) undertook to comply in so far as his frailty would permit. However,

[99] *ibid.*, 45.

[100] *ibid.*, 46-7.

[101] *Dublinensem* [an error for *dunensem*] in the printed edition, *ibid.*, 47, but described as the city 'containing the translated relics of Sts Patrick, Columba and Brigid'.

[102] the printed edition, *ibid.*, reads 'una <die>', 'die' being supplied editorially where the manuscript (British Library, Royal 10. B. IX, of the late fifteenth century) is defective. However, from the *mane facto* of the sequel it is evident that what is required is 'nocte'. The editor was probably influenced in his choice of emendation by the context, *dum . . . suo quiesceret in cubili,* to think that the knight was taking a nap, whereas the 'resting' no doubt rather implies a break in his preparatory penitential regime.

[103] *ibid.*

[104] *ibid.*

[105] *ibid.*

the knight feared for the weakness of his body, 'lest perhaps through excessive abstinence from food or drink his mental powers or senses might very well give way'.[106] The fifteen day fast was accordingly put aside and (in an elegant and pious dereliction) he maintained a fast over five days, 'in reverence for the five wounds of Christ'.[107] Then, when he had confessed to the prior and communicated, the prior, one canon and he boarded a boat and sailed south for one mile to the island where the place of the Purgatory is.

The island of the Purgatory is now described.[108] It is surrounded by a current *(flumine)* of fresh water, abundant in salmon, trout and other species of fish. The name of this current or lake *(fluminis sive stagni)* is 'Lotherge' [sc. Lough Derg] in Irish, which is explained in Latin as being 'Red Lake', a name judged particularly appropriate. The island measures one hundred and thirty paces in length by twenty paces at most in breadth. It is divided into two parts. The larger, between west and north is called in Irish 'Kernagh', explained in Latin as 'Island of Clamour'. This part is made gloomy by various types of berried shrubs and trees *(nonnullis fructuum et arborum generibus)* — Yonge gives a number of names, difficult to interpret botanically but including dogwood and elder and generally conveying a sinister impression — and is crowded with birds of extreme rapacity, crows, hawks, kites, owls and other winged predators, which nest there and screech horribly. It was long ago assigned to Satan and his satellites, 'in hereditary right', as is said to be contained in certain manuscripts in Ireland. Yonge adds that there are unclean spirits on earth and in the air as well as in hell and the implication is that these birds are demons.

In this part of the island, among other malign specimens, is frequently observed[109] a demon called in Irish 'Cornu', who apart from the wings resembles a plucked heron.[110] When he gives voice, in his usual manner, like a trumpeter, he presages the death of a

---

[106] *ibid.*, 48.

[107] *ibid.*

[108] *ibid.*, 48-50.

[109] *oculis plurimorum multociens intuetur, ibid.*, 49. In medieval Latin *intueor* is found with passive sense and I have so taken it here.

[110] or just possibly, 'a plucked heron without wings': *preter alas effigiem habens ardee dispennate, ibid.*, 49. Probability is no guide! Antonio Mannini credits him with wings. Cf. below, p. 182.

pilgrim.[111] The smaller part[112] of the island is dedicated to the angels. It is called in Irish 'Regles', explained in Latin as *Regula*, 'Rule'.[113] It is situated between east and south and comprises thirty paces in length and five and a half in breadth, a place abounding in oaks, yews and other lovely trees, filled with variety of birds echoing sweet melody. The south-western portion of this part holds a chapel founded in honour of St Patrick, four arm-lengths long and two and a half wide. Here the prior, still with some reluctance, brought the knight, who took off his own garments and shoes and was clothed by the prior in three albs belonging to the canons and in a new pair of breeches, 'as is the custom of Irish pilgrims'.[114] The knight prostrated himself and the prior and the canon said over him the litany of the dead and the exequies.[115] When this was over, the prior led the knight from the chapel, four paces in a direction between east and north, before a cave walled and vaulted with stones. There is an opening which is the entry to the Purgatory; the Purgatory itself ends up in the other, the greater, part of the island.[116] The prior and canon began chanting the *Dies irae;* the prior opened the door of the cave, until then bolted or barred, sprinkled the knight with holy water and bade him farewell. The knight entered, crossing himself and praying, 'May the Lord keep my going in and my coming out [etc.]' (Cf. Ps. 121,8) and 'Lord Jesus Christ, Son of the living God, have mercy on me a sinner'. The door was firmly shut again by the prior and the knight was on his own. He had with him a candle which on account of the restricted space of the cave he divided into nine parts, one of which he kept burning. Round his neck he had four pieces of the wood of the holy cross bound with snippets of three tunics of Jesus Christ in beryl, silver and gold, as well as other precious relics and precious stones. He also had a book with the seven penitential psalms. Yonge adds the information that the first and principal entrance to the cave is no

[111] The printed edition adds here 'Quem et miles Owain est ibidem contemplatus', *ibid.*, 49, 'Owain' being the editor's emendation of the corrupt manuscript reading *octovia*, since Delehaye judged that the author could hardly have written *miles Antonio* [sc. Mannini]. However, the account of Knight Owein does not include 'Cornu', whereas Mannini's does.

[112] The printed edition reads 'maior pars' here too. *ibid.* From the dimensions it is clear that the author intended 'minor pars'.

[113] On the significance of this, cf. above, pp. 13-14.

[114] *ibid.,* 49.

[115] The form is specified in some detail.

[116] The expression here is obscure but the general sense is clear. The entry is in the angelic part of the island but the body of the Purgatory is in the demonic part.

more than eleven palms long, three broad and four high. (A small tunnel is evidently envisaged.) The second entrance, 'versus Gerbinum', is no more than nine palms long, three broad and four high.

Laurence's Visions[117]

The knight came to the 'entrance of the second cave' about the sixth hour of St Martin's day [about 1 p.m., 11 November 1411] and remained 'until dusk of the night following' *(usque ad noctis crepusculum subsequentis*. From the details of his release it is clear that this means 'until evening of the same day'). While he was praying, two evil spirits invisibly assaulted him, dragging him by the feet three times in succession to the door of the cave and foully tearing the three albs with which he was clothed. He was not dismayed but had recourse to Christ in recollection of the five wounds, hiding in these as in secret caverns of stone from the devilish onslaught, made the sign of the cross and said his prayer 'Lord Jesus Christ [etc.]' (as above). The devils, unable to withstand the sign of the cross and the effect of meditation on the passion of Christ, retired in confusion.

Next approached from opposite the knight another devil, in the guise of an ancient pilgrim, with long beard and shaggy locks, (?)dripping wax from his burning candles.[118] Though it seemed to the knight that the new arrival was looking at him with sympathy, he was sufficiently alarmed that between his psalms he devoutly poured out a prayer concerning the incarnation, passion, resurrection and ascension of Christ. The demon then became threatening and upbraided him, 'as a man of wisdom, learned in various languages *(ydeomatibus)',* for his stupidity. Jesus was a seducer of the people and eternally condemned to the abyss. (The episode recalls similar ruses by Grissaphan's demons.) Laurence however refused to enter into debate with him and made no reply other than his prayer. The devil then spat on him and left.

---

[117] *ibid.,* 50-7.

[118] *appropinquans ex opposito militis apud suos ardentes cereos se ungebat, ibid.,* 51. If the above is the correct interpretation it implies that it was accepted that, like Laurence himself, a pilgrim in the Purgatory should be so equipped. However, the meaning here is very obscure and the text may well be corrupt as it is at many points in the manuscript. Perhaps *ungebat* is for *urebat,* in which case, understanding *suos* for *eius,* one would have: 'approaching from the opposite side of the knight, he singed himself on the latter's burning candles', thus hearking back to the long beard and hair on which emphasis has been laid.

Another devil appeared in the shape of a most beautiful noble woman, well known to Laurence, whom she addressed voluptuously, reminding him of how often he had desired her. In the past, occasion had been wanting; now place and time convened. He however rebuked her; the proposition did not accord with the role of a pilgrim and he had left the lady in question far away from Ireland. Abashed, the devil retreated. Yonge appends an exhortation on the avoidance of voluptuousness, 'the devil's sword'.

While the knight continued praying, a handsome youth appeared dressed in green and with a red stole across his shoulders, who gave him the salutation, 'Peace to you', in Hebrew.[119] To the knight's suspicious inquiry, the youth replied, 'I am your patron Michael, in whose name you have a church constructed in your own native town.'[120] The knight's lingering scepticism was overcome by the angel's orthodox statement of Christian doctrine, focussed on the incarnation. Convinced, the knight prostrated himself before the angel and asked that he show him the souls of his deceased relations and benefactors so that he might know whether they were in hell, purgatory or paradise. He followed the angel to the entrance of the cave where there appeared great, wide, square stones. The angel lifted these and another, hidden opening was revealed. The angel led him through this by circular, spiral steps for the space of a mile. At the bottom, there appeared to the knight a divine light, a cloudy sky and a flat, green meadow, the limits of whose length and breadth he could not see. The knight repeated his request and the angel showed him a valley filled with fire, in which innumerable souls, having the appearance of living people, were being tortured. Among them the knight saw all his dead relations, friends, benefactors and offspring, except for one soul. The angel explained that this was purgatory and that the tormentors were demons, though he did not see these things nor the angel himself as they were but only as was given to him. The knight wished to see the soul of

[119] At another point, St Michael uses Hebrew words — corrupt in the manuscript and perhaps originally poorly rendered — intermingled with the Greek letters alpha and omega. The intention is to create an exotically sacred effect. Probably Laurence rather than Yonge contributed this element since Yonge describes him as ornamented with the Hebrew, Greek and Latin tongues. *ibid.*, 60.

[120] *habes ecclesiasm fabricatam, ibid.*, 53: or perhaps 'you have constructed a church'. The latter would agree with the attribution elsewhere to Laurence of special devotion to St Michael. Pászthó is identified as Pastoch, north-east of Pest.

someone whom he loved[121] but the angel told him that for the
present this was hidden from him, as was hell and paradise since he
had not come with the requisite disposition, in that he did not wish
to abandon the transitory world. The knight acknowledged the
justice of this.

As to the state of purgatory, Laurence was told that twice a week,
that is, on Sunday, 'when the Son of God, God and man'[122] was
born, and again on Friday, when Christ died, St Michael himself
came to comfort the souls. (One may compare with this the episode
in Grissaphan's vision, where an angel — not St Michael —
descends and where this is described as a weekly event.) The knight
marvelled that souls on whose behalf he and others had over twenty
years performed masses, almsgiving and other pious works should
still be in torment. The angel replied that he should not be
surprised, having often read in the Apocalypse of St John that 'their
works follow them' (Rev. 14, 13). They could be further helped by
good works and especially by mass. The discussion almost certainly
has its origin in the much more academically theological treatment
of the same point in the Grissaphan account.[123] However, neither
here nor at other points where the influence of George's visions
seems probable is the correspondence such as to suggest that the
compiler was using the earlier treatise. The most likely explanation
would seem to be that Laurence was familiar with the Grissaphan
account, or at least with certain features of it, though it may be that
Yonge too knew something of it and was prompted by it to include a
documentary section in his own compilation.

Many other secret matters were discussed and revelations made,
says Yonge, 'which it was not allowed should be narrated by the
knight to the compiler of this work but [only to those to whom] they
are to be narrated by the knight on the angel's order'.[124] When all
was done, the knight was told to follow and they arrived quickly at
the cave. The knight gave thanks on his knees for his safe return and
wished to kiss the angel's feet. The angel forbade him, saying
'Touch me not, you are not worthy.' Then, standing like a prelate,
he prayed and blessed Laurence in liturgical form before

[121] *dilecti sui, ibid.*, 55.

[122] *ibid.*

[123] Cf. above, pp. 151-2.

[124] Delehaye, 'Le pèlerinage', 56. In translating I have preferred to render what I take to be
the sense of the manuscript reading here rather than the editor's emendation. The syntax is in
either case unsatisfactory.

disappearing. The prohibition here is noteworthy. One detects something of that sensitivity to physical contact as a criterion in the discernment of spirits evident among Joan of Arc's interrogators.[125] By contrast with Grissaphan, Laurence is nowhere represented as touching the angel.

Aftermath of Laurence's Pilgrimage

The prior opened the door and Laurence exited from the purgatory on the day after his entry, at about three in the afternoon. Overjoyed to see him, the prior received him in his house with honour.[126] Having thus finished his pilgrimage, Laurence returned to Dublin where he was received by many prelates, nobles and citizens. Some of these determined to have an account made for them in Latin of his pilgrimage, being the more encouraged in their resolve by the fact that Laurence, 'as was fitting', supported what he said by producing a letter from the primate, Archbishop Fleming, dated at Dromiskin, 27 December 1411, the text of which Yonge reproduces.[127] This stated, on the authority of a letter which it exemplified of Matthew, prior of Lough Derg, that Laurence entered the Purgatory, having observed all particulars of the pilgrimage, and remained there for one day. Prior Matthew's letter, dated 'On Saints' Island', 12 November 1411, is punctiliously detailed: Laurence visited 'our place', exhibited letters of the primate, performed part of the preliminary penance, entered the Purgatory with mass of the Holy Cross and other solemnities and particulars, 'attended to as no one in our time has done',[128] manfully entered the cave of St Patrick, with procession and litany,

---

[125] See the sessions of 17 March 1431 (interrogation concerning her touching of Sts Catherine and Margaret) and of 24 February 1431 (whether the voice touched her to waken her): *La Minute Française des Interrogatoires de Jeanne la Pucelle d'après le Réquisitoire de Jean d'Estivet et les Manuscrits de d'Urfé et d'Orléans*, ed. P. Doncoeur (Melun, 1952), pp. 198-9, 101. P. Champion, *Procès de Condamnation de Jeanne d'Arc Texte, Traduction et Notes*, (2 vols, Paris, 1920-1), i, 152, 45.

[126] *militem in domum suam excepit*, Delehaye, 'Le pèlerinage', 57. It is difficult to know how this should be understood. It may refer simply to the priory. It may however imply that, as so often in late medieval religious communities, the prior had his separate residence.

[127] *ibid.*, 57-8. This letter is not found among the documents calendared by Lawlor, 'Register of Archbishop Fleming'. There is no reason however to doubt its authenticity, which must have been apparent to Yonge.

[128] *audita missa de sancta Cruce et aliis solempnitatibus observatis et omnibus circumstanciis ad predictam peregrinacionem adimpletis, sicut nullus in tempore nostro adimplevit, ibid.*, 58. *sicut nullus . . . adimplevit*, is probably best taken to refer to the quality of the devotion.

naked — except for the rochets and breeches — and fasting, had remained there 'as long as practical'(?),[129] sustained, 'as we are given to understand', pains of unclean spirits and saw and heard divine revelations in the same cave as were St Nicholas,[130] George Grissaphan *(Georgius filius Grifani)* and (?)Knight Owein *(Eugenius dictus de Obrian de Anglia)*, all of whom sustained torments and pains of unclean spirits.

Yonge's account was based on conversations which he had with Laurence while the latter waited *(dum commorasset)* in Dublin for a ship. As he puts it, he 'served the said knight . . . for many days and nights in the office of writing, and . . . on multiple occasions went over all the above matters orally with him'.[131] When he had finished writing 'all and single noted above' — this need not perhaps imply the finished version — he pressed Laurence to explain the main reasons for his pilgrimage to the Purgatory and to give a written judgement on whether the visions which he had had were bodily or spiritual experiences.[132] In reply Laurence made a written statement:

> I, Laurence, knight of Hungary, visited Ireland for three reasons. First and principally, in that I heard it told both by word of mouth and in writing that if anyone had any doubt about catholic faith and entered, in due manner, the place of the Purgatory of St Patrick in Ireland he could there see [sc. clarified] all the doubt, in particular or in general. And because I had most grave error and doubt concerning the substance of the soul, what it might be and of what quality — since according to the philosophers it is said to be invisible, incorporeal and impassible — for this reason I entered the place of the Purgatory, in which by the grace of God I found the very truth concerning the said doubt. The second reason was in order that I might say to . . . my lord, the king of Hungary, that I had visited the place . . . The third reason was in order to see the marvels and the miracles of the saints of Ireland, because I heard much of them . . . As for the visions . . . , whether I saw them corporally, I say with St Paul,

---

[129] *speluncam sancti Patricii viriliter intravit et ibi commoratus fuerat, sicut eius possibilitas poposcerat, ibid.*

[130] St Nicholas is mentioned in the account of Antonio Mannini as being one of the disciples of St Patrick. Cf. *ibid.,* 58, n. 1 and below p. 171.

[131] *ibid.,* 58-9.

[132] One may compare Peter of Cornwall's reserve: 'Although it may be that all these things . . . do not happen him in reality, corporally, but in the imagination, spiritually.' See R. Easting, 'Peter of Cornwall's account', 412, ll. 35-7, and see *ibid.,* n. 1, on the theme. Cf. Dinzelbacher, *Vision und Visionsliteratur,* pp. 30, 70.

I was caught up, *whether out of the body I know not, God knows* [2 Cor. 12, 2], but it seems to me more probable that I was more truly caught up in the body than out of the body, since I lit and burned the nine pieces of my candle, one after another, until I had exited from the cave . . .[133]

The Purgatory as a solvent of doubt: well might Prior Matthew have felt concern for his high ranking, thoughtful guest.

MICHAEL HAREN

---

[133] Delehaye, 'Le pèlerinage', 59-60.

VII. The Italian Pilgrims

By the end of the twelfth century, when the fame of St Patrick's Purgatory began to spread in Europe, links between Ireland and Italy were well established. Due to the prominent position of Rome in church organisation, contacts between Italy and Ireland had been constant since the early Middle Ages. From the seventh century onwards messengers and delegations are known to have travelled between Ireland and Rome. The large volume of papal chancery material concerning Ireland, especially after the eleventh century, indicates a network of contacts which made the ecclesiastical correspondence between the two countries possible.[1] Also, in northern Italy, the Irishman Columbanus had founded a monastery at Bobbio at the beginning of the seventh century, starting a circulation of men and manuscripts which continued in the following centuries.[2] In addition to the old contacts within the organisation of the church, new links were formed after the Anglo-Norman conquest. Italian merchants, especially from Florence and Lucca, began to trade with Irish towns such as Cork, Dublin, Wexford and Drogheda and some settled there. By the end of the thirteenth century Italian families controlled an important part of the banking, money-lending and tax collecting in Ireland.[3] Their financial operations took place within a network based on personal acquaintance with other Italian merchants and bankers in the various European countries. Large Florentine firms like the Frescobaldi or the Bardi with agents in England and Ireland represented powerful financial forces in the thirteenth century.[4] Living in a Christian world these merchants had an interest in church matters. We have no evidence of their possible interest in Lough Derg in the early times of the pilgrimage but by the fifteenth century St Patrick's Purgatory *(Purgatorium sancti*

---

[1] M. Sheehy, *Pontificia Hibernica: Medieval papal chancery documents concerning Ireland 640-1261* (2 vols, Dublin, 1962-65).

[2] See the acts of the 1951 Bobbio colloquy, *San Columbano e la sua opera in Italia* (Bobbio, 1953).

[3] See M. D. O'Sullivan, *Italian merchant bankers in Ireland in the thirteenth century* (Dublin, 1962).

[4] *ibid.*, 77-86.

Patricii) was mentioned on maps of Ireland used by Italian traders.[5]

Apart from trade there were also literary contacts. The wealth of medieval manuscript material of Irish interest in Italian libraries bears witness to the importance of these contacts.[6] As in other European countries vision literature attracted great interest. Irish vision literature seems to have been well known in Italy before Dante composed his *Divine Comedy* in the years 1312-1320. The role played by the accounts of visions set in Ireland in the composition of the *Divine Comedy* has often been highlighted.[7] St Patrick's Purgatory is also mentioned in another fourteenth century vernacular text, the romance of *Guerino Meschino* written by Andrea da Barberino at the end of the fourteenth century.[8] These borrowings and allusions are not isolated phenomena. By the fourteenth century Italian readers of the learned classes had access to the original accounts of these stories in various texts. Those unable to read Latin could enjoy the translations or adaptations in Italian which still survive in fourteenth and fifteenth-century manuscripts. The visionary experiences of several Irish saints were included in the popular collections of saints' Lives. Originally called *Nauigatio Brendani,* the tale of the voyage of St Brendan to the otherworld was widely known and its supernatural content advertised in titles such as 'How St Brendan went to the paradise of delights' *(Come san Brandano andoe al paradiso dilitiano)*.[9] The vision of the seventh century Irish monk Fursa was related in the *Storia di Furseo monaco*.[10] In the various

[5] See T. J. Westropp, 'Early Italian maps of Ireland from 1300 to 1600, with notes on foreign settlers and trade', *Proceedings of the Royal Irish Academy,* xxx (1912-13), [361-428] 426. See Figure 1.

[6] See R. J. Hayes, *Manuscript sources for the history of Irish civilisation* (14 vols, Boston 1965-79) under the names of Italian towns.

[7] See P. Villari, *Antiche leggende e tradizioni che illustrano la Divina Commedia* (Pisa, 1865); Boswell, *An Irish precursor of Dante.*

[8] Guerino, born in a noble Italian family, is captured as an infant by the Saracens to become a slave. Having reached adulthood, he leaves his masters and goes around the world in search of his real father. His travels bring him to strange countries inhabited by giants and monsters, and finally to the other world. Both the Christian and the pagan tradition are included in this tale, with references both to the Sibyl's cave and St Patrick's Purgatory. See E. Levi, *I cantori leggendari del popolo italiano nei secoli XIV e XV* (Turin, 1914). See above p. 92 and note 21.

[9] Florence, Bibliotheca Nazionale Centrale, Conventi soppressi C. II. 1550 (saec. XIV-XV); Florence, Bibliotheca Nazionale Centrale, Magliabecchi XXXVIII, 10 (saec. XV); Bologna, Bibliotheca Universitaria, Lat. 997 [1513] (saec. XV, A.D. 1461).

[10] Florence, Bibliotheca Nazionale Centrale, Principale II.II.89 [Magliabecchi XXI, 123] (saec. XV); Florence, Bibliotheca Riccardiana, 1340 (saec. XV); Venice, Bibliotheca Nazionale Marciana, 5644 [It. V. 28] (saec. XV); Venice, Civico Museo Correr, Cod. Cic. 2242 (saec. XV).

versions of the *Visione di Tundale* or *Istoria di Tugdalo d'Ibernia* the readers could learn about the vision of the Munster knight Tnugdal which took place in the city of Cork in 1148.[11] St Patrick's Purgatory and the Vision of Knight Owein were known through the various adaptations of H. de Saltrey's *Tractatus* under the title of *Il Purgatorio di San Patrizio*.[12]

Without a doubt, the fame of St Patrick's Purgatory in Italy was enhanced by the inclusion of a chapter devoted to it in the *Golden Legend (Legenda Aurea)*, one of the most popular works of the late Middle Ages. This text had been written in Latin shortly before 1264 by Jacobus de Varagine, a native of Varraze near Genoa, who later became a bishop of that city. The text in the *Golden Legend* is loosely based on the tale of Owein related in the *Tractatus*. However, the hero is not Owein but a nobleman called Nicholas. As a result, this character appears in later tradition as Lord Nicholas or even St Nicholas, a disciple of St Patrick.[13] One example of this can be seen in the Todi Fresco, a magnificent depiction of St Patrick's Purgatory seen through the eyes of a fourteenth-century artist.[14] The small figure which stands below St Patrick in the fresco is labelled *Dominus Nicolaus* (Lord Nicholas). The Todi Fresco is an important witness to the impact of the legend of St Patrick's Purgatory in northern Italy. The

[11] Florence, Bibliotheca Nazionale Centrale, Palatino, Panciatico 40 [*olim* 75] (saec. XIV); Florence, Bibliotheca Nazionale Centrale, Magliabecchi XXXV, 173 (saec. XIV); Florence, Bibliotheca Nazionale Centrale, Magliabecchi XXIV, 158 (saec. XV); Florence, Bibliotheca Nazionale Centrale, Principale II. II. 71 [Magliabecchi VII, 22] (saec. XV); Florence, Bibliotheca Riccardiana, 1408 [P. III. 23] (saec. XV); Rome, Bibliotheca Apostolica Vaticana, Chigi Latino M. V. 118 (saec. XV). On the Latin original see Picard and Pontfarcy, *The Vision of Tnugdal*.

[12] Florence, Bibliotheca Riccardiana, 1294 e 2760 (saec. XIV); Rome, Bibliotheca Corsiniana, Rossi 30 [44. C. 5] (saec. XIV); Florence, Bibliotheca Nazionale Centrale, Magliabecchi XXXV, 3 (saec. XV); Florence, Bibliotheca Nazionale Centrale, Principale II. IV. 64 [Magliabecchi XXXIX, 68] (saec. XV); Florence, Bibliotheca Nazionale Centrale, Conventi soppressi G. III. 676 (saec. XV); Rome, Bibliotheca Corsiniana, Rossi 298 [43. A. 23] (saec. XV); Rome, Bibliotheca Apostolica Vaticana, Vaticani Latini 13072 (saec. XV), fos 86v-104v in Italian; Venice, Bibliotheca Nazionale Marciana, 5023 [It. I. 30] (saec. XV); Venice, Bibliotheca Nazionale Marciana, 4947 [It. I. 66] (saec. XV).

[13] A fifteenth-century visitor to St Patrick's Purgatory, Antonio Mannini, begins the legend of the evil bird Corna thus: 'Al tempo che Messer Iddio mostrò a San Patrizio questo purgatorio, dopo lui e uno de' suoi discepoli si chiamò S. Niccolò, v'entrarono molti . . . (At the time when God our Lord showed the Purgatory to Saint Patrick, many men entered there after the saint and one of his disciple called St Nicholas . . .)'. On Mannini see below pp. 180-189. Nicolaus is also mentioned in connection with Saint Patrick's Purgatory by Domenico di Bandino in his *Fons memorabilium universi* (see below p. 175 and note 27).

[14] On the recently rediscovered Todi Fresco, see Mac Tréinfhir, 'The Todi Fresco and Saint Patrick's Purgatory, Lough Derg.' The Fresco is reproduced below, Figure 6.

Sienese artist who painted the fresco in 1346 has adapted the tale of Owein to a wider tradition of visions of the otherworld. It deviates from the text of H. de Saltrey in presenting the torments of purgatory associated with the seven deadly sins, each torment being the punishment for a specific sin. In this respect it is similar in approach to the representation of the purgatory found in Marcus's *Vision of Tnugdal (Visio Tnugdali)*. The influence of this text is shown in the depiction of sloth *(accidia)* illustrated by a soul walking on a bridge covered in nails as described in chapter seven of the *Vision of Tnugdal*.[15] Confusion or assimilation of elements drawn from the *Tractatus* and the *Vision of Tnugdal* is a feature of several manuscripts of Italian origin.

One of these texts is the *Vision of Louis d'Auxerre* found in two manuscripts from northern Italy.[16] The pilgrimage of the French knight to Lough Derg seems to have originated in Italy under the influence of a Franciscan from Rome.[17] There may have been a Louis d'Auxerre who went to St Patrick's Purgatory in 1358 or 1360 as the conflicting evidence of the two manuscripts implies, but the text of his visions is clearly a literary description of the Purgatory including episodes borrowed from the *Vision of Tnugdal*. An example of this is the account of the crossing of the bridge, an episode found in most tales of travel to the other world, but with features specific to each. The crossing of the bridge is found both in H. de Saltrey's *Tractatus* and in the *Vision of Tnugdal* but the version found in the *Vision of Louis d'Auxerre* is more akin to the latter. Unlike Owein, Tnugdal has to cross a very narrow bridge driving an untamed cow and finds it impossible as he meets in the middle a man carrying sheaves on his back. Similarly, as Louis tries to cross a narrow bridge, his progress is impeded by a man driving a reluctant horse. Another borrowing from the *Vision of Tnugdal* can be found further on in the text as Louis is shown a room in a castle where a king is seated on a golden throne surrounded by magnificent objects and receiving

---

[15] A. Wagner (ed.), *Visio Tnugdali* (Erlangen, 1882), 19-23; English translation in Picard and Pontfarcy, *The Vision of Tnugdal*.

[16] A first manuscript comes from the region of Padua and is now in Austria: Vienna, Österreichischen Nationalbibliothek 3160 (saec. XV). The text, entitled here *Visio Lodoyci de Sur,* is found at folios 259a-261b. The major part of the work is written in Latin with some Italian words inserted here and there but the end is written only in Italian. The second manuscript is found in Venice, Civico Museo Correr, Correr 1508 [I, 384] (saec. XIV), fos. 1-24. It is wholly written in Italian and beautifully illustrated with coloured drawings. The Latin text has been edited by K. Strecker in Voigt, *Beiträge,* 226-45.

[17] See below pp. 176-7 and note 32.

many presents from pilgrims. For three hours every day the king sits on this throne but for three hours every night he has to live in a bed of fire as a punishment for the sin of lust. This account corresponds to the description of king Cormac's mansion in the *Vision of Tnugdal*.[18] While the subject matter of the vision concerns a French knight, the redactors of the texts were definitely Italian and their works show how well acquainted they were with Irish vision literature.

The fame of St Patrick's Purgatory was so wide in fifteenth century Italy that the legend appears even in didactic texts. Among the works translated from Latin to Italian was the *Treatise on the sevenfold fear (Tractatus de septemplici timore)* attributed to Humbert de Romans (c1200-†1277), General of the Dominican order. This work is closely related to another treatise, *The seven gifts of the Holy Ghost (De septem donis spiritus sancti)*, also written by a contemporary Dominican writer, Etienne de Bourbon (c.a. 1200-†c.1261).[19] These treatises demonstrate the necessity and usefulness of fear for all Christians. Beside the fear of God, they devote long chapters to fear of the devil, of the last judgment, hell and purgatory. The Italian translation of the *Treatise on the sevenfold fear* is found in a copy made in 1438 under the title *Treatise on the seven types of fear (Trattato de'sette modi del timore)*.[20] But unlike the Latin version, the Italian text in chapter 10, which deals with the fear of the devil, includes an account of St Patrick's Purgatory. This account which is presented as a letter concerning the whereabouts of St Patrick's Purgatory written to Andrew, 'abbot of Sas' by a brother Nicholas, 'the least of the monks of Satiria',[21] is in fact a close translation of the full version of H. de Saltrey's *Tractatus*. It includes the prologue and the episodes of the old Irishman's confession and the old prior with only one tooth.[22] The attribution to Nicholas is due to a garbling of

---

[18] *Vision of Tnugdal,* chapter 17. L. Frati has edited this episode and compared the Latin and the Italian version in 'Tradizioni storiche del Purgatorio di San Patrizio', *Giornale Storico,* xvii (1891), [46-79] 77-8.

[19] On the relationship between these two works, see Frati, 'Il purgatorio di S. Patrizio secondo Stefano di Bourbon e Uberto da Romans', 163-7.

[20] Florence, Bibliotheca Nazionale Centrale, Magliabecchi XXV, 3 (saec. XV [27 December 1438]).

[21] *Ibid.,* fo. 96r: '*Inchominciasi il prologho cioè l'epistola del modo como si trovo il Purgatorio di San Patricio.* See Hayes, *Sources,* xi, 368.

[22] On the specificity of these episodes and their place in the work of H. de Saltrey, see Pontfarcy, 'Le *Tractatus de Purgatorio sancti Patricii*', 471-2.

the opening sentences of the *Tractatus*.[23] The inclusion of this translation in the *Treatise on the seven types of fear* shows another function of the story of Owein which explains its diffusion. Beyond its narrative and literary value the *Tractatus* provided an example well suited to the theological needs of the time. The visits of Italian travellers to Lough Derg must be understood in the context of these commercial and literary connections.

The fourteenth-century travellers

The first two Italian pilgrims to Lough Derg are known to us from letters patent of King Edward III dated 24 October 1358, where the king testifies that the knight Malatesta Ungaro *(Malatesta Ungarus de Arminio miles)* and a young gentleman from Lombardy, Nicholas Beccari of Ferrara *(Nicholaus de Beccariis de Ferraria, domicellus natione lumbardus)* have been to St Patrick's Purgatory and have remained locked underground for one day and one night, as the custom requires, and have endured many sufferings in the body. The king was able to verify the accounts of the Italian travellers from letters written by Amaury de Saint Amand, his justiciar in Ireland, and by the prior of St Patrick's Purgatory.[24] The surname *'Ungaro'* given to Malesta, together with the scribal error *Arminio* for *Arimino*, have led to confusion.[25] He was not a Hungarian nobleman, but a member of the powerful Malatesti family who ruled at Rimini. The son of Malatesta 'Guastafamiglia' and nephew of the famous Galeotto

---

[23] A comparison between the two passages shows the dependence of the *Epistola* on the *Tractatus*.

Tractatus de Purgatorio sancti Patricii, British Library, Royal 13 B viii (saec. XII), fo. 100b.	*Epistola del modo como si trovo il Purgatorio di San patrizio,* Florence, Bibliotheca Nazionale Centrale, Magliabecchi XXV, 3 (saec. XV), fos. 96r-96v.
Patri suo in Christo preoptato domino H. abbati de Sartis frater H. monachorum de Saltereia minimus cum continua salute patri filius obedientie munus.	Al suo padre principio in Christo misse Andrea abate di Sas frate Nicholao minimo da monaci di Satiria continua savio al padre figliuolo dono d'obidienza.

[24] The Latin text of the royal letters can be found in T. Rymer, *Foedera, conventiones, litterae, et cujuscunque generis acta publica* (4 vols., London, 1816-1869), iii, 274-5.

[25] See Frati, 'Tradizioni storiche' 49 and note 4.

Malatesta,[26] he had acquired the surname 'Ungaro' after being knighted by Louis the Great, king of Hungary, in 1347. Following the submission of the Malatesti to the papacy, he went to Avignon in 1358 to give allegiance to pope Innocent VI. He then went on travelling to Flanders, England and Ireland where he decided to enter the Purgatory. The visit of Malatesta to Lough Derg is also recorded by Domenico di Bandini of Arezzo in his *Book on islands (Liber de insulis)*, which is part of the encyclopedic work he wrote between 1374 and 1415 *(Fons memorabilium universi)*.[27] Bandini seems slightly doubtful about the story of Malatesta's descent and safe return from the cave, or rather pit as the Latin text has it *(a dicto puteo se redisse)*. However, he confirms that the event was widely known and talked about. On the other hand the letter written by Cecco Meletti of Forlì to Malatesta is full of praise for the courage of the man who, having gone nearly to the end of the world, dared to enter the cave 'where a night thick with darkness and tenebrous clouds surround the black opening of hell'.[28] Malatesta is also mentioned in the *Vision of Louis d'Auxerre*.[29]

[26] The genealogy of the Malatesti in the fourteenth century can be reconstructed thus:

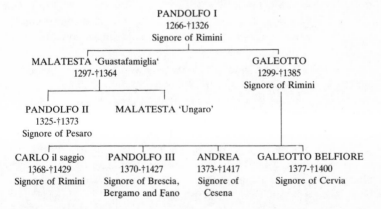

See P. Zama, *I Malatesti* (Faenza, 1965); J. Larner, *The lords of Romagna* (London, 1965); P. J. Jones, *The Malatesta of Rimini and the papal state* (Cambridge, 1974).

[27] On the career and writings of Domenico di Bandino see A. T. Hankey, 'Domenico di Bandino of Arezzo', *Italian Studies*, xii (1957), 110-128; *ibid*. 'The successive revisions and surviving codices of the "Fons memorabilium universi" of Domenico di Bandino', *Rinascimento*, xi (1960), 3-49.

[28] This letter is found in a manuscript of the Bibliotheca Ambrosiana in Milan, MS P. 256 sup., fo. 76 r.

[29] See above p. 92.

Near the end of the vision, as Louis emerges from the Purgatory, he sees Malatesta 'with a large retinue and going in procession with the monks of St Patrick'. The historical value of this last testimony is doubtful since, as I have suggested above, the account attributed to him is probably a literary fabrication. But even if Louis was not at Lough Derg in 1358, the mention of Malatesta in later tradition attests the fame of his adventures.

The second person mentioned in the patent roll, *Nicholaus,* is identified as an Italian from Lombardy. He was in fact Niccolò Beccari or del Beccaio from Ferrara (a town formerly included in the province of Lombardy), and a brother of the poet Antonio Beccari better known as Antonio da Ferrara.[30] Their father, Tura, was a butcher *(beccaio)* who had his sons educated and Niccolò was sent to university. He became one of these Italian courtiers who were both men of arms and men of letters. He liked the company of poets and was himself a poet. Petrarch was among his close friends. As a young man he joined the retinue of Malatesta Ungaro and followed him in his travels to France, Flanders and the British isles. He was later to join the court of Charles IV, King of Bohemia, in Prague where he made his name as a court poet. His presence at Lough Derg in 1358 is interesting as he had a critical mind and did not hesitate to express his opinions, even on church matters. He is known as the author of a pamphlet against the holy see *(Regulae singulares).*[31]

Around the time when Malatesta was in Ireland, probably shortly afterwards, another Italian is said to have gone to Lough Derg. He was Taddeo Gualandi from Pisa, a Franciscan friar, reader at Sancta Maria in Ara Celi at Rome. Our source for the visit is the beginning of the account of the pilgrimage of Louis d'Auxerre given in the Museo Correr manuscript mentioned above. According to the narrator, Louis was inspired by Taddeo Gualandi's experience at St Patrick's Purgatory — which is said to be in Britain — and decided to follow his example on 25 April 1360

---

[30] His collected works have not yet been published but isolated ballads and sonnets can be found in various publications. See bibliography compiled by Mario Marti in the *Dizionario Biografico degli Italiani* (Rome 1960-in progress), vii, 437-40. The two brothers are celebrated in the *Leandreide* written in the 1380's and attributed to Giangirolamo Natali from Venice: see *Leandreide,* Canto 7, lines 53-54 in C. del Balzo, *Poesie di mille autori intorno a Dante Alighieri* (15 vols, Rome 1889-1909), ii, 257-456.

[31] The biography of the two Beccaris has been studied by E. Levi, 'Antonio e Niccolò da Fèrrara, poeti et uomini di corte del trecento', *Atti e memorie della deputazione ferrarese di storia patria,* xix. 2 (1909), 41-405.

in order to do penance for his sins.[32] We have no other information about Taddeo, not even the date of his visit to the Purgatory. If there is some historical truth behind the *Vision of Louis d'Auxerre,* we can only assume that Gualandi's visit happened between 1357 and 1360.

The last Italian pilgrim to Lough Derg in that century was Guido Cissi. His name is found in a letter of recommendation written at Downpatrick by Milo Sweetman, archbishop of Armagh, on 15 March 1365. In his letter the archbishop asks the prior of St Patrick's Purgatory and all the clergy and laymen in the province of Armagh to welcome and help John Bonham and Guido Cissi, on their way to St Patrick's Purgatory for the salvation of their souls.[33] Nothing more is known about Guido Cissi's precise origin and background.

The accounts of the pilgrimage of these fourteenth-century Italian travellers tells us very little about Lough Derg, the island, the inside of the cave or the visions they may have had there. On the other hand they are of interest for the contemporary background to the pilgrimage. First, it may not be fortuitous that these visits take place in the 1350's and 60's. The mid-fourteenth century is a particularly unhappy period in a century full of disasters. In the midst of political instability and violence, the Black Death had arrived at Genoa in 1348 and quickly spread to other cities. The death toll was especially heavy in Venice and Florence with about 100,000 people dying in each city. As a result of the plague, many merchant families suffered bankruptcy. Such a climate would have been conducive to reflection on death and the otherworld. In the circumstances, the preachers' warnings and exhortations to do penance in order to avoid the torments of hell had an immediate relevance. In Italy, as in the other European countries, the period of the plague saw a renewed interest in pilgrimages. But Lough Derg was far removed from the European

[32] Venice, Civico Museo Correr, Correr 1508 (I. 384), fo. 1 'Un pezo nei nostri tempi, corando l'anno del nostro signior miser Jhesu Christo MCCLX (= MCCCLX), a di XXV de avril, lo excelentisimo chavaliero miser Lodovico de Franza de la città de Anchisodia . . . abiando molte persone ditoli fra Tadio di Gualandi da Pissa, indegno fra menor, letor de Santa Maria de Aracelli, partito de Roma, essere stato nel Purgatorio di San Patrizio in Bertania, el dito chavaliero fu preso dal desiderio d'imitare l'esempio di fra Taddeo Gualandi andando al Purgatorio di San Patrizio per penitenza de' suoi peccati'. See above p. 172.

[33] H. J. Lawlor, 'A calendar of the register of Archbishop Sweteman' *Proceedings of the Royal Irish Academy,* xxix (1911), [213-310] 274. The entry in the original document (Armagh, Metropolitan Registry, Diocesan Register of Primate Sweteman, now deposited in the Public Record Office of Northern Ireland, Belfast) can be found at folio 41v.

centres of pilgrimage and was not likely to attract many continental pilgrims. However, in the 1350's, it had been the object of a publicity campaign organised by the archbishop of Armagh, Richard FitzRalph.

During his stay at the papal court in Avignon (1349-1351) FitzRalph had been active in promoting the cult of St Patrick. In a sermon given before pope Clement VI on 14 February 1350 he had used as an *exemplum*[34] the story of the angel's apparition to Patrick sending him on his mission to Ireland.[35] The following year he petitioned and obtained from the pope permission to grant indulgence to all pilgrims who visited the cathedral of Armagh on the saint's feast day, 17 March.[36] In 1353 when George Grissaphan came back from Lough Derg, FitzRalph issued him with letters authenticating his visions.[37] These letters are important in the history of the dissemination of the fame of St Patrick's Purgatory as they began to circulate in Europe as part of the legal dossier accompanying the text of the *Visions of George.*[38] Considering that the archbishop's nephew, also called Richard FitzRalph, was in residence at Avignon in 1354 at the time of George Grissaphan's arrival at the papal court, Archbishop FitzRalph was in a position not only to arrange a proper reception for the knight at Avignon but also the publication of a written account of his visions.[39] If this is so, the publication of the *Visions of George* is part of FitzRalph's campaign to promote the cult of St Patrick, establish the renown of the province of Armagh and develop St Patrick's Purgatory as an important place of pilgrimage.

In the case of Malatesta the adventures of 'Ritter Georg' were certainly a deciding factor since the two men had a lot in common. Both had taken part in the Italian campaign of Louis the Great, king of Hungary. Louis, a descendant of the Angevin rulers of Naples, had kept an interest in Italy, not only in the north where he fought against the Venetians over their Dalmatian territories, but in the south where he made two expeditions in 1347 and 1350.

[34] An exemplum was a short moralized narrative used to illustrate the abstract theme of a sermon. It became part of the preaching tradition in the twelfth century and was a favourite device among thirteenth and fourteenth century preachers.

[35] *FitzRalph's Sermon Diary* (Oxford, Bodleian Library, Bodl. 144), fo. 211v. On *FitzRalph's Sermon Diary*, see A. Gwynn, 'The Sermon Diary of Richard FitzRalph, archbishop of Armagh', *Proceedings of the Royal Irish Academy*, xliv (1937), 1-57.

[36] *Calendar of entries in the papal registers*, iii, 387.

[37] See above pp. 120-1.

[38] Walsh, *A Fourteenth-Century Scholar*, pp. 304-318.

[39] See Hammerich, 'Eine Pilgerfahrt', 37.

George Grissaphan took part in the first of these and remained in charge of the garrison of Trani, near Bari.[40] According to the testimony of the *Visions of George,* he undertook his long pilgrimage in order to expiate the sins of cruelty, murder and robbery against the people of the surrounding territories. Malatesta had also campaigned with Louis the Great and had retained his nickname from his association with the Hungarian king. Together with his father and his uncle Galeotto he took part in the incessant wars between the cities of the Marches and Romagna. Like other *signori* in the region, the Malatesti also controlled papal territories. However, the arrival in Italy of Cardinal Albornoz in 1353 was to restore papal authority in these provinces. A native of Castile, Cardinal Albornoz was not only a great churchman but also a statesman and a brilliant general.[41] Having secured an alliance with the Visconti in Milan, he recovered Rome and the neighbouring Patrimony in 1354 and then moved on to the Marches. He isolated the Malatesti from their neighbours by having them excommunicated on 12 December 1354. The chief of the rebels, Galeotto Malatesta was finally taken prisoner and Albornoz set siege before Rimini. Beaten, Galeotto made his submission and his family swore allegiance to the pope. The visit of his nephew, Malatesta 'Ungaro', to pope Innocent VI in Avignon must be understood in the context of these events. When he reached the papal city the fame of George Grissaphan and of St Patrick's Purgatory must have been well established there. It is not surprising that, once in northern Europe, Malatesta should have wished to visit the Purgatory. If one can judge from the mention of his name in the *Vision of Louis d'Auxerre* or the warm praise of his friend Cecco Meletti, the visit of Malatesta to Ireland must have been an important factor in the renewed interest in the pilgrimage to Lough Derg in subsequent years.

The fifteenth-century travellers

In contrast to the paucity of details about Lough Derg in the accounts concerning Italian travellers in the fourteenth century, the beginning of the following century provides us with a wealth of details concerning St Patrick's Purgatory. It is the account of the

[40] *Ibid.*, 36.

[41] On Cardinal Egidio d'Albornoz see the large bibliography following the entry Albornoz in the *Dizionario biografico degli Italiani,* ii, 45-53.

pilgrimage of Antonio di Giovanni Mannini in 1411. The document is in a collection of memoirs of Florentine families, formerly in the papers of Senator Strozzi, but now in the National Library in Florence.[42] The penultimate item in the manuscript is the book of family records of three of the sons of Giovanni Mannini: Alamanno, Luigi and Salvestro. The Mannini family was involved in trade and they travelled frequently outside their city. They had friends and probably business interests in Paris and show special concern about the political situation in France in the 1410's. The visit to Lough Derg by a fourth son, Antonio, is recorded by his brother Salvestro who transcribed a letter by Antonio Mannini to a friend of his in London named Corso di Giovanni Rustichi.[43] The letter was written in Dublin on 25 February 1412 and entrusted to Laurence Rathold for safe delivery in London. Corso then sent it to Salvestro Mannini in Florence where it arrived on 12 April 1412. From this letter and the accompanying introduction and postscript by Salvestro the circumstances of Antonio's pilgrimage can be reconstructed.

Antonio Mannini came to Ireland in 1410 for business purposes. He must have been quite an important merchant, rich enough to pay for the construction of a church as he promises at the end of his letter and powerful enough to mix with local magnates in Ireland such as the Earl of Kildare.[44] He knew of the existence of St Patrick's Purgatory and had hoped to go there on pilgrimage while in Ireland but had been dissuaded by a priest from Rome called Antonio da Focha who had returned from the Purgatory.

[42] Florence, Bibliotheca Nazionale Centrale, II, IV, 380 [Magliabecchi XXV, 595] (saec. XVII). See G. Mazzatinti & al., *Inventi dei manoscritti delle bibliothece d'Italia* (Forli 1890-in progress), xi, 45. On the fashion of writing memoirs among Florentine merchants, including the Manninis, see F. Pezzarossa, 'La traditizione fiorentina della memorialistica' in G. M. Anselmi, F. Pezzarossa, L. Avellini, *La "memoria" dei mercatores* (Bologna 1980), 41-149. The text of Antonio Mannini's letter as copied by his brother Salvestro has been edited by Frati, 'Il Purgatorio di S. Patrizio', Appendix I, 154-162. An English translation of this text can be found in Seymour, *St Patrick's Purgatory*, 54-61.

[43] Corso Rustichi was back in Italy in 1424 where he was imprisoned in Piacenza as is recorded in a letter addressed to Rinaldo degli Albizzi by his brother Betto asking for his liberation. See C. Guasti, *Commissioni di Rinaldo degli Albizzi per il comune di Firenze dal 1399 al 1433* (3 vols, Florence 1867-73), ii, 13, 24, 26 and 36.

[44] E. Gamurrini in his *Istoria genealogica delle famiglie nobili toscane et umbre* (4 vols, Florence 1668-73), ii, 111-2, records a conversation between Antonio Mannini and Gerald, fifth earl of Kildare, during which Gerald told Mannini about the Italian origins of the Geraldine family in Ireland and their links with the Gherardini in Florence. See A. Fitzgibbon, 'Appendix to the unpublished Geraldine documents — the Gherardini of Tuscany', *Journal of the Royal Society of Antiquaries of Ireland*, xiv (1876-78), [246-64], 247.

Thus, Mannini's testimony provides us with the name of yet
another Italian pilgrim to Lough Derg. Da Focha told Mannini
that the pilgrimage was too much of an ordeal for the merchant's
weak constitution and added other negative reasons on which
Mannini prefers to remain silent. In the meantime his business
must have turned out badly as he complains that after a year in
Ireland he was without money. This is hardly surprising in view of
the political and economic situation in Ireland at that time. In the
midst of serious financial difficulties, the lord lieutenant, Thomas
of Lancaster, second son of King Henry IV, had returned to
England in March 1409 and left Thomas Le Botiller, prior of the
Hospitallers at Kilmainham, as his deputy. The government of Le
Botiller was so poor that the Irish Council, gathered at Naas at the
end of 1411, decided to send the archbishops of Dublin and Cashel
to the King to complain about the state the country was in.[45]
Antonio Mannini had been trying to leave Ireland for some time
but without success. He mentions a first letter sent to Corso
Rustichi on 8 June 1411 together with a casket containing other
letters, including a letter of authorisation by the mayor of Dublin,
all attesting to his intention to depart. At that date he hoped to be
in England before Michaelmas of the same year but, due to lack of
wind and money, he was still in Dublin when Laurence Rathold
made his remarkable entrance in the capital.[46] Mannini visited the
Hungarian lord and had a long interview with him. He was so
impressed by his devotion that he decided to join him on his
pilgrimage to Lough Derg:

> When I saw his holy resolve and devotion, he who had come from
> the leading city in the whole of christendom to the end of the world
> for the salvation of his soul while I just stood here near this
> Purgatory, I considered, in much pain and suffering, what my life
> had been in the past, that of a sinner and a man always intent on
> worldly matters; but, comforted by good hope, I turned myself to
> God and inspired by his mercy, I took the decision and formed the
> plan to go to this Purgatory for the salvation of my soul . . .

The two pilgrims left Dublin on Friday 25 September 1411.
Mannini had hoped to complete his pilgrimage within three weeks
at most but 'on account of the dangerous road and many other

[45] See A. J. Otway-Ruthven, *A History of medieval Ireland* (London 1968), pp. 345-7.
[46] See above p. 159.

causes' it took three and a half months before their return to
Dublin. The account of the visit of Laurence Rathold by James
Yonge is more explicit on the various 'causes' for the lengthy
journey. They had to stop in Armagh or at Dromiskin to visit the
Primate and obtain the customary letter of introduction for the
prior of St Patrick's Purgatory. Another custom for the pilgrims
was to stop at Downpatrick to venerate the relics of Patrick, Brigid
and Columba. Rathold stayed there for several days, praying and
fasting. They finally reached Lough Derg on 4 November 1411.
Mannini describes their arrival in very precise terms:

> The place where the Purgatory lies is a lake surrounded by very high
> mountains which is exactly like a well. It measures ten miles in
> circumference and contains thirty four islands, both big and small.
> We arrived at this lake safe and sound on Thursday [=Wednesday]
> 4 November and came to the island where the priory stands, which
> is distant from the island where the Purgatory lies by one mile
> across water. The island of the Purgatory is 129 paces long and 30
> paces large and set exactly in the middle of this lake.

Upon his arrival Mannini made his confession to the prior and
started the customary fast on bread and water 'according to the
rules of the pilgrimage'. Although he wanted to fast for the usual
fifteen days, the prior would not allow him to continue beyond
three days on account of the great cold of that winter. Mannini
entered the Purgatory on Saturday 7 November 1411 after a very
precise ritual. He rose before daybreak and the prior heard his
confession, said mass for him and gave him holy communion. He
then heard a second mass, that of the Annunciation of Our Lady,
said by a canon of the community called Brother John. After the
habitual warnings and last attempts to discourage the pilgrim, the
prior led him to the water, kissed him and gave him his
benediction. The crossing to the island of the Purgatory took place
in a little boat 'which was made like a kind of hollow tree trunk,
roughly dug out and where four people would hardly have fitted',
and rowed by Canon John with two small oars. For the occasion
Mannini was wearing a long riding tunic and a waistcoat over his
shirt but was barefoot and bareheaded.

On the way to the island he saw a first manifestation of the devil
in the form of a large black bird similar in shape to a heron and
with no feathers except four or five on each wing. Having blessed

himself several times to ward off the evil, the canon told Mannini the legend attached to this particular bird. In the time of St Patrick, most people who entered the Purgatory used to perish there and disappear for ever. Patrick soon discovered that responsibility for this lay with a perverse demon called Corna who successfully tempted all the pilgrims. The saint obtained from the Lord that the demon be transformed into a bird bound to live forever on this lake but compelled to leave the island of Purgatory every time a Christian landed there. However, the canon added that whenever the wicked bird Corna sounded the horn with his beak like a man, it was a sign of perdition for the person about to enter the Purgatory. The same legend is related by James Yonge in his account of Laurence Rathold's visit. In his description of the lake and the island, Yonge remarks on the noise and great number of birds of prey, ravens, hawks, rooks, owls and other predatory birds nesting there. He associates these birds with Satan and his satellites and mentions the existence of a demon called *Cornu* in Irish, in the shape of a heron without feathers except on the wings, who foretells the death of pilgrims by giving a call similar to the sound of a trumpet.[47] Nevertheless, the bird did not utter a sound for the coming of Antonio Mannini and the pilgrim was glad to escape with only his fright.

On their arriving at the island a second incident occurred. As the two travellers stood up, ready to land the boat, Mannini was projected into the water and plunged head first to a depth of three fathoms. As he touched the bottom of the lake he was able to feel grass there. But having invoked the name of Jesus Christ as instructed by the prior, he rose to the surface where the canon caught his hand and, rowing with his free hand, dragged him to the shore. Strangely enough, although his tunic was wet on the outside, all his clothes were dry inside and so was a little book that he kept in his pocket.

Notwithstanding such a strange landing, Mannini proceeded with his project despite the canon's efforts to discourage him. They entered a small chapel situated at the east end of the island and measuring thirty feet by fifteen. Mannini was asked to kneel in front of an altar on which there was a carved crucifix, a picture of

[47] J. Yonge, *Memoriale*, c. 6 (in Delehaye, 'Le pèlerinage', 48-9). According to John Richardson, *The great folly*, 3, eighteenth-century pilgrims to Lough Derg were shown a stone carving representing a monster called 'Caoranach'. On the later legends concerning Corna/Caorthannach, see MacNeill, *The Festival of Lughnasa*, 503-11 and above p. 37.

the Virgin holding her infant son in her arms and a picture of St Patrick. While the pilgrim was on his knees, the canon removed his tunic and waistcoat and covered him instead with a long white garment similar to a dalmatic which he had first blessed with holy water. After many prayers and another aspersion of holy water, the canon asked him to get up and, with a crucifix in his hand, led him by the right hand to the door of the chapel for another ritual. Mannini was asked to lie on his back on the floor, his hands crossed over his chest and his eyes closed and the canon recited the vigil and the office of the dead over him, together with the proper aspersions as if the pilgrim was already dead. He then asked him to get up and gave him the cross to carry in his right hand. By then Mannini was so weak that he could hardly stand. So, helped by the canon, he went outside and the two of them walked around the chapel in procession three times, the canon saying the litanies and Mannini providing the responses. When the litanies and prayers were finished the canon led him to the door of the Purgatory 'which is outside this chapel, at about five paces from there on the north side'. Mannini knelt in front of the door and the canon made a last attempt to dissuade him but, faced by the pilgrim's determination, he sprinkled him with holy water, blessed him three times, kissed him and allowed him to enter the cave. Mannini entered on his knees, still holding the crucifix, and the canon locked the door after him and left the island. As he entered the dark cave, Mannini had a further frightening experience in the shape of an enormous black spider, bigger than the palm of his hand, which disappeared when the name of the Lord was invoked. Again, the description of the cave given by the Italian pilgrim is most precise:

> 'The place is three feet wide, nine feet long and high enough for a man to remain on his knees but not to stand upright. For it is exactly like a sepulchre, vaulted overhead and towards the south, that is towards the chapel, there is a return measuring three feet long where the prior told me to remain, saying my prayers and waiting there'.

Kneeling in this return Mannini started praying as the prior had asked him: the seven penitential psalms and the litanies, one Salve Regina and fifteen Ave Marias for the fifteen joys of the Virgin Mary. But while praying he fell asleep so that he could not tell if his experiences were felt by his body or only by his soul. In any

case he does not give any information about his visions as he is at
liberty to do so only in confession. He reveals only that he had
many visions and temptations.

Mannini remained only five hours in the Purgatory instead of
the usual twenty-four hours. Worried about the extreme cold
(according to Mannini the Lough Derg area was the coldest place
he had ever been), the prior sent the canon to collect him. When
the priest opened the door, he found him unconscious, with his
face, body and limbs as cold as ice. He had to shake him hard in
order to wake him up. Leaving the cave they went back to the
chapel for the concluding rites: he had to kneel in front of the altar
and the cross and white dalmatic were removed from him. By
then, he was sufficiently recovered to dress himself. The last ritual
before leaving the island was that of the *sortes sacrae*:[48] the canon
put an ancient psalter on the altar and asked Mannini to open it
and read a verse at random. The pilgrim chanced upon Psalms 85,
13 'For great is your mercy towards me and you have delivered my
soul from the lowest Hell', an amazing coincidence which
prompted the canon to recite the Te Deum. When he returned to
the main island the prior and the community were waiting for him.
They all kissed him and, rejoicing with him, they led him to the
church where a last Te Deum was recited.

Since Mannini returned to Dublin with Laurence Rathold he
probably remained at Lough Derg at least until Thursday 12
November, date of the prior's certificate given to Rathold and
presented to Primate Fleming.[49] At the end of December the two
pilgrims were probably at Dromiskin as the Primate's letter
authenticating Laurence's visit is dated 27 December 1411 at his
manor.[50] Mannini was back in Dublin by mid-January 1412 and
hoped to stay there for a while. Comforted by his experience, he
was confident in his good fortune and renewed prosperity in
business. He even asked his brother Salvestro to come to Ireland
and to bring his wife Maddalena and son Giovanni to join him.
From Salvestro's silence, one can assume that this voyage never
took place. In any case, Antonio returned to Florence a year later,

---

[48] Also called *sortes biblicae,* the *sortes sacrae* denote a method of divination by chance
selection of passages from the Bible. The practice was common in medieval Europe.

[49] J. Yonge, *Memoriale,* c. 12 (in Delehaye, 'Le pèlerinage', 58): 'Datum in Insula
Sanctorum, feria quinta post diem sancti Martini anno Domini millesimo C.C.C.C.mo XImo'.
The feast of St Martin was on Wednesday 11 November in 1411.

[50] *Ibid.:* 'Datum in manerio nostro de Dromeskyn XXVII die decembris anno Domini
supradicto et nostre consecrationis octauo'.

Station Island from Thomas Carve, *Lyra; sive Anacephalaeosis Hibernica* (Sulzbach 1666).

on 12 October 1413, with a gentleman from Ireland.[51] There were other Irishmen in Florence in October 1413. Antonio d'Ottaviano di Rossellino Gherardini recalls in his *Book of Records* that in the same month an Irish bishop passed through Florence and that he met a priest of his retinue from the chapter of Ardfert Cathedral called Maurice, belonging to the Geraldine family in Ireland, who explained how the Gherardini of Florence were related to his family.[52] Antonio may have travelled with the bishop's suite but this cannot be established with certainty. If one can judge by the care that Salvestro Mannini took to relate the adventures of his brother, one can imagine the impact of his story made among his friends in Florence, thus strengthening the reputation of St Patrick's Purgatory in that city.

Can we rely on Mannini's testimony as a genuine historical source? While Laurence Rathold *(Lorenzo Rattoldi)* is mentioned twice in Mannini's letter, James Yonge's account of Rathold's visit does not state that the hero of the story had a travelling companion. Indeed, there is no reason why Yonge should have mentioned a person of a lower social status who completed a pilgrimage in the shadow of the Hungarian lord. Also, if the account was written several years after Rathold's experience, the minor figure of Mannini would have left little or no impression. However, without explaining who he is, Yonge alludes to Mannini in the episode concerning the evil bird Corna. As a further proof of the existence of the bird, Yonge adds that 'even the knight Antonio saw it there'.[53] This Antonio is more than likely Mannini:

[51] Florence, Bibliotheca Nazionale Centrale, II. IV. 380 (Magliabecchi XXV. 595), fo. 448 r 'Nota che questo dì 12 ottobre 1413 tornò Antonio Mannini nostro fratello dalle parti d'Irlanda, il quale era stato in dette parti d'anni tre, e menò seco un gentilhuomo di quelle parti . . .'.

[52] See E. Gamurrini, *Istoria genealogica,* ii, 111; English translation in A. Fitzgibbon, 'Appendix to the unpublished Geraldine documents', 247. The priest who talked to Antonio Gherardini could possibly have been Maurice FitzMaurice, precentor of Ardfert Cathedral, who obtained a deanery from the Pope Alexander V in February 1410. See *Calendar of entries in the papal registers,* vi, 164-5.

[53] London, British Library Royal 10.B.IX (saec XV²), fo. 39r: 'Quem et miles octo via est ibidem contemplatus.' In his edition of this manuscript Delehaye ('Le pèlerinage', 49) renders the strange form *octo via* by *Owain.* This reading is a guess which has no paleographical foundation. Furthermore there is no mention of the bird Corna in the story of the knight Owein. Delehaye himself is unsure about his guess and suggests a possible reading *Antonius* in his critical notes. As there is no mark for s in the manuscript, I would suggest that *octo via* in the manuscript results from two common mistakes in late medieval manuscripts: the confusion between *a* and *o* on the one hand and *u* and *n* on the other. The late fifteenth-century scribe would have supplied two familiar Latin nouns for the elements of the proper name he could not read: *octo* for *anto* and *via* for *nio*.

he is the only pilgrim known to us who claims to have seen the bird
and his letter contains a full account of the legend of Corna in
contrast to the scant information given by Yonge. Since Mannini's
letter was intended for a limited circulation among relatives and
friends, it is unlikely that Yonge or any intervening scribe knew
about him from a written source and the most plausible
explanation for the mention of his name in connection with Corna
is that Rathold himself told Yonge about it. In this case the Corna
episode in Yonge's account would be an indication that Mannini
was actually at Lough Derg with Rathold. Further evidence of
Mannini's presence at St Patrick's Purgatory is found in the letter
itself when the pilgrim mentions a three foot long return at the end
of the Purgatory cave going towards the chapel. This feature could
be an echo of Rathold's second entrance *(secundus introitus),* but
its description is more precise and corresponds exactly to the
accounts of other travellers to Lough Derg. It is found both in
Perellós[54] and in later, and perhaps more objective, descriptions of
the far end of the cave: the report of Chiericati a century later
(1517),[55] the drawing given in the seventeenth century edition of
Thomas Carve's map[56] or the account of John Richardson in
1727.[57] The mention of this architectural feature is important: it
shows that Mannini is an independent witness who did not rely on
the Rathold accounts which might have circulated in Dublin early
in 1412. It also shows that far from having been destroyed in 1497
the part of the cave where Antonio Mannini had his vision of
Purgatory was still visited by pilgrims 300 years later.

Through its simplicity and honesty, Mannini's account proves to
be a prime document for assessing the reality of the medieval
pilgrim's experience at Lough Derg. Not only does he give us

---

[54] See above p. 114.

[55] Chiericati, papal nuncio at the court of Henry VIII, gave his account in a letter to Isabella
d'Este written from Middelburg in Holland on 28 August 1517. A copy of this letter is now in
Mantua, Archivio di Stato, Archivio Gonzaga, Serie B xxxiii. 10, Busta 85. See below p. 00 and
note 00.

[56] Thomas Carve, *Lyra; siue anacephalaeosis hibernica* (Sulzbach 1666), see Figure 5.

[57] J. Richardson, *The great folly,* 8: 'The cave commonly called St Patrick's Purgatory . . . is
about 10 foot distant from the church. It is 22 foot long, 2 foot and 1 inch wide and 3 foot high.
It hath a bending within 6 feet of the far end . . .'.

valuable topographical details about St Patrick's Purgatory,[58] but
…sion of the account is worthy of note. The
…ge are essentially religious: Mannini does
…ut of curiosity but because he is in need of
…in his life. Neither does he try to hide his
…le experience he was frightened, scared to
…ked towards his feeling of fright: the
…Focha before his departure, the cautions
…im of the many who died or became mad
…le of the canon and his story about the
…he rituals of death preceding the entrance
…nention the black spider. To this feeling of
…ysical discomfort of hunger and cold and,
…an, a plunge into the waters of the lake.
…he cave Mannini fell asleep out of physical
…In these conditions one can imagine the
…have had and which he refused to tell his
…the emphasis of the pilgrimage was on
…y explains to us how pilgrims were
conditioned to have visionary experiences. With hindsight it helps
to understand the nature of the changes made after the destruction
of 1497. As the post-1497 descriptions mentioned above show, the
cave of the Purgatory was restored to its former shape and even
extended, but its function was changed. Instead of a solitary
visionary experience, pilgrims were brought there in groups[59] and
an opening was made to provide light in the end recess, allowing
prayer to take place without the terrors suffered in the previous
centuries.

JEAN-MICHEL PICARD

[58] The evidence concerning the physical surroundings of the pilgrimage can be summarised
thus: Mannini confirms the existence of two islands for the purpose of the pilgrimage. Pilgrims
were first brought to a bigger island where a priory stood and spent up to fifteen days fasting
and praying there. The certificate given by the prior to Mannini's travelling companion clearly
identifies this island as Saints' Island. Then they were brought to a smaller island (about 200
yards long by 50 wide) where the Purgatory lay. Mannini mentions two structures on the east
side of this island: one small chapel (about 30 feet long by 15 wide) and a tomb-like structure
closed by a door (9 feet long, 3 feet wide and about 3 feet high) lying 8 yards away from the
chapel towards the north. The end of this cave was a sort of alcove, three feet long, set on the
south side, towards the chapel.

[59] Chiericati notes that twelve pilgrims were able to fit in the first chamber of the cave.

VIII. The Close of the Medieval Pilgrimage: the Papal Suppression and its Aftermath

The chronological scope of 'the Middle Ages' is increasingly vague. 'Medieval' has one significance, even then not simply stated, for the historian of artistic and intellectual movements, another in the political, social and economic contexts, another in the ecclesiastical. The significance varies also from one country to another and, within countries, between region and region. In Ireland, more especially in Gaelic Ulster, the 'middle ages', conceived in political, cultural and social terms, had a powerful half-life through the sixteenth century. The limits are more than any other those constituted by the progress of Reformation and Counter-Reformation, of conquest and plantation. While absolute historical statements are hazardous, it can be asserted confidently that for St Patrick's Purgatory at least, the fall of Constantinople — the traditional dating of the end of the middle ages — is without implication. The Purgatory had its own fall. It proved not to be final. However its coincidence with other changes makes it a suitable conclusion to the history of the medieval pilgrimage.

As presently understood, the immediate prelude to this fall was as follows. A regular canon of the Augustinian house of Eymstadt, in the Netherlands, of the Congregation of Windesheim, although he had been long in the order and was a meticulous observer of its rule, applied day in and day out to his superiors for licence to enter a stricter order or to wander through the provinces as a poor mendicant. What he required, evidently was a life of more heroic asceticism. The account is printed, from an unacknowledged source, in the Bollandist *Acta Sanctorum*[1] and dated, at least in its inception, to the year 1494:

---

[1] *Acta Sanctorum*, Martii, ii (Paris and Rome, 1865), 588. Leslie, *St Patrick's Purgatory*, p. 63, states that the source of this account was a codex in the Royal Brussels Library, entitled *de destructione purgatorii Patricii*. I have so far failed to identify this manuscript from the catalogues of that collection, which contains a large mass of material both hagiographical and relating to the Congregation of Windesheim. There is no reason for doubting the authenticity of the account, which is wholly verisimilitudinous, but prudence dictates that it should not be treated as though our source for it were a record of established date and provenance.

Having obtained his desire, he proceeded begging to various countries and regions of Christendom and came at last to the kingdom of Ireland, in order that he might see and enter the Purgatory of St Patrick, of which many things are told. And when he came to the place and the monastery, where its entrance is said to be, he spoke to the person in charge (*cum praesidente loci illius*), unfolding to him his desire. He sent him to the diocesan, telling him that it was unlawful for him to admit anyone without assent of his bishop. The canon went to the bishop; and since he was a poor man and without money, he was scarcely admitted by the servants; and falling down at the bishop's knees, he sought that licence be given him to enter the Purgatory of St Patrick. The bishop, however, sought a certain sum of money, which he said was due to him by right from those entering. The brother replied that he was a poor man and had no money, but that even if he had he would not dare to pay, on account of the contagion of simony arising.[2] After many entreaties he finally prevailed on the bishop and the latter furnished certain letters of admission, sending him to the prince of that territory to obtain his licence too. The prince also pressed for money, but since he could not extract any from him who did not have, in the end he admitted him, although with difficulty. Returning to the prior of the place of the Purgatory, he presented to him the letters of the bishop and the prince. When the prior had read them he said to him, 'Brother, it is necessary that you make the customary payment to our monastery also', specifying to him a certain sum. The brother replied that he was a beggar and had no money but that it was illicit for him to pay for such because it would be simoniacal; that he was seeking for God's sake and for the salvation of his soul to be admitted to that most famous place. The prior therefore ordered his sacrist to admit him to it. When the brother had made confession and received the most holy body of the Lord, as he had read in manuscripts that others had done in the past before entry to the pit *(ante introitum laci illius),* he was lowered by the sacrist on a rope into a deep pit *(in lacum quemdam profundum).* Then, when he was already in, he tendered him on the rope a little bread and a flask of water as refreshment when he came to do battle with the demons.

There he sat in the pit all night, trembling and in fright, but offering fervent prayers to the Lord and terrified from one minute almost to another that the demons would come. And when he had sat from evening until morning, after sunrise the sacrist came to the mouth of the pit *(ad orificium laci),* hailing him and letting down the rope for his removal. The brother was now full of astonishment in that he had

[2] Simony — the offence of Simon Magus in the Acts of the Apostles — was the purchase or sale of ecclesiastical office or of spiritual benefit.

seen nothing, had heard nothing and had suffered no inconvenience nor distress; and he turned over in his mind various thoughts about what he had read and heard of this Purgatory; for he did not know that the ancient miracle, once the faith was established, had ceased: the inhabitants of the place were nonetheless asserting to visitors, for financial gain, that purgation of sins was still taking place there. Having therefore examined everything and desirous that this delusion of the simple be abolished, the said brother, leaving Ireland, made his way to Rome, and since he could not get access to the supreme pontiff, he recounted to the latter's penitentiary, a man of sound morality and ecclesiastical outlook, all that had befallen, with the request that he notify it to the lord pope. He readily agreed to do so, having received most firm assurance or oath from the brother that matters were as described. The penitentiary therefore approached the supreme pontiff and laid the whole affair before him. He took it badly that the simple were being deceived in this manner and ordered the penitentiary to send letters authenticated with the apostolic seal to the bishop, prince and prior of the place, ordering them to overturn from its foundation the place in which the entry to the Purgatory, said to be of St Patrick, once had been *(ut locum illum, in quo quondam introitus fuerat ad Purgatorium, quod S. Patricii dicitur, funditus everterent),* and to certify by their letters and seals, through the same bearer of their letters,[3] that it had been overturned. The said brother was accordingly sent back by the pope to Ireland, carrying the apostolic rescript by force of which thus the prince of the province, together with the bishop and prior, destroyed that place of deceit[4] and notified its destruction by their writings to the supreme pontiff, the said messenger bringing the same to the curia.

During this period, Clogher was without a resident bishop, since the Munster Franciscan, John Edmund de Courcy, who had been provided to the see by Sixtus IV in 1484, had failed to establish himself in the face of local opposition. This does not however impugn the veracity of the canon of Eymstadt's complaint. The 'bishop' to whom he was sent was, as Professor Aubrey Gwynn proposed, in all probability the *de facto* vicar general of the diocese, Cathal Óg MacManus, compiler of the contemporary *Annals of Ulster* and chief ecclesiastical representative of the opposition to Bishop Edmund.[5] With less confidence one may speculate on the identity of the prior and prince. The priory of Lough Derg seems to

---

[3] *per eumdem suarum litterarum portitorem, ibid.* This seems to mean the canon.

[4] or possibly 'the place of the deceit', *locum illum fallaciae, ibid.*

[5] A. Gwynn, *The Medieval Province of Armagh* (Dundalk, 1946), p. 174.

have suffered decline in the second half of the fifteenth century and the most likely explanation is that this was due to its having become an object of contention between rival interests.[6] In 1479, Nellanus MacGrath obtained a mandate from Sixtus IV to have dissolved a union, which he described as having been made by ordinary authority, at a time immemorial, of the rectory of Templecarne [co. Donegal] to the priory of Lough Derg. As grounds for the dissolution of the union and the collation of the rectory to himself he pleaded that 'there is at present no rector and no prior or convent in the said monastery, divine offices are not celebrated there and the fruits of the said monastery are in the possession of divers clerks'.[7] Here as so often with papal provisions to Ireland, the historian is presented with a snapshot. The contours of the scene which it represents are not easily determined in isolation and in interpreting it allowance must be made for the effect of the filter through which it has been taken. That said, Nellanus' manoeuvre may be understood as a recognition by the MacGraths that control over the priory itself had become so uncertain that it was time to detach from it such assets as might be separately preserved. That reading of the situation is strengthened by the fact that in 1490, 'Terence' Maguire proposed to Innocent VIII a radically new tenure of the priory. The rectory of Derryvullan [co. Fermanagh] was to be erected in his favour as a simple prebend of Clogher cathedral and the priory, which he said was detained by Patrick MacGrath, was to be united to the prebend.[8] The 'Terence' of the papal letter is Turlough Maguire — son of Bishop Piers (res. 1447) — whom the *Annals of Ulster* record as having died from a fall down a stone staircase at Athboy 'about the feast of St Patrick', 1504.[9] Since he is described in the obit as prior of Lough Derg he had evidently managed to retain some lien on the Purgatory. Was he then the president alias prior to whom the canon of Eymstadt applied? Until the full range of papal archival material has been explored — supplications, briefs

[6] In 1455 it was in dispute between Raymund Maguire. prior by papal provision, and Donal MacGrath. See *Registrum Iohannis Mey The Register of John Mey Archbishop of Armagh, 1443-1456*, ed. W. G. H. Quigley and E. F. D. Roberts (Belfast, 1972), pp. 342-3.

[7] *Calendar of Entries in the Papal Registers relating to Great Britain and Ireland, Papal Letters*, xiii, ed. J. A. Twemlow (London, 1955), 667.

[8] *Calendar of Entries in the Papal Registers relating to Great Britain and Ireland, Papal Letters*, xv, *Innocent VIII Lateran Registers (1484-1492)*, ed. M. J. Haren (Dublin, 1978), 315-6.

[9] *The Annals of Ulster*, ed. B. MacCarthy, iii (Dublin, 1895), 466-7. It does not seem to me that his identification with Thomas, abbot in 1470 of Sts Peter and Paul, Armagh, is well founded. *De Annatis Hiberniae*, i: Ulster, ed. M. A. Costello (Dublin, 1912), 38.

and penitentiary business as well as Lateran and Vatican registers — judgement must be interim. It may be assumed that the MacGrath interest remained alive. Turlough may only ever have been 'prior' with opposition. If the description of 1479 was at all accurate and continued to hold true, neither he nor anyone else could have been prior in more than name and it is clear from the arrangement of 1490 that Turlough in particular did not envisage a close association with Saints' Island. However, as the evidence stands at present the most plausible construction is that the canon was received by Prior Turlough, who may even have attended at or near the Purgatory for such an occasion, and was referred by him in traditional manner to the local ordinary. The metropolitan has now disappeared from the formalities — no doubt, as Professor Gwynn suggested, because he was identified with the excluded bishop.[10] Whether his role as a licensing authority had devolved as a matter of routine on the 'prince of the territory' or whether this was a stratagem resorted to for the particular circumstance and in the face of the canon's embarrassing punctiliousness is impossible to say. In either case, on the premises, the prince is most likely to be Maguire (or his representative), who would thus complete a cosy triumvirate in extraction.[11] The imposition of a formal admission charge, of which there is no earlier note (though perhaps no one was as sensitive on the point as the high-minded canon), may simply indicate that the Purgatory's fame had made it something of a tourist trap. But the novelty may equally represent the determination of new management, untramelled by *noblesse oblige,* to derive whatever additional profit it might from a recently acquired and impoverished asset. At all events, out of greed, compounded perhaps in indeterminable measure by ignorance, indifference and spite, the ceremony for entering the Purgatory has now quite altered from that described previously. The prior no longer rejoices at the sight of the licences for entry; he demands his

[10] Gwynn, *Medieval Province*, p. 174.

[11] Whether the 'prince of that territory' is identical with the 'prince of the province' in the *Acta Sanctorum* account is unclear. Though he may well have been incorrect on the point, the writer thought that the papal commission had been directed to the 'bishop, prince and prior of the place', which though not impossible would have been rather like directing the burglars to investigate a robbery. At the point of execution, the agents are said to be 'the prince of the province, together with bishop and prior'. Dr Art Cosgrove suggested to me that 'prince of the province' if referred to O'Neill would recall his acknowledged role as secular arm to the metropolitan in the Gaelic parts of the province of Armagh. If O'Neill was acting on behalf of metropolitan authority, this might explain the prominent reference to the prince in the details of the execution.

cut. He no longer assures himself of the quality of the postulant's faith nor recites the office for the dead nor sees to it that the pilgrim is properly dressed nor accompanies him assiduously to his immurement.[12] Much less does he attend, with trepidation giving way to glad transports, his restoration to the world. He delegates to his sacrist — whoever he may be — the job of letting him down a hole on a rope and retrieving him by the same means in due course. Confession and communion there is — but was that only because the canon had read about it in books? Strange that he had not also read about the fifteen days of fasting!

So far, no record is known of these events from a papal source.[13] There is however all important confirmation in the *Annals of Ulster,* under the year 1497, that 'The Cave of the Purgatory of St Patrick on Loch Gearg was broken this year by the Guardian of Donegal and by the representatives of the Bishop in the Deanery of Lough Erne by authorisation of the Pope about the feast of St Patrick . . .: it being understood by everyone in general from the History of the Knight and other old books that this was not the Purgatory Patrick got from God although they were, everyone, visiting it.'[14] Is this to be taken at face value? Such ready compliance with a mandate running counter to local interests comes as a surprise to the student of Hiberno-papal relations in the period. The standard reaction was to counterplead and at least postpone the evil day. Means had not been lacking to circumvent Bishop de Courcy's papal provision when he attempted on the strength of it to take possession of his diocese. One possible reading of the circumstances is that the canon was not admitted to the real Purgatory and that the destruction was accordingly of the surrogate Purgatory. However, the *Annals* refer to a Purgatory which was being generally visited; they are very specific in the title which they give it and the manner of its destruction does not imply the filling in of a pit: 'The cave . . . was

---

[12] It is true that this last office and the retrieval of the pilgrim was delegated in the case of Mannini but the prior is represented as accompanying the latter to the water's edge and his diligence otherwise cannot be faulted.

[13] It is not found in *Calendar of Entries in the Papal Registers relating to Great Britain and Ireland, Papal Letters,* xvi, *Alexander VI Lateran Registers Part One (1492-1498),* ed. A. P. Fuller (Dublin, 1986). In view of the *Acta Sanctorum* account the most likely archival series in which to expect to find notice of the transaction from the papal side is the recently opened Sacred Penitentiary material.

[14] *Annals of Ulster,* iii, 416-7.

destroyed/broken' ('Uaim Purgadoire Patraig . . . do briseadh').[15]
There was much that differentiated the canon's dismal experience
from the appointments described in the tale of Knight Owein. But
was not the crucial difference — it is certainly that to which the
canon's displeasure is specifically referred — that the one context
raised demons and the other did not? It was not until he realised that
there were going to be no demons that the canon is said to have
reflected on what he had read. His reasoning seems to have been,
no demons, no Purgatory. This may have been the point which
established to the satisfaction of all who heard the story that the
ancient miracle had ceased and, whether mediated through the
papal letter or not, may be sufficient to explain the bibliographical
content of the *Annals* entry.[16] Moreover, in addition to the specific
reference of the *Annals,* there is some evidence that the Purgatory
had markedly altered its appearance between the last firm
description, that of Rathold-Mannini and 1517, the date of the next
detailed account of it, by the papal nuncio at the court of Henry
VIII, Francesco Chiericati. In a letter to Isabella d'Este, Chiericati
gives a very lively report of his trip through Ulster to Lough Derg
and of what he found there.[17] What he found is unexpected in view
of much that has gone before. When he arrived, all that he had to do
was to blow a horn and signal with an improvised flag for the two

[15] *ibid.* Professor Próinséas Ní Chatháin tells me that 'briseadh' is compatible with 'broken'
and 'destroyed'. How one interprets the breaking or destruction depends on how one envisages
the structure of the cave alias pit — or at least the first 'chamber' of it. For this one is wholly
dependent on written descriptions. In the absence of archaeological evidence the problems
which arise both in reading the individual accounts and in comparing them are incapable of
resolution. Of particular relevance to the 'destruction' is the question whether the structure was
man-made or natural or a combination. Rathold's description, which is the last before 1497 —
if one discounts the narrative of the canon of Eymstadt in view of the peculiar difficulties which
it poses — and is among the more sober, implies one tunnel-like chamber, apparently vaulted
and therefore perhaps man-made, which he calls a 'first entrance', followed by a 'second
entrance'. A possible interpretation of the 1497 'destruction' and the one to which I incline is
that it involved the bringing down partially or totally of Rathold's 'first entrance'.

[16] It is impossible on the evidence to determine where the canon was brought. However if, as
the *Acta Sanctorum* account implies, he attended at the destruction, there is a presumption in
favour of Station Island since what was destroyed is likely in those circumstances to have borne
some relation to what he had first visited.

[17] The letter is printed in B. Morsolin, *Francesco Chiericati Vescovo e Diplomatico del
Secolo Decimosesto Lettura del Prof. Morsolin (Dagli Atti 1⁰ semestre 1873 dell' Academia
Olimpica di Vicenza* (Vicenza, 1873), pp. 87-92. J. P. Mahaffy, 'Two early tours in Ireland',
Hermathena, xl (1914), [1-16], 10-15, published a translation by Professor J. G. Smyly. M.
Purcell, 'St Patrick's Purgatory: Francesco Chiericati's letter to Isabella d'Este', *Seanchas
Ardmhacha,* xii, 2 (1987), [1-10] 3-10, prints the text published by Morsolin, with a new
translation. I am grateful to Professor John Barnes and Mrs Corinna Lonergan for checking my
rendering on the points where my interpretation differs from the published versions.

servants of the three regular canons 'who are at the Purgatory' *(che stano al Purgatorio)* to ferry him and his party across one by one, at 'uno dinaro' a head: the system was evidently well established. He was brought to one island only. The island had two habitations, 'a small dwelling house made of planks *(una picol casupola facta de tavoli)* for the three resident canons' and, close by, another small dwelling house of similar construction for the pilgrims. The dimensions which Chiericati gives for the island, twenty paces long and sixteen wide, are so impossible as to be useless as a point of reference and the presence of habitations would more readily suggest that this was Saints' Island than Station Island. However, apart from the fact that the only stone building which he saw was a small church like an oratory, one feature in his description of the inside of the cave — 'At the back, the cave turns aside for two cubits *(la grotta si volta per due brazza)*' — recalls that two chamber arrangement on Station Island as described by Rathold. The return at the back of the cave was evidently the real Purgatory. It was said, according to Chiericati, that there St Patrick used to sleep and its terror was such as to deter him, renaissance man though he was, from looking into it. At the return there was 'a round platform' *(una preda tonda),* resembling a mill-stone, which gave an echo when struck. Chiericati adds, 'They say there is a well there and that this is the origin of the stories which are told of the well of St Patrick.' This is an aspect missing from the Rathold-Mannini account, though gigantically represented in Grissaphan. In the present context, however, the important feature on which Chiericati wholly departs from the information of Rathold-Mannini is the size of the ante-chamber or the cave up to the return. In Chiericati's description, this appears to be quite narrow — two and a half cubits (or possibly arm-lengths) wide *(due brazza e mezzo)* (the door, by comparison, is said to be three cubits — *tre brazza* — from the ground) — but it is otherwise such as to allow twelve persons to be there at their ease *(penetra entro tanto che a suo comodo li pol stare dodici persone).*[18] While the measurements of 1411 are not necessarily as reliable as they are explicit, they constitute evidence which is unlikely to be improved on and they convey a quite different impression from that conveyed by Chiericati.

It is with the greatest diffidence that one may venture a hypothesis to cover the various pieces of evidence so far available.

[18] *stare* does not necessarily mean 'to stand' though that might be thought implicit in Chiericati's saying that they may be there at their ease.

Let us suppose that the entry in the *Annals of Ulster* is factual, in which case it may be thought to refer to the destruction of the first chamber, up to the return. This would have necessitated, in order for the Purgatory to be reopened, the reconstruction of the ante-chamber, and in its reconstruction it was enlarged. How then to account for the destruction and the reconstruction? The 'Maguire' party (as represented, minimally and leaving aside altogether the identification of the prince, by Turlough and by Cathal MacManus) may not have seen the cave of the Purgatory as a vital concern. It is difficult to imagine that had they done so they would have capitulated so readily. If it were not a vital concern then perhaps there was an argument for complying with the papal mandate rather than adding to the troubles of a diocese the see of which was in contention. On reflection even, the mandate may not have been unwelcome. The *Annals* certainly present a brave face to the cataclysm. The cave was broken 'by authorisation of the Pope' ('a hudaras an Phapa'). Is there a positive note here? If the tenure of the priory was to be in new hands perhaps the mystique of the Purgatory, with its MacGrath associations, had as well be dispelled. Is this the explanation for the presence of the Guardian of Donegal? Had Turlough and Cathal wished to perform a token destruction they could surely have better managed that themselves. If they were serious in the business they may have wished to lend maximum authority to proceedings which might otherwise appear partisan not to say wanton. But this line of speculation must be treated coolly: the Guardian may be the representative of the Franciscan Bishop de Courcy who might have suggested him to Rome as a suitable person to monitor the implementation of the commission. In that case, Cathal MacManus' hand may have been forced, the more so if O'Neill too was involved, as representing metropolitan authority. The pleading of papal authority would then be face-saving formula.

As to the reconstruction, even if the Maguire party had been merely a compliant agent in the execution of the papal mandate it can hardly have summoned sufficient enthusiasm to reverse the damage. In fact, the sequel shows that the Maguire hold on the priory was precarious. On the inopportune death of Turlough it reverted to MacGrath hands. One cannot be certain at present that it did so immediately nor can one say by what mechanism — that is, whether or not by papal provision, as is not improbable. Whatever the mechanism, the crucial factor, both in the original acquisition of the priory by Turlough and in its reversion to a

MacGrath, is likely to have been a shift of relationship between Maguires and O'Donnells. The earliest evidence for a reversion is also the earliest evidence for the restoration of the pilgrimage. This is the survival of an original testimonial and credence, dated 12 August 1507, by 'Master Donatus Magrahe',[19] prior 'of the Purgatory', in favour of an Irish priest, Nylanus O'Ledan, who has 'performed all the pilgrimages of the island of the said Purgatory and has stayed in the ditch of the same St Patrick *(in fossa eidem* [sic] *sancti patricii)* for a natural day' where 'he sustained in his body such pains [and] torments as he saw or had *(penas tormenta si quas vidit vel habuit ibidem corporaliter sustinuit)'*.[20] It may be suggested that the reconstruction of the Purgatory, as proposed above, was taken in hand by this Donatus as soon as he secured the priory, which he probably held until about 1511. When, in December 1511, Julius II appointed Thomas Halsey, priest, doctor of both laws, papal chaplain and minor penitentiary in St Peter's Basilica 'for the English, Scottish and Irish tongue *(pro lingua Anglica, Scota et Ibernica)'* to the priory of St Patrick's Purgatory *(putei seu stagni sive lacus Rubei sancti Anneoch* [recte *Daveoch*]), it was described as being vacant by the death of Donatus MacGrath, former prior of the same.[21] What happened as a result of Halsey's provision remains to be discovered. It is most unlikely that he ever tried to secure personal possession. His provision, however, though bizarre, is interesting in that implies a certain level of recognition of the special penitential status of the priory which rendered it a suitable benefice to be held, at least in title, by a papal penitentiary. Further papal letters or supplications may be expected to throw light on these and other points which are still obscure. An important aspect of Prior Donatus' letter is that it advertises a share 'in all the indulgences of divers Roman pontiffs and other bishops, namely ten thousand, six hundred and seven years in sum, granted to our place' as well as in the suffrages of the Augustinian order to all assisting the pilgrim.[22] The indulgences

---

[19] 'Master' suggests that he was a university graduate.

[20] See L. Bieler, 'Letter of credence by Donatus Magrahe, prior of Lough Derg, for Nylanus OLedan, priest and pilgrim', *Clogher Record* (1958), 257-9. The pilgrim was visiting 'all the approved places of pilgrimage of the whole of Ireland'.

[21] Archivio Segreto Vaticano, *Regesta Lateranensia* 1266 fos. 61r-62v. This letter will appear in my edition of papal chancery registers for the second part of the pontificate of Julius II (Calendar of Papal Registers — Papal Letters, xix, in preparation). Halsey was provided to the see of Leighlin in 1513 but seems not to have resided.

[22] See Bieler, 'Letter of credence', 257, 259.

are an aspect on which one would like more precise information. The perception of the Purgatory as a formally privileged centre would certainly help to explain its vitality in the period. It is clear that by the time of Chiericati's visit the pilgrimage was not merely alive but was flourishing as perhaps never before. This is implied by the well established system of ferrying and the size of the ante-chamber. Moreover, Chiericati tells us that five others, presumably Irish, entered the cave with his two companions. There had also been re-established some degree of regular life on the Lough. How much is a question which again one may expect to have illuminated by further papal documentation.

Visions were continuing. Chiericati says that two of those who entered the cave while he was there were so affected. In other respects, what he describes seems to give a new importance to the penitential disciplines preceding immurement. Besides fasting, doing a round of (?) cells *(tre campane* — literally 'three bells') dedicated respectively to St Brigid, St Patrick and St Columba, with prayers, pilgrims are said to stand in the lake as far as the neck for some hours of the day *(per tante ore del iorno)*. There seems to be an indication of an established round also in Prior Donatus' reference to O'Ledan's having performed 'all the pilgrimages of the island'. As the pilgrimage continued, penitential exercises came to replace otherworldly visions as its principal focus. The age of visionary literature was long over. Yonge-Rathold's is the last example of the genre. Although there are other known foreign pilgrims between Laurence's time and Chiericati's[23] the fascination exercised for several centuries by the Purgatory on the European imagination was passing. Various influences may be adduced in explanation. A prominent strand of

---

[23] Known foreign pilgrims in the period were: Ghillebert de Lannoy (1430); a Swiss pilgrim (c. 1446) referred to in a note printed by Leslie, *St Patrick's Purgatory,* p. 40; the knight of Bruges, Sir John de Banste (see above, p. 80); the two priests of Lyons, with their servant, who had testimonial from Archbishop Octavian as having visited the Purgatory and Croagh Patrick (Armagh Registers, Octavian, fo. 172r; cf. Leslie, *St Patrick's Purgatory,* p. 61, and above, p. 96); John Bermyngham, squire, and William Bramery, members of the household of King Henry VII, who had a safe-conduct from Octavian, dated 27 August 1489, while visiting Armagh, Downpatrick and the Purgatory (Armagh Registers, Octavian, fo. 294v); and the French knight (1516), who was handsomely entertained by ODonnell and who handsomely repaid his entertainment by a gift of the ordnance with which Sligo castle was attacked in that year *(Annals of Ulster,* iii, 520-1; *Annals of Loch Cé,* ed. W. M. Hennessy, ii (London, 1871), 225; cf. Leslie, *St Patrick's Purgatory,* pp. 63-4, and above, p. 96). My references to Octavian's register I owe to Mr Anthony Lynch, who kindly supplied me with photocopies of a typescript in his possession of the Reeves transcripts from the Armagh register series.

the spirituality of the later middle ages was inimical to pilgrimages, emphasising that God was more readily found at home and in the recesses of the soul than by wandering abroad. Later, this quietism merged with a sceptical reserve in the face of all religious extravagance. The prince of Christian humanists, Erasmus, in his best-selling *Adages,* urbanely poked fun at this latter-day version of the classical cave of Trophonius (who, being swallowed up by the earth, was consulted as an oracle and whose clients invariably returned despondent).[24] Then, aside from this shift in religious sentiment, it is unlikely that the appeal of the Purgatory could have been unaffected by the geographical discoveries of the late fifteenth century. Some of its attraction and of its plausibility as an entrance to the otherworld must have lain in its marginal location, a point of which its custodians seem to have been conscious or on which at least they were certainly self-conscious: 'in the monastery of St Patrick our patron, in the ends or final parts of the world', is how the prior dates his testimonial for George Grissaphan, and 'bishop of Clogher, by the ends of the world', is the style of Nicholas MacCathasaigh on the same occasion. It may only be guessed at how far this exoticism was responsible for the astonishing longevity of the ancient miracle. In fact, as we know, the ancient miracle was less ancient than was supposed. The purely penitential pilgrimage which survived its cessation was, in its imitation of the flight to the desert, the more authentic continuation of the early Christian history of the Purgatory.

MICHAEL HAREN

---

[24] Erasmus, *Adagia,* i. 7. 77. Cf. M. M. Phillips, *The Adages of Erasmus* (Cambridge, 1964), p. 15. On the theme of despondency in the medieval tradition, see above, pp. 47, 61, 86.

IX. The Later Pilgrimage —
Irish Poetry on Loch Derg

Sources in late medieval and early modern Irish attribute an ancient origin to St Patrick's Purgatory:

> Loch Dearg aon Róimh na hÉireann
> mar fuair sinn sa seinléigheann

'Lough Derg the one shrine of Ireland as we have found in the old learning', so said the sixteenth-century poet Tuileagna Ó Maol-chonaire.[1] A century earlier the *Annals of Ulster* in recording the destruction of one site, cite the authentic sources as coming *as sdair an Ridire agus a seinlebraib eile* 'from the History of the Knight and from other old books'.[2] The metrical instructions for pilgrims in the form of a poem of 19 stanzas are said to be derived from *Psaltair Caisil,* the Psalter of Cashel, a lost manuscript originally attributed to Cormac mac Cuileannáin (+908):[3] *Turas Locha Deirge do réir Psaltrach Chaisil.* The third Irish Life of Kevin gives *Uaim Phádraig a nUltaibh* 'Patrick's Cave in Ulster' as a *príomhthuras,* one of the four chief pilgrimages of Ireland.[4]

In the mid-seventeenth century Bishop Henry Jones, having quoted many witnesses to a cult of the Purgatory adds this coda:

> To all which, I will in the last place adde one of the ancient *Irish Rhymes* concerning this supposed to be by *S. Patrick* himselfe, in a *vision* delivered to *one sleeping in this Purgatory,* and that to this end, that it should be everywhere divulged, which concludeth with the former: the words are these.

> Awake thou man, and remember my Rhyme in haste. Let it spread East and West, and be written with a pen. I am Patrick, chiefe, or head of the Clergie who have obtained from god no small thing: A gift large and liberall which was never found till I came to it; A Purgatory for punishment here, and no other Purgatory to be after.

---

[1] Leslie, *Saint Patrick's Purgatory,* p. 168.
[2] *Annals of Ulster,* 1497.
[3] R. Flower, *Catalogue of Irish Manuscripts in the British Museum,* (1953), iii, p. 46. Teresa Condon, *Lia Fáil* 1 (Dublin, 1926), p. 44.
[4] Plummer, *Bethada Náem nÉrenn. Lives of Irish Saints,* i, p. 161; ii, p. 156.

He gives the original in the margin from *Mss. Hibern. Derm. mac Egan,* one of the Irish Manuscripts of Diarmuid Mac Aodhagáin. While the quotation has little literary merit, it is perhaps worth reprinting as a *curiosum* since the book is virtually unobtainable:

> Eregh a giolla so this, agus meabhruigh go dian mo ran
> siolthar e soir 7 siar, agus sgriobhthar e le peann
> Is me Padruig ceann na gcliar, fuarus o dhia ni nach gann
> teaghlach fairsing fiali nach bhfríoth riamh go ttanagh ann
> Purgadoir a bhfus chum pian, agus gan na diaidh purgadoir thall.[5]

This is popular verse, propagandist, and with some of the triumphalism of later hagiographical works. It is interesting that this inferior work appears to be all Jones had to hand but it may be that he meant it to be derisory. The metre is the sub-literary *amhrán* and the spirit is somewhat removed from the soul-searching and humility of the Irish classical poets in their contemplation of Patrick's Purgatory.

The poems in classical verse are not numerous. There are several problems and complexities associated with them but nevertheless they are very interesting.[6] Most of the material comes from Gaelic MS. 64 in the National Library of Scotland in Edinburgh. E. C. Quiggin appears to have been the first to record the five poems in this manuscript relating to Patrick's Purgatory in his description of the contents of Gaelic MS. LXIV in the Advocates' Library as it was then.[7]

Osborn Bergin deciphered the poor manuscript text and Lambert McKenna edited and translated them. Eleanor Knott thought that they were a 'group of poems on the Loch Derg cave apparently in commemoration of a pilgrimage thereto by the composers'.[8] Fr Lambert McKenna suggested they might be 'a collection made by different poets'.[9] As we shall see, their transmission is not straightforward. Some extraneous stanzas would seem to have been included and there are metrical

---

[5] Jones, *Saint Patrick's Purgatory,* p. 19, 1.4 and margin.

[6] Printed by Leslie, *St Patrick's Purgatory,* p. 163 ff.

[7] 'Prologomena to the study of the later Irish Bards 1200-1500', *Proceedings of the British Academy* v, 1911. Reprints in Irish Studies Number 2 from the American Committee for Irish Studies, n.d., p. 53 1.18 ff. The contents of this Edinburgh MS. are almost all poems of a religious nature.

[8] E. Knott, *The Bardic Poems of Tadhg Dall Ó Huiginn* (2 vols., London, 1926), ii, p. 292.

[9] Leslie, *St Patrick's Purgatory,* p. 163.

anomalies, but there is still a definite unity and homogeneity in the subject matter.

We may speculate that the poets of the North-West, members of the learned families of Ó Huiginn, Mac an Bhaird and Ó Maol-chonaire went to Loch Derg as a spiritual exercise, that they took part in a poetry contest on a set subject, or were commissioned by one or more ecclesiastical patrons. We cannot be sure how this mini-anthology came about.

The most popular of all the Loch Derg poems is not found in the Edinburgh group. It has been copied into many more manuscripts and edited more often in modern times than any other. It was invested with the greatest antiquity in the manuscript tradition where it is ascribed to Donnchadh Mór Ó Dálaigh (+1244) who is buried in Boyle Abbey, Co. Roscommon.

The poem *Truagh mo Thuras ar Loch Dearg* 'Alas, for my journey to Loch Derg', is quoted in translation by Douglas Hyde in his Literary History of Ireland in which the first quatrain is printed.[10] It was edited by Énrí Ó Muirgheasa from a manuscript written at Antwerp in the 1770's by Brian Ó Cathalán, later the parish priest of Enniskeen, Co. Monaghan.[11]

The Archbishop of Dublin, John Carpenter, who is so closely associated with Irish manuscripts and scribes in eighteenth-century Dublin, owned the Trinity College Dublin MS. H.5.13 written about 1700. He has inscribed his name *Seaan Mac a'tSaoir* and the date 1745, on the page following our poem.[12]

Although *Truagh mo thuras ar Loch Dearg* occurs in so many manuscripts and its prestige, no doubt, rested on its ascription to Donnchadh Mór, it is probable that he did not compose it.[13] He was held in great regard and long after the decline of the bardic tradition orally transmitted poetry was fathered on him. Douglas

---

[10] Douglas Hyde, *A Literary History of Ireland* (London, 1899). New edition with introduction by Brian Ó Cuív (London, 1967), p. 466 f. Hyde's translation was based on the edition in *The Gaelic Journal* iv (1893), p. 190 f. from a Maynooth MS. The poem was also printed in *Timthire* vi 2, p. 40; Leslie, *St Patrick's Purgatory, p. 166.*

[11] Énrí Ó Muirgheasa, *Dánta Diadha Uladh*, (Baile Átha Cliath, 1936), p. 149-51. This is from MS. A 39 in the Franciscan Library, Killiney, Co. Dublin and another MS.

[12] E. J. Gwynn, T. K. Abbott, *Catalogue of the Irish manuscripts in the Library of Trinity College, Dublin* (Dublin, 1921), p. 245 ff. See also Donn Piatt, *Cois Life Fadó*, (Baile Átha Cliath, 1985), p. 47-8.

[13] Lambert McKenna edited the poems of Donnchadh Mór Ó Dálaigh. In the preface we read: 'His name evidently carried with it a great prestige among the scribes to judge by the enormous number of poems attributed to him many of them demonstrably by other authors', *Dán Dé* (Dublin, 1922), p. viii-ix.

Hyde himself heard his verses being recited by native Irish speakers in Roscommon and Mayo.[14] There was another fourteenth-century Donnchadh Mór Ó Dálaigh from the Burren in Co. Clare and this also occasioned some confusion in the manuscript tradition.[15]

The poem itself was written by the poet 'on his unexpectedly finding himself unable to shed a tear after his arriving at Loch Derg on a pilgrimage' in the opinion of Hyde. It is a forlorn cry to God for repentance while buried alive in the grave, naked and hungry. Contemplation of the wounds of Christ will not bring a tear to the eye. A dialogue with the wilfully sinful body and an ominous reminder of the loud cries of all — both clergy and laity — on Judgement Day are all to no avail when the heart is harder than a stone.

Were it not for this hardness of heart in time of penance *Muna bheath cruaidhe cridhe* another poet tells us we need not leave the house of Patrick in the state of sin.[16] He is going to enter the dark black cave with bare walls; for fear of the heart's sleeping he begs Patrick's presence in the cave. Christ's descent into hell at Easter is recalled with his victory over the demons. His own parallel descent and his emergence after a night and day in the narrow dwelling of stone leaves him without sin. In the morning early the clear *linn* 'lake' for cleansing sin looks like the venerable River Jordan, an obvious allusion to the belief in the baptismal effect of the Loch Derg *turas* in the washing away of all sin.

It is *Linn Pádraig na bport solas* 'the lake of Patrick of bright havens', for Fearghal Óg Ó hUiginn who is determined to enter the saint's *uaimh*.[17] The sinner who has lain in *Linn Pádraig* will leave the stream in the state in which he was after baptism:

> fágbbhaidh an sruth . . .
> sa chruth i m-bí ar n-a bhaisteadh.

God has left Patrick to remedy original sin, *do leigheas locht ar*

[14] Hyde, *loc. cit.*
[15] *Dán Dé, loc. cit.*
[16] Leslie, *St Patrick's Purgatory*, p. 176-9. He is apparently a member of the Ó Huiginn family but most of the name is illegible.
[17] Leslie, *St Patrick's Purgatory*, p. 179-80. This poem from the Edinburgh group is a *memento mori* to the poet himself. Eleanor Knott suggests that he may have been a sixteenth-century contemporary of Tadhg Dall Ó Huiginn, TD, ii, p. 313, 1.29. Here the use of the word *Ifreann* may simply reflect the older usage where the word stood for both Hell and Purgatory. The dark cave may also be a metaphorical image of this world.

sinsear, and may the love of Patrick from heaven light up this cave of Hell.

This supreme confidence in Patrick is echoed in *Mo chean théid i dteaghais Phádraig.* He is fortunate who enters Patrick's dwelling. This complicated composition is ascribed to Aonghus Mac Aodha Ruaidh, an Ó Huiginn who was active in the 1590's in North Connacht.[18] It appears to be a short piece with two quatrains interpolated, followed by a complete poem of invocation to Patrick and other saints.

The opening rejoices in the release from fear of the day of judgement which is given to him who arises from the *teach luighe* 'grave' of the saint who is the *gell* 'pledge' against that day of assembly.

While the (?) additional poem[19] is not of any great literary excellence, it is of particular interest in that it names the saints of the Loch Derg beds. The poet begins *Gabaim comairce Pádraig* 'I take the protection of Patrick' and goes on to ask Colum Cille, Brendan, Brigid, Molaise, M'Aodhóg and Caitiriona to intercede for him. With the exception of M'Aodhóg, these correspond to the *Lectus vel Circulus* titulars of Thomas Carve's 1666 map.[20] Here Daibéoc has become *Abogi* in a Latinised genitive form. *D'Aibheóg* would be interchangeable in early Irish hagiographical usage with M'Aibheóg and it would also be confused in later language with Mobhéog. It is more than likely that we have here a scribal transformation to M'Aodhóg, or perhaps a popular transposition of an obscure earlier saint to the patron saint of Ferns, Maedóc of Drumlane, Co. Cavan and Rossinver, Co. Leitrim, whose *Vita* brings him into relations with Molaisse of Devenish as Charles Plummer has pointed out.[21]

Next Caillín of Fenagh, Co. Leitrim, Tighearnach of Clones, Ciarán of Clonmacnois and Sinell (? Loch Erne) are asked for help while the poet is still

> *i n-iomdhaidh Phádraig fheartaigh*
> *ca bhfuil leabaidh as cruaidhe*
> 'in the couch of Patrick of miraculous powers — where is there a harder bed?'

Though Patrick's Bed is hard and cold, the great Tadhg Dall Ó

---

[18] Leslie, *St Patrick's Purgatory,* p. 174-5. E. Knott, TD, ii, p. 306, 1.15 ff.

[19] From quatrain 6 to the end.

[20] See above, p. 186.

[21] *Vitae Sanctorum Hiberniae* (Oxford, 1910), vol. i, p. lxxviii.

Huiginn (+1591) calls it a healer's house, *Teach leagha, leaba Phádraig.* Patrick is the *liaigh cabhartha* 'the helping physician' as well as a *Fáidh adhartha d'Éireannchaibh* 'the venerated prophet of Irishmen'.[22] His theme is the fact and process of healing. His description might be simply recounting a visit by sick pilgrims to an ancient holy well. His vocabulary is that of physical illness and its cure. The *maor uamha* 'steward of the cave' is the *buachaill othair* 'servant attending the sick'. An attack of illness *taom d'easláinte,* an injury *lot,* any kind of wound *éanghuin, cneadh, créacht,* will be healed *i n-uaimh éarluimh an einigh* 'in the cave of the hospitable patron saint'. After 'leaving their garment of sickness' *fágbháil a n-éadaigh othair* the pilgrims confront a pool outside the cave on the far side. It is styled 'a lake-spring to bathe all from their wounds' and all wounds are healed in it.

Eleanor Knott thought this 'piece seems principally concerned with the "circle or cell" known as Patrick's Bed'.[23] This poem can be taken as allegorical with the different types of wound corresponding to the infinite variations of sin. The word sin is not mentioned at all nor is there any reference to penance but the essence of the Purgatory was repentance and expiation. It is of course tempting to see in the 'garment of sickness' the profusion of 'rags' which so obsessed one of the foreign observers — the remnants from a pilgrimage for the sick. The *fothragadh* 'bathing of the whole body' in the lake-spring, *lochthobar,* recalls the parallel with the River Jordan in the poem *Muna bheath cruaidhe cridhe* as we have already seen.

The metaphorical washing is clearly shown in *Loch Dearg aonRóimh na hÉireann* ascribed to Tuileagna Ó Maol-chonaire.[24]

---

[22] First edited and translated by Eleanor Knott, TD ii, p. 289-92; Leslie, *St Patrick's Purgatory,* p. 163-5. It is perhaps worthy of note here that Tadhg Dall uses *Éireannach* the 'common name of Irishman' here, probably *metri causa,* but could it be also because St Patrick's Purgatory was not exclusive to the old native religious tradition?

[23] Knott, TD ii, p. 293, 1.1. Eleanor Knott also prints two and a half quatrains with a defective first line on *Uaimh Pádraig,* extolling the fame and virtues of the Cave of Patrick. This is tantalising because we cannot know whether Tadhg Dall Ó Huiginn composed other poems on the Purgatory, or whether the poem on the *Leaba* and this fragment on the *Uaimh,* were part of a kind of *Dinnseanchas* or series of topographical poems on Loch Derg (*ibid.* p. 288, 290; Leslie, *St Patrick's Purgatory,* p. 165).

[24] As note 1 above. He was styled Tuileagna mac Torna and was probably a brother of Torna mac Torna, the early sixteenth-century scribe. This poem is found in other MSS; in R.I.A. Ms. 24 L 28, p. 232, it begins *Loch Derg aonrogha na h-Éireann;* in T.C.D. H.4.4, p. 46 it is attributed to Aonghus Ó Dálaigh but Eleanor Knott is dubious about this ascription, TD ii, p. 292. However, there are two or three poems or parts of poems mixed up here, and they are very difficult to disentangle.

Instead of a purgatory the island is *Pardhas na sreabh milis* 'paradise of the sweet streams'. The poet enters a dialogue with his unclean body and threatens it that he will not purify it again after this visit to the house where Patrick fasted. However, immediately we are told since he could not find a tear of repentance he must lie again in the Saint's cave. Like a good doctor he must bathe his soul *fothrogadh m'anma is éigean.*

In what may be the beginning of a different piece[25] we read that Patrick the Patriarch of Ireland visited the territories and routed the Devil:

> *cuairt neamhlag os cionn na gcríoch*
> *dar liom do dhearmad Dáibhíoth.*

This has been translated by Father McKenna as 'over all the land — which, one would think, has forgotten (the story of) David'. This is still not very clear. Could it be an echo of the underlying cult of Dabéoc and could *Dábhíoth* be a reflex of the earlier hypocoristic form? If so, it cannot be said to make much more sense by saying that Daibheóg had forgotten those lands or conversely that they had forgotten him.

The poet begs Patrick to draw away the strength of the Devil from himself. He meditates on Christ's testament of love through His suffering and begs the Blessed Virgin to come and watch over him.

Fearghal Óg Mac an Bhaird bids farewell to Patrick's Island, *Slán uaim ag oiléan Pádraig.*[26] It is a joyful happy poem. *Eaglais an uird* 'the church of the order' is *Róimh gach anma d'fhóiridhin* 'the shrine that succours every soul'. He bids a reluctant good-bye to the beds *ag an hiomdhadhaibh* as he ruefully remarks that his suffering in them is no hearsay, *ní sgéal sgeoil.* He mentions a yew tree — perhaps a repository for the sick-clothes and rags. The *uaimh* is angelic, love for it has penetrated his heart. At Patrick's Lake *Linn Pádraig* he suffered pain but it is *ceann oilithre na hÉireann* 'the chief pilgrimage of Ireland'. Finally he bids farewell to Patrick who has ever willingly helped every sufferer.

Robin Flower drew attention to two other poems in the British

---

[25] Leslie, *St Patrick's Purgatory,* p. 169, quatrain 21.

[26] Leslie, *St Patrick's Purgatory,* p. 172-3. This has been written *Slán uaim ag oilithre Pádraig* '. . . Patrick's Pilgrimage' in other MSS. See R.I.A. No. 61 (front flyleaf) and No. 84, p. 345 1.22. This is also ascribed to Aonghus Ó Dálaigh in T.C.D. MS. H.4.4, p. 86. See above note 24.

Library MS. Add. 30512.[27] There is a note on St Patrick's
Purgatory followed by two poems on folio 17:

1. *An coimgidh atá ar nim 7 ar lár*
   'The Lord who is in heaven and on earth;

2. *Eisdigh [a] aos cumtha caoin*
   'Listen, fair poet companions'.

These poems have not yet been edited or discussed but the second
one which the colophon tells us gives instructions to the pilgrim
may well be similar to *A dhuine théid go Loch Dearg*. The latter as
we have seen was believed to derive from the Psalter of Cashel.

Teresa Condon as an addendum to her edition of the prose text
Purgadóir Phádraig Naomhtha, an Irish translation of the
seventeenth century, edited the text of this composition. It
comprises nineteen quatrains giving minute details of the *Turas*:

1 You who go to Loch Derg
   Do not recall resentful hate or anger
   Preserve these verses as a pack of provisions
   The gentle cure for every misfortune

2 A Pater, an Ave and the Creed
   On your knees as the first course
   At the great altar, having crossed the wave
   To the stronghold of Patrick son of Calpurnius

3 On your knees — I am certain
   Where the sacrifice of the Mass is made
   Three Paters, three Aves and the Creed
   In honour of him of bright aspect

4 In honour of the Passion which the king bore
   Your seven decades are the third thing
   With each decade say a Pater
   Until you make up the right number

5 Seven penitential beds — without a lie
   In the rough land of Patrick on the island

---

[27] As note 3 above, ii, 476-7. Flower prints a colophon showing that these pieces were
written in Cahir for Pierce Butler in 1561 and invoking a prayer for him. It has not been
possible to examine these texts, but an edition would be a *desideratum*. Trinity College, Dublin
MS. H.1.11, f.117a-118a contains a copy of them from this British Library MS. A translation
has been attempted here since the original is not easily available of Teresa Condon's *Lia Fáil*
text.

The obligation of each bed and its spoken prayer
From the Bed of Brendan to Aibheóg

6   Three Paters outside
At each bed of penance
Three Aves and the Creed
As prescribed by the blessed clergy

7   The same again — and it is no lie
On your knees in hardship
At the entrance to each bed
According to Patrick's rule.

8   The same again inside
Before we go on our knees
Three times going around
On bare bare flagstones

9   Three Paters, three Aves and the Creed
On the floor of every bed always sharp
On your knees we recall
It is not unknown to us

10 I must cross the wave
To the black stone of Patrick
Where there are sharp-hard paths
Full of obstacles which draw blood (?)

11 Five Paters, five Aves and the Creed
Around the fully sharp flags
Three hours with too many stones
In the pool with bare feet

12 Five Paters, five Aves and the Creed
The obligation of each rugged bed
On your knees on the fair flag
Be guided by me O Christian!

13 We proceed to the Flag of the Footmarks
Where the fainthearted is consoled
A Pater Ave and Creed
Are said in its honour

14 From that flag we go on
To the great altar of Patrick
One Pater, Ave and Creed
On your knees without excuse

15 Let us go from there in
To the house for cleansing sinners

Let us recite our psalter there
On our knees at Mass

16   Eighteen days our time there[28]
With absence of food and common meals
Once a day great our distaste
For one portion of water and bread

17   In the morning we are called
By the bell of the Mass priest
After preparing for death (?) and praying
With the household of angelic Patrick

18   Twenty-four hours without sleep
In a cold narrow prison
Without being able to leave it quickly
The . . . cave of Patrick

19   We make the end of our journey
With three waves across the lake
Until we come to our house
Without hatred, without envy, without ill-will.

This guide to the pilgrimage may confuse us the more but it
might be useful to compare the instructions with the accounts in
the guide-books and with the experiences of pilgrims.[29]
It is axiomatic that the sixteenth century was a most troubled
time for the Irish church. Aodh mac Aingil, writing in 1618 writes
of *an mhaith mhór thigeadh do na hanmannuibh tréna thathuighi 7
an díoghbháil tig dhóibh fána thoirmiosg orra* 'the great benefit
that used to come to souls through visiting it [Loch Derg] and the
harm *that comes* to them through prohibiting them'.[30] This may
reflect a more widespread concern and perhaps the Loch Derg
pieces of the North-Western poets record some of the Irish
reaction to the depredations of Henry VIII and their aftermath.[31]

PRÓINSÉAS NÍ CHATHÁIN

[28] *Tráth* is a difficult word to translate, it originally meant the canonical hour; in the later
langauge it can mean twenty-four hours. In view of some of the accounts of nine-day periods it
has been translated as 'day'.
[29] For instance, Father Dominick Brullaughan (1735) and the Nuncio Francesco Chiericati
(1517).
[30] The Franciscan Archbishop of Armagh (+1626). His *Scathán Shacramuinte na hAithridhe*
was first published in 1618. It was edited by Cainneach Ó Maonaigh, O.F.M., Dublin 1952. See
ibid. p. 208, l.6864.
[31] For these learned families see especially Father Paul Walsh, *Irish Men of Learning*
(Dublin, 1947).

Bibliography

Manuscripts and incunabula

Auch, Archives Départementales du Gers, Auch, MS I - 4066.

Barcelona, Biblioteca de Catalunya, Barcelona, BON.10.V.II (1486).

Bologna, Bibliotheca Universitaria, MS Lat. 997 [1513] (saec. XV, A.D. 1461).

Cambridge, University Library, MS Ee.6.11.

Dublin, Franciscan Library, Killiney, Co. Dublin, MS A 39.

Dublin, Royal Irish Academy, MS 24 L 28.

Dublin, Royal Irish Academy, MS 61.

Dublin, Royal Irish Academy, MS 84.

Dublin, Trinity College, MS H.1. 11.

Dublin, Trinity College, MS H.4.4.

Dublin, Trinity College, MS 951.

Edinburgh, National Library of Scotland, MS Advocates' 19.2.1 (saec. XIV).

Edinburgh, National Library of Scotland, Gaelic MS 64.

Florence, Bibliotheca Nazionale Centrale, Conventi soppressi, MS C. II. 15 50 (saec. XIV-XV).

Florence, Bibliotheca Nazionale Centrale, Conventi soppressi, MS G. III. 676 (saec. XV).

Florence, Bibliotheca Nazionale Centrale, MS II, IV, 380 [Magliabecchi XXV, 595] (saec. XVII).

Florence, Bibliotheca Nazionale Centrale, MS Magliabecchi XXIV, 158 (saec. XV).

Florence, Bibliotheca Nazionale Centrale, MS Magliabecchi XXV, 3 (saec. XV).

Florence, Bibliotheca Nazionale Centrale, MS Magliabecchi XXXV, 3 (saec. XV).

Florence, Bibliotheca Nazionale Centrale, MS Magliabecchi XXXV, 173 (saec. XIV).

Florence, Bibliotheca Nazionale Centrale, MS Magliabecchi XXXVIII, 10 (saec. XV).

Florence, Bibliotheca Nazionale Centrale, MS Palatino, Panciatico 40 [olim 75] (saec. XIV).

Florence, Bibliotheca Nazionale Centrale, MS Principale II. II. 71 [Magliabecchi VII, 22] (saec. XV).

Florence, Bibliotheca Nazionale Centrale, MS Principale II II 89 [Magliabecchi XXI, 123] (saec. XV).

Florence, Bibliotheca Nazionale Centrale, MS Principale II. IV. 64 [Magliabecchi XXXIX, 68] (saec. XV).

Florence, Bibliotheca Riccardiana, MSS 1294 and 2760 (saec. XIV).

Florence, Bibliotheca Riccardiana, MS 1340 (saec. XV).

Florence, Bibliotheca Riccardiana, MS 1408 [P. III. 23] (saec. XV).

London, British Library, MS Additional 30512 (saec. XVI).

London, British Library, MS Additional 34193 (saec. XV).

London, British Library, MS Cotton Domit. A.IV (saec. XV).

London, British Library, MS Lansdowne 383 (saec. XIII).

London, British Library, MS Royal 10 B ix (saec. XV[2]).

London, British Library, MS Royal 13 B viii (saec. XII[2]).

London, British Library, MS Royal 17 B xliii (saec. XV).

London, Lambeth Palace Library, MS 51 (saec. XIII[1]).

Mantova, Archivio di Stato, Archivo Gonzaga, MS Serie B xxxiii. 10, Busta 85.

Oxford, Bodleian Library, MS Laud Misc. 108.

Oxford, Bodleian Library, MS Bodl. 144.

Milan, Bibliotheca Ambrosiana, MS P. 256 sup.

Paris, Bibliothèque Nationale, MS fr. 15210.

Paris, Bibliothèque Nationale, MS fr. 25549.

Paris, Bibliothèque Nationale, Rés. p.Y[2] 49.

Rome, Bibliotheca Corsiniana, MS Rossi 30 [44. C. 5] (saec. XIV).

Rome, Bibliotheca Corsiniana, MS Rossi 298 [43. A. 23] (saec. XV).

Rome, Bibliotheca Apostolica Vaticana, MS Vat. Lat. 13072 (saec. XV).

Rome, Bibliotheca Apostolica Vaticana, MS Chigi Latina M. V. 118 (saec. XV).

Toulouse, Bibliothèque Municipale, Toulouse, MS 894.

Venice, Bibliotheca Nazionale Marciana, MS 4947 [It. I. 66] (saec. XV).

Venice, Bibliotheca Nazionale Marciana, MS 5023 [It. I. 30] (saec. XV).

Venice, Bibliotheca Nazionale Marciana, MS 5644 [It. V. 28] (saec. XV).

Venice, Civico Museo Correr, MS Cod. Cic. 2242 (saec. XV).

Venice, Civico Museo Correr, MS Correr 1508 (I. 384).

Vienna, Osterreichischen Nationalbibliothek, MS 3160 (saec. XV).

Modern Printed Works

Acta Sanctorum (Brussels, 1863-1940).

Agallamh na Seanórach, ed. N. Ní Shéaghda (3 vols, Dublin, 1942-45).

Anderson, A. and M. O. Anderson (eds and trs), *Adomnán's Life of Columba* (2 vols, London, 1961).

Annala Rioghachta Eireann: Annals of the Kingsdom of Ireland by the Four Masters, ed. J. O'Donovan (7 vols, Dublin, 1848-1851).

Annala Uladh: Annals of Ulster: a chronicle of Irish affairs from A.D. 431 to A.D. 1540, eds W. Hennessy and B. Mac Carthy (4 vols, Dublin, 1887-1901).

Annals of Loch Cé, ed. W. M. Hennessy, Rolls series, 54 (London, 1871).

Artmann, H. C., *Der Schlüssel des heilige Patrick: religiöse Dichtungen der Kelten* (Salzburg, 1959).

Atkinson, Jenkins, T., *The Espurgatoire Seint Patriz of Marie de France with a text of the Latin original* (Chicago, 1903).

Balzo, C. del (comp.), *Poesie di mille autori intorno a Dante Alighieri* (Roma, 1889-1909).

Bar, F., *Les Routes de l'Autre Monde: descente aux enfers et voyages dans l'au-delà* (Paris, 1946).

Bartrum, P. C., *Early Welsh Genealogical Tracts* (Cardiff, 1966).

Baudry, P., 'L'église paroissiale de S. Patrice . . . Description des vitraux', *Revue de Rouen et de Normandie,* Aug. 1849 - Jan./Feb. 1850 (Rouen 1850).

Bayley, A. R., 'Patrick's Purgatory', *Notes and Queries,* clxxxii (1942), 67-68.

Becker, E. J., *A Contribution to the Comparative Study of the Medieval Visions of Heaven and Hell, with Special Reference to the Middle-English Versions* (Baltimore, 1899).

Bede, *A History of the English Church and People,* translated by L. Sherley-Price, revised by R. E. Latham (Harmondsworth, 1968).

Bergin, O. and R. I. Best (eds and trs), 'Tochmarc Étaíne', *Ériu*, xii (1938), 137-196.

Bethell, D., 'English monks and Irish reform in the eleventh and twelfth centuries', *Historical Studies: papers read before the Irish Conference of Historians*, viii, ed. T. D. Williams (Dublin, 1971) 111-135.

Bieler, L., *The Life and Legend of St Patrick: problems of modern scholarship* (Dublin, 1949).

— (tr.) *The Works of St Patrick* (London, 1953).

— 'Letter of credence by Donatus Magrahe, prior of Lough Derg, for Nylanus O'Ledan, priest and pilgrim', *Clogher Record* (1958), 257-259.

— 'St. Patrick's Purgatory: contributions towards an historical topography', *Irish Ecclesiastical Record*, xciii (1960), 137-144.

— (ed.), *The Irish Penitentials* (Dublin, 1963).

Bieler, L. (ed.) and F. Kelly, *The Patrician Texts in the Book of Armagh* (Dublin, 1979).

Binchy, D. A. (ed. and tr.), 'The saga of Fergus Mac Léti', *Ériu*, xvi (1952), 33-48.

Bolton, C. A., 'The saint on Croagh Patrick', *Irish Ecclesiastical Record*, lxx (1948), 681-686.

Boswell, C. S., *An Irish Precursor of Dante: a study on the vision of Heaven and Hell ascribed to the eight-century Saint Adamnán, with translation of the Irish text* (London, 1908).

Bouillon, F., *Histoire de la Vie et du Purgatoire de S. Patrice* (Paris, 1676).

Brady, I., 'The development of the doctrine of the Immaculate Conception in the fourteenth century after Aureoli', *Franciscan Studies*, xv (1955), 175-202.

Brandes, H. (ed.), *Visio Sancti Pauli. Ein Beitrag zur Visionslitteratur mit einem deutschen und zwei lateinischen Texten* (Halle, 1885).

Breatnach, P. A., 'The origins of the Irish monastic tradition at Ratisbon (Regensburg)', *Celtica*, xiii (1980), 58-77.

Brunel, C., 'Sur la version provençale du voyage de Raimon de Perillos au Purgatoire de Saint Patrice', *Estudios dedicados a R. Menéndez Pidal*, vi (Madrid, 1956), 1-21.

Burton, Robert, *The Anatomy of Melancholy*, ed. H. Jackson (London, 1932).

Byrne, F. J., 'Ireland before the Norman invasion', *Irish Historical Studies*, xvi (1968), 1-14.

— *Irish Kings and High-Kings* (London, 1973).

— 'The trembling sod: Ireland in 1169', in *A New History of Ireland,* ed. A. Cosgrove (Oxford, 1987), 1-42.

Caerwyn Williams, J. E., 'Welsh versions of Purgatorium s. Patricii', *Studia Celtica,* vii-ix (1973-74), 121-194.

Calendars of Entries in the Papal Registers relating to Great Britain and Ireland. Papal Letters, iii, ed. W. H. Bliss and C. Johnson (London 1897); xiii, ed. J. A. Twemlow (London, 1955); xv, *Innocent VIII Lateran Registers (1484-1492),* ed. M. J. Haren (Dublin, 1978); xvi, ed. A. P. Fuller (Dublin, 1986).

Carve, Thomas, *Lyra; sive Anacephalaeosis Hibernica* (Sulzbach, 1666).

Carville, G., 'The Cistercian settlement of Ireland (1142-1541)', *Studia Monastica,* xv (1973), 23-41.

Castellane, le Marquis de, 'Voyage au Purgatoire de Saint Patrice', *Mémoires de la Société Archéologique du Midi de la France,* i (1832-1833) 51-72; iii, 33-51.

Catalogue of Irish Manuscripts in the British Museum, i, comp. S. O'Grady; ii and iii, comp. R. Flower (London, 1926-1953).

Catalogue of the Irish Manuscripts in the Library of Trinity College, Dublin, eds E. J. Gwynn and T. K. Abbott (Dublin, 1921).

Catalogue of Romances in the Department of Manuscripts in the British Museum, ed. H. L. D. Ward (London, 1893).

Champion, P., *Procès de Condamnation de Jeanne d'Arc. Texte, traduction et notes* (2 vols, Paris 1920-1).

Chartreux, F. A. S., *La Vie admirable du grand S. Patrice d'Hibernie* (Brussels, 1637).

Chaucer, *The Works of Geoffrey Chaucer,* ed. F. N. Robinson, 2nd ed. (London, 1957).

Colgan, J. (ed.), *Acta Sanctorum* (Louvain, 1640).

— *Trias Thaumaturgae* (Louvain, 1647).

Colon, G., *El léxico catalán en la Romania* (Madrid, 1976).

— *La llengua catalana en els seus textos* (2 vols, Barcelona, 1978).

Condún, T., 'Purgadóir Pádraigh Naomhtha', *Lia Fáil,* i (Dublin, 1926), 1-48.

Connolly, A. G., 'Clogher in Celtic and Anglo-Norman Ireland', *St Macartan's Seminary Centenary Souvenir* (Drogheda, 1940).

Contributions to a Dictionary of the Irish Language, M. E. Byrne and M. Joynt: degra-dodelbtha (Dublin, 1959); M. Joynt: R (Dublin, 1944); D. Greene and E. G. Quinn: to-tu (Dublin, 1948).

Cosgrove, A., *Late Medieval Ireland, 1370-1541* (Dublin, 1981).

Costello, S., 'The Life of Ramon de Perellós, Viscount of Roda and Perellós' (unpublished M.A. thesis, Queen's University, Belfast, 1930).

Cunningham, J. B., *Lough Derg. Legendary Pilgrimage* (Monaghan, 1984).

Curtayne, A., *Lough Derg, St Patrick's Purgatory* (London/Dublin, 1947).

Davenport, A., 'Patrick's Purgatory', *Notes and Queries,* clxxxi (1941), 67.

De Annatis Hiberniae, i: Ulster, ed. M. A. Costello (Dublin, 1912).

Delehaye, H., 'Le pèlerinage de Laurent de Pászthó au Purgatoire de s. Patrice', *Analecta Bollandiana,* xxvii (1908), 35-60.

Desonay, F., *Antoine de la Sale. Le Paradis de la Reine Sybille* (Paris, 1930).

Dinzelbacher, P., *Jenseitsbrücke im Mittelalter* (Vienna, 1973).

— 'Die Visionen des Mittelalters. Eins geschichtlicher Umriss, *Zeitschrift für Religions- und Geistesgeschichte,* xxx (1978), 116-128.

— 'Mittelalterliche Vision und moderne Sterbeforschung', *Psychologie in der Mediävistik: Gesammelte Beiträge des Steinheimer Symposions,* ed. Jürgen Kühnel and others (Göppingen, 1985), 9-49.

— *Vision und Visionsliteratur im Mittelalter,* Monographien zur Geschichte des Mittelalters 23 (Stuttgart, 1981).

— 'La littérature des révélations au Moyen Age: un document historique', *Revue Historique,* cclxxv (1986), 289-305.

Dizionario Biografico degli Italiani (20 vols, Rome, 1960-).

Dixon, V. F., 'Saint Patrick of Ireland and the dramatists of golden age Spain', *Hermathena,* cxxi (1976), 142-158.

Doble, G. H., *The Saints of Cornwall* (Oxford, 1970).

Dolley, M., *Anglo-Norman Ireland (1100-1318)* (Dublin, 1972).

Doncoeur, P. (ed.), *La Minute Française des Interrogatoires de Jeanne la Pucelle d'après le Réquisitoire de Jean d'Estivet et les Manuscrits de d'Urfé et d'Orléans* (Melun, 1952).

Dottin, G. (ed.), *Louis Eunius ou le Purgatoire de saint Patrice. Mystère breton en deux journées* (Paris, 1911).

Droz, E., *Le Recueil de Trepperel* (Paris, 1935).

Duerr, H. P., *Dreamtime: concerning the boundary between wilderness and civilization,* translated by Felicitas Goodman (Oxford, 1985).

Dunaire Finn, Part I, ed. Eoin MacNeill, Irish Texts Society vii (Dublin, 1908); Parts II and III, ed. Gerard Murphy, Irish Texts Society xxvii (Dublin, 1933) and vol. xliii (Dublin, 1941).

218 BIBLIOGRAPHY

Dunning, P. J., 'The Arroasian Order in Medieval Ireland', *Irish Historical Studies*, iv (1945), 297-315.

Easting, R., 'An Edition of *Owayne Miles* and other Middle English texts concerning St Patrick's Purgatory' (D.Phil. thesis, University of Oxford, 1976); parts to be published as *St Patrick's Purgatory: two versions of 'Owayne Miles' and 'The Vision of William of Stranton' together with the long text of the 'Tractatus de Purgatorio Sancti Patricii'*, Early English Text Society, forthcoming.

— 'The date and dedication of the *Tractatus de Purgatorio sancti Patricii*', *Speculum*, liii (1978), 778-783.

— (ed.), 'Peter of Cornwall's account of St Patrick's Purgatory', *Analecta Bollandiana*, xcvii (1979), 397-416.

— 'Owein at St Patrick's Purgatory', *Medium Aevum*, lv, 2 (1986), 159-175.

— 'Purgatory and the Earthly Paradise in the *Tractatus de Purgatorio sancti Patricii*', *Cîteaux: Commentarii Cistercienses*, xxxvii (1986), 23-48.

— 'The *South English Legendary* "St Patrick" as translation', forthcoming in Leeds Studies in English.

Eckleben, S., *Die alteste Schilderung vom Fegefeur des heil. Patricius* (Halle, 1885).

Endres, J. A., *Honorius Augustodunensis* (München, 1906).

Farcy de Pontfarcy, Y. de, 'L'Espurgatoire Seint Patriz de Marie de France' (unpublished doctoral thesis, Université de Rennes, 1971).

— See also under Pontfarcy.

Félice, Ph. de, *L'Autre Monde, Mythes et Légendes. Le Purgatoire de Saint Patrice* (Paris, 1906).

Fitzgibbon, A., 'Appendix to the unpublished Geraldine documents- the Gherardini of Tuscany', *The Journal of the Royal Society of Antiquaries of Ireland*, xiv (1976-78), 246-264.

Flanagan, M-Th., 'St Mary's Abbey, Louth and the introduction of the Arrouaisian Observance into Ireland', *Clogher Record*, x (1980), 223-234.

Flint, V. I. J., 'The "Elucidarium" of Honorius Augustodunensis and Reform in the late eleventh century England', *Revue Bénédictine*, lxxxv (1975), 178-198.

— 'The place and purpose of the works of Honorius Augustodunensis', *ibid.*, lxxxvii (1977), 97-127.

Flynn, L. J., *St Patrick's Purgatory, Lough Derg county Donegal*, The Irish Heritage Series, 54 (Dublin, 1986).

Foulet, L., 'Marie de France et la légende du Purgatoire de saint Patrice', *Romanische Forschungen*, xxii (1908), 599-627.

Frati, L., 'Il Purgatorio di S. Patrizio secondo, Stefano di Bourbon e Uberto da Romans', *Giornale Storico della Letteratura Italiana* viii (1886), 140-179.

— 'Tradizioni storiche del Purgatorio di san Patrizio', *ibid.*, xvii (1891), 46-79.

Froissart, *Chroniques de Froissart*, ed. J. B. M. C. Kervyn de Lettenhoeve (25 vols, Brussels, 1867-77); *The Chronicles of Froissart translated by John Bourchier, Lord Berners*, The Globe Edition, edited and reduced into one volume by G. C. Macauley (London, 1913).

Fuhrmann, J. P., *Irish Medieval Monasteries on the Continent* (Washington, 1927).

Gamurrini, E., *Istoria Genealogica delle Famiglie Nobili Toscane et Umbre* (Florence, 1671).

Gerson, Jean, *Oeuvres Complètes*, ed. P. Glorieux, iii *L'Ouevre Magistrale* (Paris, Tournai, Rome, New York, 1962).

Giraldus Cambrensis, *Opera*: v. *Topographia Hibernica et Expugnatio Hibernica*, ed. J. F. Dimock (London, 1867); see tr. J. J. O'Meara.

Gougaud, Dom Louis, *Ermites et Reclus* (Vienne, 1928).

Gregory of Tours, *The History of the Franks*, tr. L. Thorpe (Harmondsworth, 1974).

Gregory the Great, *Dialogues*, tr. O. J. Zimmerman (Washington, 1959).

Grosjean, P., 'S. Patricius in monte Cruachan Aighle', *Analecta Bollandiana*, 1 (1932), 346-357.

Guasti, C. (ed.), *Commissioni di Rinaldo degli Albizzi per il comune di Firenze dal 1399 al 1433* (2 vols, Firenze, 1867-73).

Gwynn, A., Review of A. Curtayne, *Lough Derg, St Patrick's Purgatory*, in *Studies: an Irish Quarterly Journal*, xxxiii (1944), 550-554.

— *The Medieval Province of Armagh* (Dundalk, 1946).

— 'The sermon diary of Richard FitzRalph, archbishop of Armagh', *Proceedings of the Royal Irish Academy*, xliv C (1937), 1-57.

— 'Archbishop FitzRalph and George of Hungary', *Studies: an Irish Quarterly Journal*, xxiv (1935), 558-572.

— 'St Malachy of Armagh', *ibid.*, lxx (1948), 961-978; lxxi (1949), 134-148, 317-331.

— 'The centenary of the Synod of Kells', *ibid.*, lxxvii (1952), 161-176, 250-164.

— 'Armagh and Louth in the 12th century', *Seanchas Ardmhacha*, i (1954), 1-11; ii (1955), 17-37.

— 'Raphoe and Derry in the 12th and 13th centuries', *Donegal Annual*, iv (1959), 84-100.

— *The Twelfth-Century Reform*, A History of Irish Catholicism ii (Dublin/Sydney, 1968).

— and R. N. Hadcock, *Medieval Religious Houses. Ireland* (London, 1970).

Hammerich, L. L., 'Eine Pilgerfahrt des XIV. Jahrhunderts nach dem Fegfeuer des hl.Patrizius', *Zeitschrift für deutsche Philologie*, liii (1928), 25-40.

— 'Le pèlerinage de Louis d'Auxerre au Purgatoire de S. Patrice', *Romania*, lv (1929), 118-124.

— (ed.), *Visiones Georgii: Visiones quas in Purgatorio sancti Patricii vidit Georgius Miles de Ungaria A.D. MCCCLIII* (Det Kgl. Danske Videnskabernes Selskab. Historisk-filologiske Meddelelser, xviii, 2, Copenhagen, 1930).

Hankey, A. T., 'Domenico di Bandino of Arezzo', *Italian Studies*, xii (1957), 110-128.

— 'The successive revisions and surviving codices of the "Fons memorabilium universi" of Domenico di Bandino', *Rinascimento*, xi (1960), 3-49.

Haren, M., *Medieval Thought. The western intellectual tradition from antiquity to the thirteenth century* (London, 1985).

Hayes, R. J. (ed.), *The Manuscript Sources for the History of Irish Civilisation* (14 vols, Boston, 1965-75).

Healy, J., *Life and Writings of St Patrick* (Dublin, 1905).

Hennig, J., 'Medieval Ireland in Cistercian records', *Irish Ecclesiastical Record*, lxxiii (1950), 226-242.

Hogan, E., *Onomasticon Goedelicum* (Dublin/London 1910).

Hughes, K., 'The distribution of Irish scriptoria and centres of learning from 730-1111', in *Studies in the Early British Church* (Cambridge, 1958), 243-272.

— 'The changing theory and practice of Irish pilgrimage', *Journal of Ecclesiastical History*, xi (1960), 143-151.

— *The Church in Early Irish Society* (London, 1966).

— *Early Christian Ireland: introduction to the sources* (London, 1972).

Hyde, D., *A Literary History of Ireland* (London, 1899); new edition with introduction by Briain Ó Cuiv (London, 1967).

— *Legends of Saints and Sinners* (Dublin, 1915).

Jacob, E. F., *The Fifteenth Century 1399-1485* (corrected reprint Oxford, 1969).

Jacobus de Voragine, '*The Golden Legend,* translated by William Caxton (3 vols, London, 1892).

James, M. R., *The Apocryphal New Testament* (Oxford, 1969).

Jeanroy, A. and A. Vignaux, *Voyage au Purgatoire de St Patrice, Visions de Tindal et de St Paul,* Textes Languedociens du quinzième siècle (Toulouse, 1903).

Jocelin of Furness, *Vita sancti Patricii:* see Colgan, *Trias Thaumaturgae* and tr. E. Swift, *The Life and Acts of Saint Patrick* (Dublin, 1809).

Jones, Bishop Henry, *St Patrick's Purgatory: containing the description, originall progresse and demolition of that superstitious place* (London, 1647).

Jones, P. J., 'The Malatesta of Rimini and the papal state', *Italian Studies,* xii (1957), 110-128.

Joyce, P. W., *The Origin and History of Irish Names of Places* (2 vols, Dublin, 1871).

Keating, G., *Foras feasa ar Éirinn: The History of Ireland,* eds and trs D. Comyn and P. S. Dinneen, Irish Texts Society iv, viii, ix, xv (4 vols, London 1902-14).

Keen, M., *Chivalry* (New Haven and London, 1984).

Kenney, J. F., *The Sources for the Early History of Ireland, I: Ecclesiastical* (New York, 1929).

Knott, E., *The Bardic Poems of Tadhg Dall Ó Huiginn* (2 vols, London, 1926).

Knowles, D., *The Monastic Order in England* (London, 1948).

— C. N. L. Brooke, V. London (eds), *The Heads of Religious Houses, England and Wales, 940-1216* (Cambridge, 1972).

Kölbing, E., 'Zwei mittelenglische Bearbeitungen der Sage von s. Patrick's Purgatorium', *Englische Studien,* i (Breslau, 1876), 57-121.

Krapp, G. P., *The Legend of Saint Patrick's Purgatory: its later literary history* (Baltimore, 1900).

Krappe, A. H., 'St Patrick and the snakes', *Traditio,* v (1947), 323-330.

— 'La Cailleach Bheara. Notes de Mythologie Gaélique', *Etudes Celtiques,* i (1936), 292-302.

Labande, E. R., 'Recherches sur les pèlerins dans l'Europe des XIe et XIIe siècles', *Cahiers de Civilisation Médiévale,* i (1958), 158-169, 339-347.

Lacy, B., *Archaeological Survey of County Donegal* (Lifford, 1983).

Lanigan, J., *An Ecclesiastical History of Ireland* (4 vols, Dublin, 1822).

Larner, J., *The Lords of Romagna* (London, 1965).

Lawlor, H. J. (ed.), 'A calendar of the register of Archbishop Sweteman', *Proceedings of the Royal Irish Academy*, xxix, C (1911), 213-310.

— 'A calendar of the register of Archbishop Fleming', *ibid.*, xxx, C. (1912-3), 94-190.

Leclercq, J., 'Monachisme et pèrégrination du IXe au XIIe siècle', *Studia Monastica*, iii (1961), 33-52.

Le Don, G., 'Structures et significations de l'imagerie médiévale de l'enfer', *Cahiers de Civilisation Médiévale*, xxii (1979), 363-372.

Lefèvre, Y., *L'Elucidarium et les Lucidaires. Contribution, par l'histoire d'un texte, à l'histoire des croyances religieuses en France au Moyen Age* (Paris, 1954).

Le Goff, J., *La Naissance du Purgatoire* (Paris, Gallimard 1981), translated by A. Goldhammer, *The Birth of Purgatory* (London, 1984).

Leire Guimaraens, F. da, 'La doctrine des théologiens sur l'Immaculée Conception de 1250 à 1350', *Etudes Franciscaines*, new series ii (1952) 181-203; iv (1953) 23-51.

Leslie, S., *St Patrick's Purgatory. A record from history and literature* (London, 1932).

Levi, E., *I Cantori Leggendari del Popolo Italiano nei Secoli XIV e XV* (Turin, 1914).

— 'Antonio e Niccolò da Ferrara, poeti et uomini di corte del trecento', *Atti e Memorie della Deputazione Ferrarese di Storia Patria*, xix, 2 (1909), 41-405.

Livingstone, P., *The Fermanagh Story* (Enniskillen, 1969).

Locke, F. W., 'A new date for the composition of the *Tractatus de Purgatorio sancti Patricii*', *Speculum*, xl (1965), 641-646.

Loomis, L. H., 'Chaucer and the Auchinleck manuscript: *Sir Thomas* and *Guy Warwick*', in *Essays and Studies in Honor of Carleton Brown* (New York, 1940), pp. 111-128.

Lucas, A. T., 'Souterrains: the literary evidence', *Béaloideas*, xxxix-xli (1971-73), 165-191.

Luce, S., *Chronique des quatre premiers Valois (1327-1393)* (Paris, 1862).

Ludovico Ariosto 'Orlando Furioso', translated into English Heroical Verse by Sir John Harington (1591), ed. with an introduction by Robert McNulty (Oxford, 1972).

Lynch, J., *Cambrensis Eversus* (St Omer, 1662), ed. and tr. M. Kelly (3 vols, Dublin 1848-1852).

Mac Aingil, Aodh, *Scathán Shacramuinte na hAithridhe,* ed. Cainneach Ó Maonaigh (Dublin, 1952).

MacBride, P., 'St Patrick's Purgatory in Spanish literature', *Studies: an Irish Quarterly Journal,* xxv (1936), 277-291.

MacNeill, E., see *Dunaire Finn.*

MacNeill, M., *The Festival of Lughnasa* (Oxford, 1962).

Mac Ritchie, D., 'A note on St Patrick's Purgatory', *The Journal of the Royal Society of Antiquaries of Ireland,* xxx (1900), 165-167.

— 'An additional note on St Patrick's Purgatory', *ibid.,* xxxi (1906) 85-86.

Mac Tréinfhir, N., 'The Todi fresco and St Patrick's Purgatory, Lough Derg', *Clogher Record,* xii, 2 (1986), 141-158.

Mahaffy, J. P., 'Two early tours of Ireland', *Hermathena,* xi (1914), 1-16.

Malone, S., *Church History of Ireland from the Anglo-Norman Invasion to the Reformation* (2 vols, Dublin, 1880).

Martyrology of Donegal, eds J. Todd and W. Reeves (Dublin, 1864).

Martyrology of Oengus, ed. W. Stokes (Dublin, 1905).

Martyrology of Tallaght, ed. M. Kelly (Dublin, 1857).

Mall, E., 'Zur Geschichte der Legend vom Purgatorium heil. Patricius', *Romanische Forschungen,* vi (1891), 139-197.

Malory, Sir Thomas, *Works,* ed. Eugene Vinaver (Oxford, second edition, 1971).

Massaut, J-P., 'La vision de l'au-delà au Moyen Age', *Moyen Age,* xci (1985), 75-86.

Mazzatinti, G. & al., *Inventi dei Manoscritti delle Bibliothece d'Italia,* vol. 11 (Forli 1901).

McCone, K., 'Clones and her neighbours in the early period: hints from some Airgialla Saint's Lives', *Clogher Record,* xi, 3 (1984), 305-325.

McCullough, J. A., *Early Christian Visions of the Other World* (Edinburgh, 1912).

McKenna, L., *Dán Dé* (Dublin, 1922).

McNamara, M., *The Apocrypha in the Irish Church* (Dublin, 1975).

Mearns, R., *The Vision of Tundale,* Middle English Texts, 18 (Heidelberg, 1985).

Messingham, *Florilegium Insulae Sanctorum seu Vitae et Acta Sanctorum*

Hiberniae . . . (Paris, 1624); tr. *A Brief History of St Patrick's Purgatory and its Pilgrimage* (Paris, 1718).

Millet, B., 'Dioceses in Ireland up to the 15th century', *Seanchas Ardmhacha,* xii (1986), 1-42.

Milligan, S. F., 'Descriptive sketch of places visited in connection with the Ulster Meeting: Ballyshannon', *Journal of the Royal Society of Antiquaries of Ireland,* xxvi (1896), 294-297.

Miquel y Planas, R., *Llegendes de l'Altra Vida. Viatges del Cavaller Owein y de Ramon de Perellós al Purgatori de San Patricii;* . . . (Barcelona, 1914).

— (ed.), *Viatge al Purgatori de Sant Patrici per Ramon de Perellós (1397) seguit de les Visions de Tundal* . . . Històries d'altre temps X (Barcelona 1917).

Mitjà, M., 'Procés contra els consellers domèstics i curials de Joan I . . .', *Boletín de la Real Academia de Buenas Letras de Barcelona,* xxvii (1957-58) (Barcelona, 1958), 375-417.

Mollat, M., 'Innocent VI et les tentatives de paix entre la France et l'Angleterre', *Revue d'Histoire Ecclésiastique,* x (1909), 729-43.

Molloy Carpenter, D., 'The Journey of Ramon de Perellós to Saint Patrick's Purgatory: the Auch Manuscript' (unpublished M.Phil. thesis, N.U.I. (U.C.D.) 1984).

Mörner, M. (ed.), *Le Purgatoire de Saint Patrice par Berol* (Lund, 1917).

— *Le Purgatoire de Saint Patrice du Manuscrit de la Bibl. Nat. fonds fr. 25545* (Lund/Leipzig, 1920).

Morsolin, B., *Francesco Chiericati Vescovo e Diplomatico del Secolo Decimosesto. Lettura del Prof. Morsolin (Dagli Atti 1 semestre 1873 dell' Academia Olimpica di Vicenza* (Vicenza, 1873).

Moschus, F. (ed.), *Jacobi de Vitriaco libri duo quorum prior Orientalis sive Hierosolymitanae, alter Occidentalis Historiae nomine inscribitur* (Douai, 1597).

Mulligan, P., 'The diocese of Clogher in brief', *Clogher Record Album,* ed. J. Duffy (Monaghan, 1975), pp. 9-12.

Murphy, G., see *Dunaire Finn.*

— *The Ossianic Lore and Romantic Tales of Medieval Ireland* (Dublin, 1961).

Murphy, M. J., *At Slieve Gullion's foot* (Dundalk, 1949 and 1975 reprint).

O'Connor, D., *St Patrick's Purgatory Lough Derg* (Dublin, 1903).

Ó Fiaich, T., 'The Kingdom of Airgialla and its Sub-Kingdoms' (unpublished M.A. thesis, N.U.I. (U.C.D.) 1950).

— 'Irish Peregrini on the Continent', *Irish Ecclesiastical Record,* ciii (1965), 233-400.

Ó Gallachair, P., 'Patrician Donegal', *Donegal Annual,* v, 1 (1962), 70-79.

Ó hÓgáin, D., ' "Moch amach ar maidin dé Luain!" Staidéar ar an seanchas faoi ollphiasta i lochanna na hÉireann', *Béaloideas,* li (1983), 87-125.

— *Fionn mac Cumhaill. Images of the gaelic hero* (Dublin, 1988).

O'Kelleher, A. and G. Schoepperle (eds and tras), *Betha Colaim Chille: Life of Columcille* (University of Illinois, 1918).

O'Kelly, J. J., *Leabhar na Laoitheadh* (Dublin, 1913).

O'Meara, J. J. (tr.), *Gerald of Wales' The History and Topography of Ireland,* revised edition (Harmondsworth, 1982).

— (tr.), *The Voyage of St Brendan. Journey to the Promised Land* (Dublin, 1976).

Ó Muirgheasa, É., *Dánta Diadha Uladh* (Baile Átha Cliath, 1936).

Ó Muraíle, N., 'The barony-names of Fermanagh and Monaghan', *Clogher Record,* xi (1984), 387-402.

Ó Riain, P., 'Boundary association in early Irish society', *Studia Celtica,* vii (1972), 12-29.

— *Corpus Genealogiarum Sanctorum Hiberniae* (Dublin, 1985).

Ó Riain-Raedel, D., 'Aspects of the promotion of Irish saints' cults in medieval Germany', *Zeitschrift für Celtische Philologie,* xxxix (1982), 220-234.

Os, A. B. van, *Religious Visions. The development of the eschatological elements in mediaeval English religious literature* (Amsterdam, 1932).

O'Sullevan Beare, Philip, *Patritiana Decas* (Madrid, 1629).

O'Sullivan, M. D., *Italian Merchant Bankers in Ireland in the Thirteenth Century* (Dublin, 1962).

Ó Tuathail, É. (ed.), *Sgéalta Mhuintir Luiningh: Munterloney folk-tales* (Dublin, 1933).

Otway, A. C., *Sketches in Ireland* (Dublin, 1827).

Otway-Ruthven, A. J., *A History of Medieval Ireland* (London/New York, 1968).

Owain Miles and other Inedited Fragments of Ancient English Poetry, ed. D. Laing and W. B. D. D. Turnbull and others (Edinburgh, 1837).

Owen, D. D. R., *The Vision of Hell: infernal journeys in medieval French literature* (Edinburgh/London, 1970).

Papon, J-P., *Histoire Générale de Provence* (4 vols, Paris, 1776-1786).

Patch, H. R., *The Other World according to Descriptions in Medieval Literature* (New York, 1970 reprint of 1950 ed.).

Paterson, T. G. F., *Country Cracks. Old tales from the county of Armagh* (Dundalk, 1939).

Perroy, E., 'Quatre lettres du Cardinal Guy de Boulogne (1352-1354)', *Revue du Nord,* xxxvi (1954), 159-164.

Pezzarossa, F., 'La traditizione fiorentina della memorialistica' in G. M. Anselmi, F. Pezzarossa, L. Avellini, *La 'Memoria' dei Mercatores* (Bologna, 1980), pp. 41-149.

Phillips, M. M., *The Adages of Erasmus* (Cambridge, 1964).

Piatt, D., *Cois Life Fadó* (Baile Átha Cliath, 1985).

Picard, J-M., 'The marvellous in Irish and continental saints' lives of the Merovingian period', in *Columbanus and Merovingian Monasticism,* eds H. B. Clarke and M. Brennan, BAR International Series 113 (Oxford, 1981), 91-103.

Picard, J-M. (tr.) and Y. de Pontfarcy, *St Patrick's Purgatory. A twelfth century tale of a journey to the Other World* (Dublin, 1985).

— *The Vision of Tnugdal* (Dublin, forthcoming, 1989).

Plummer, C. (ed.), *Vitae Sanctorum Hiberniae* (2 vols, Oxford, 1910).

— (ed. and tr.), *Bethada Náem nÉrenn: Lives of Irish Saints* (2 vols, Oxford, 1922).

Plutarch, *Moralia,* eds and trs P. H. de Lacy and B. Einarson, The Loeb Classical Library (London, 1959), vii, 'On the Delays of the Divine Vengeance', pars 22-33: *Vision of Thespesius.*

Pontfarcy, Y. de, 'Le *Tractatus de Purgatorio sancti Patricii* de H. de Saltrey, sa date et ses sources', *Peritia: Journal of the Medieval Academy of Ireland,* iii (1984), 460-480.

— See also under Farcy de Pontfarcy.

Purcell, M., 'St Patrick's Purgatory: Francesco Chiericati's letter to Isabella d'Este', *Seanchas Ardmhacha,* xii, 2 (1987) 1-10.

Quiggin, E. C., 'Prologomena to the study of the later Irish bards 1200-1500', *Proceedings of the British Academy,* v (1911). Reprinted in *Irish Studies,* ii (n.d.).

Ranulph Higden, *Polychronicon,* Rolls Series 41 (9 vols, London, 1865-86).

Registrum Iohannis Mey. The Register of John Mey Archbishop of Armagh (1445-1456), ed. W. G. H. Quigley and E. F. D. Roberts (Belfast, 1972).

Richardson, J., *The great folly, superstition and idolatry of pilgrimages in Ireland; especially of that to Patrick's Purgatory* (Dublin, 1727).

Riquer, M. de, *História de la Literatura Catalana,* revised edition (3 vols, Barcelona, 1980).

Robinson, J. L., 'On the ancient deeds of the parish of St John, Dublin, preserved in the Library of Trinity College Dublin', *Proceedings of the Royal Irish Academy,* xxxiii, C (1916-7), 175-224.

Roger of Wendover's Flower of History, translated by J. A. Giles, Bohn's Antiquarian Library (3 vols, London, 1849).

Ryan, J., 'St Patrick's Purgatory', *Studies* xxi (1932), 443-460.

— 'St Patrick's Purgatory, Lough Derg', *Clogher Record Album,* ed. J. Duffy (Monaghan, 1975), pp. 13-26.

— *Irish Monasticism. Origins and early development,* 2nd ed. (Shannon, 1972).

Rymer, T., *Foedera, Conventiones, Litterae, et cujuscunque generis Acta Publica . . .* ed. A. Clarke and F. Holbrooke (4 vols, London, 1816-1869).

San Colombano e la sua opera in Italia, Acts of the 1951 Bobbio Colloquy (Bobbio, 1953).

Scott, A. B., *Malachy* (Dublin, 1976).

Selmer, C. (ed.), *Navigatio Sancti Brendani Abbatis* (University of Notre Dame, Indiana, 1959); see tr. O'Meara.

Seymour, St J. D., *St Patrick's Purgatory: a mediaeval pilgrimage in Ireland* (Dundalk, 1918).

— 'Irish versions of the Vision of St Paul', *The Journal of Theological Studies,* xxiv (1922), 54-59.

— *Irish Visions of the Other-World. A contribution to the study of mediaeval visions* (London, 1930).

Shackford, M. H., *Legends and Satires from Medieval Literature* (Boston, 1913).

Sheehy, M., *Pontificia Hibernica. Medieval papal chancery documents concerning Ireland 640-1261* (2 vols, Dublin, 1962-65).

Shields, H. E., 'An old French Book of Legends and its Apocalyptic Background' (unpublished Ph.D. thesis, Trinity College, Dublin 1967).

— 'Légendes religieuses en ancien français, MS 951 de la Bibl. de Trinity College à Dublin', *Scriptorium,* xxxiv, 1 (1980) 59-71.

Silverstein, T., *Visio sancti Pauli. The history of the apocalypse in Latin together with nine texts* (London, 1935).

— 'The Vision of St Paul: new links and patterns in the western tradition', *Archives d'Histoire Doctrinale et Littéraire du Moyen Age*, xxxiv (1959), 199-248.

Simms, K., 'The medieval kingdom of Lough Erne', *Clogher Record*, ix (1977), 126-141.

— 'The origins of the diocese of Clogher', *ibid.*, x (1980), 180-198.

Southern, R. W., *Western Society and the Church in the Middle Ages* (Harmondsworth, 1973).

— Review of J. Le Goff's *La Naissance du Purgatoire*, in *Times Literary Supplement*, 18 June 1982, 651-2.

Spencer, T., 'Chaucer's hell: a study in mediaeval conventions', *Speculum*, ii (1927), 177-200.

Stanford, M. A., 'The Sumner's Tale and Saint Patrick's Purgatory', *Journal of English and Germanic Philologie*, xix (1920), 377-381.

Stephanus Forcatulus, *De Gallorum Imperio et Philosophia Libri VII* (Paris, 1580).

Stokes, W. (ed. and tr.), *Bethu Phátraic. The Tripartite Life of St Patrick with other documents relating to that saint* (2 vols, London 1887).

— 'Cuimmin's poem on the saints of Ireland', *Zeitschrift für Celtische Philologie*, i (1897), 59-73.

Strachan, L. R. M., 'Patrick's Purgatory', *Notes and Queries*, clxxxii (1942), 111.

Strecker, K. (ed.), 'Literarische Nachfolge des "Georg von Ungarn' . . . "Visio Ludovici de Francia",' in M. Voigt, *Beiträge zur Geschichte der Visionenliteratur im Mittelalter*, i (Leipzig, 1924), 226-52.

Szöverffy, J., 'The Anglo-Norman conquest of Ireland and St Patrick, Dublin and Armagh in Jocelin's Life of St Patrick', *Repertorium Novum*, ii (1957-60), 6-16.

Tasis, R., *Pere el Ceremoniós i els seus Fills* (Barcelona, 1957).

— *Joan I. El rei caçador i músic* (Barcelona, 1959).

The Auchinleck Manuscript, with an Introduction by D. Pearsall and I. C. Cunningham (London, 1977).

The Pricke of Conscience, ed. R. Morris (Berlin, 1863).

The South English Legendary, ed. Charlotte d'Evelyn and Anna J. Mills, Early English Text Society, ccxxxv (1956), 85-110.

Thompson, E. M., 'The vision of Edmund Leversedge', *Notes and Queries for Somerset and Dorset*, ix (1904), 19-35.

Thurneysen, R., *A Grammar of Old Irish* (Dublin, 1946).

Tischendorf, C., *Apocalypses Apocryphae* (Leipzig, 1866).

Transactions of the Ossianic Society, ii ed. N. O'Kearney (Dublin, 1855); vi ed. J. Daly (Dublin, 1861).

Veinant, A. and Giraud de Savines eds, *Le Voyage du Puys Sainct Patrix* (Lyon, 1506, réimpression Paris, 1839).

Vendryes, J., *Lexique Etymologique de l'Irlandais Ancien. Lettres RS* (Dublin/Paris 1974).

Verdeyen, R. and J. Endepols, *Tondalus' Visoen en St Patricius' Vagevuur* (2 vols, Ghent, 1914-1917).

Villari, P., *Antiche Leggende e Tradizioni che illustrano la Divina Commedia* (Pisa, 1865).

Vising, J., *Le Purgatoire de Saint Patrice des Mss Harleien 273 et fonds fr. 2198* (Göteborg, 1916).

Vogel, C., 'Le pèlerinage pénitentiel', *Revue des Sciences Religieuses*, xxxviii (1964), 113-153.

Voigt, M., *Beiträge zur Geschichte der Visionenlitteratur im Mittelalter* (Leipzig, 1924).

Waddel, H., *Beasts and Saints* (London, 1934).

Wagner, A. (ed.), *Visio Tnugdali* (Erlangen, 1882); see tr. Picard.

Wahl, O. (ed.), *Apocalypses Esdrae. Apocalypses Sedrach. Visio Beati Esdrae,* Pseudo epigraphia veteris testamenti Graece 4 (Leiden, 1974).

Walsh, K., *A Fourteenth-Century Scholar and Primate. Richard FitzRalph in Oxford, Avignon and Armagh* (Oxford, 1981).

Walsh, P., *Irish Men of Learning* (Dublin, 1947).

Ware, Sir James, *The Whole Works of Sir James Ware concerning Ireland,* ed. W. Harris (2 vols, Dublin, 1746).

Warnke, K., *Das Buch vom Espurgatoire S. Patrice der Marie de France und seine Quelle,* Bibliotheca Normannica, IX (Halle/Saale, 1938).

Waterhouse, G., 'St Patrick's Purgatory: a German account', *Hermathena*, xliv (1926), 30-51.

Watt, J., *The Church in Medieval Ireland* (Dublin, 1972).

Weston, J. L., *The Chief Middle English Poetes* (Boston, 1914).

— *From Ritual to Romance* (Cambridge, 1920).

Westropp, T. J., 'Early Italian maps of Ireland from 1300 to 1600, with notes on foreign settlers and trade', *Proceedings of the Royal Irish Academy,* xxx (1912-13), 361-428.

Wylie, J. H., *The Reign of Henry the Fifth,* I (1413-1415) (Cambridge, 1914).

Wright, T., *St Patrick's Purgatory. An essay on the legends of Purgatory, Hell and Paradise, current during the Middle Ages* (London, 1844).

Zaleski, C., 'St Patrick's Purgatory: pilgrimage motifs in a medieval otherworld vision', *Journal of the History of Ideas,* xlvi (1985), 467-85.

— *Otherworld Journeys: accounts of near-death experience in medieval and modern times* (New York and Oxford, 1987).

Zama, P., *I Malatesti* (Faenza, 1965).

Zanden, C. M. van der, 'Autour d'un Ms latin du Purgatoire de Saint Patrice de la Bibl. de l'Université d'Utrecht', *Neophilologus,* x (1925), 243-249.

— 'Un chapitre intéréssant de la *Topographia Hibernica* et le *Tractatus de Purgatorio sancti Patricii*', *Neophilologus,* xii (1927), 132-137.

— *Etude sur le Purgatoire de Saint Patrice accompagnée du texte latin d'Utrecht et du texte anglo-normand de Cambridge* (Amsterdam, 1927).

Zumkeller, A., 'Die Augustinerschule des Mittelalters: Verterter und philosophischtheologische Lehre', *Analecta Augustiniana,* xxvii (1964), 167-262.

YOLANDE de PONTFARCY

Index